FORENSIC CREMATION

Recovery
and
Analysis

Scott I. Fairgrieve

2008

CRC Press
Taylor & Francis Group
Boca Raton London New York

CRC Press is an imprint of the
Taylor & Francis Group, an informa business

to the use of many analytical avenues in order to pursue a positive identification. It is equally clear that a team approach to the identification of disaster victims, particularly when cremated, will enhance the chances of arriving at an identification. For cremains that have reached Crow–Glassman Stage V, the use of DNA will be a foregone conclusion. However, morphological comparisons to antemortem records may still be possible.

8.6 IMPLANTS AS A MEANS OF IDENTIFICATION

As with dental restorations, surgical procedures may also require the implantation of materials in the body that may be of assistance in the identification of cremains. The usefulness of orthopedic devices, due to manufacturer logo and a means of tracking these devices to specific patients through unique serial and lot numbers, has been documented as a likely source of information for positively identifying associated human remains (Ubelaker and Jacobs, 1995). Pacemakers have been a commonly traced implant in the identification of remains (Sathyavagiswaran et al., 1992).

Although there are many forms of implants, one would have to consider the likelihood of survival of such implants in cremation contexts. Fixative devices, screws, and surgical plates are ideal candidates for examination in cremains. However, even more complicated devices, such as an osteostimulator, an implanted device that is used to induce the regeneration of bone tissue by means of a stimulating electrical current, have been of assistance in the identification of cremains (e.g., Bennett and Benedix, 1999).

All materials that are directly associated with human cremains that can possibly be a component of an implanted device must be explained in the analysis of recovered materials. The challenge is to recognize these cremated components from amongst other fire-altered materials associated with, or around, the human cremated material.

8.7 IDENTIFYING CREMAINS OF HISTORIC FIGURES

On occasion human cremains are recovered in a context that is consistent with an expected or purported individual. The challenge is no less difficult in attempting to identify these remains as with many others. To serve as examples of the challenges of such identifications, I have chosen to summarize the cases of attempting to identify the charred remains once purported to be those of King Philip II of Macedonia, father of Alexander the Great (Andronicos, 1994; Bartsiokas, 2000), and the attempts to identify the cremains of Adolf Hitler (Laurier et al., 1994; Kaleka, 1993).

The cremated remains of what was subsequently identified as belonging to an adult male were discovered in "Royal Tomb II" at Vergina, Greece, in 1977 by Andronicus (1994). The richness of the grave goods and the context (ca. 336 B.C.) served to identify the tomb as that of King Philip II of Macedonia. As noted by Bartsiokas (2000), this conclusion has been challenged due to another estimated date of 317 B.C. and, hence, belonging to King Philip III Arrhidaeus, a half-brother of Alex-

ander the Great. As Philip II is said to have suffered an arrow wound to his right eye, the detection of evidence of such an injury on the cremains would be thought to have served as a strong indicator of the identity of these cremains. In a forensic context, if a pathology is noted in a medical record with accompanying radiographs, one would be more confident of utilizing a pathology as a basis for identification. The strongest possible conclusion that could be made in this case, should the cremains provide unequivocal evidence of an antemortem eye injury that is consistent with that reported in history, would be that we failed to exclude Philip II as the identity of the cremains. Examination of the margins of the supraorbital margin of the right eye did not yield any evidence of a healed fracture or callus formation (Bartsiokas, 2000). However, is it possible for an arrow to enter the right orbit and result in the loss of an eye without leaving any evidence on the bone? The obvious answer is yes. Although it may not seem likely, documentation of the incident is not sufficient to say one way or the other. Another point of consideration is the interval of time that has passed from the incident to the time of death. A lack of evidence of a callus formation on the bone may indicate that sufficient time has passed for resorption of the bony callus. Although Bartsiokas (2000) concludes that there is no evidence to support traumatic injuries to the face, and any asymmetries can be attributed to the warping and shrinkage associated with the cremation process. It is true that cranio-facial skeletal elements are highly susceptible to the aforementioned heat-induced changes. However, given the above, it cannot be categorically stated one way or another that the cremains are, or are not, those of Philip II of Macedonia. A rigorous forensic approach would prevent us from rendering a conclusion one way or another. Hence, the cremains should be considered as unidentified.

In the twentieth century, the most infamous person whose charred remains were under severe scrutiny for identification were those of Adolf Hitler. In spite of such interest, the purported cranial and dental fragments held by Russian authorities still have questions related to identification issues (for a review, see Marchetti et al., 2005). The issues surrounding Hilter's remains lie in the fact that the remains recovered were subjected to fire, using gasoline as an accelerant. According to Bezymenski (1968), the charred remains recovered represented an adult male of approximately 50–60 years of age with a stature of approximately 165 centimeters. Enough soft tissue was present in order for there to be an examination of internal organs, even to note the absence of the left testicle. The skull consisted of an occipital, left temporal, "lower cheek bones," nasal bones, and the mandible and maxilla. The dental remains are of significance due to the presence of bridgework, artificial teeth, crowns, and fillings. Given the above condition of the remains, this would put them into either level 2 or 3 of the Crow–Glassman Scale.

A reexamination of documents concerning the discovery of the grave containing the corpses of a man and a woman outside of Hitler's Berlin bunker yielded a reference to two fragments from a skull found at a depth of 50 to 60 centimeters (Petrova and Watson, 1996). One fragment is noted as having a bullet hole. This hole, interpreted as being an exit wound, is from a close contact gunshot through the mouth or the chin. The original autopsy report, cited by Bezymenski (1968) makes no mention of such fragments. However, mention was made of splinters from a glass ampule in the mouth of the male body (presumably containing cyanide). Further,

FORENSIC CREMATION

Recovery
and
Analysis

FORENSIC CREMATION

Recovery
and
Analysis

Scott I. Fairgrieve

CRC Press
Taylor & Francis Group
Boca Raton London New York

CRC Press is an imprint of the
Taylor & Francis Group, an informa business

CRC Press
Taylor & Francis Group
6000 Broken Sound Parkway NW, Suite 300
Boca Raton, FL 33487-2742

International Standard Book Number-13: 978-0-8493-9189-7 (Hardcover)

Library of Congress Cataloging-in-Publication Data

Fairgrieve, Scott I.
   Forensic cremation recovery and analysis / Scott I. Fairgrieve.
      p. ; cm.
   "A CRC title."
   Includes bibliographical references and index.
   ISBN-13: 978-0-8493-9189-7 (hardcover: alk. paper)
   1. Dead--Identification. 2. Fire--Casualties--Identification. 3. Cremation. I. Title.
   [DNLM: 1. Forensic Anthropology--methods. 2. Mortuary Practice. 3. Cadaver. W 822 F169f 2008]

RA1055.F35 2008
614'.17--dc22
                                                 2007019366

Visit the Taylor & Francis Web site at
http://www.taylorandfrancis.com

and the CRC Press Web site at
http://www.crcpress.com

Dedication

This work is dedicated to my colleagues and students in the Department of Forensic Science at Laurentian University.

Contents

PREFACE

The objective of this book is to provide forensic professionals and students a synopsis of the challenges and practicalities of recovering and analyzing human remains that have undergone extreme levels of damage in fire contexts. Forensic anthropologists are often confronted with decomposing and fragmentary human remains that require analysis for identity and trauma. Human remains that have been burned to the point of little to no soft tissue remaining require special consideration by the analyst. The special consideration of which I speak begins right at the scene with the recovery of the cremated remains (or cremains). Many professionals who attend fire scenes, such as fire service personnel, fire investigators, forensic identification/ crime scene investigators, coroners, and medical examiners, have a collective interest in the remains as well as the context in which the remains occur. Their collective expertise is needed for the successful interpretation of such fire scenes. However, the literature in this area, in general, does not consider the potential contributions of a forensic anthropological analysis. This book is to remedy this situation and provide an opportunity for forensic professionals to consider the recovery and interpretation of cremains from the point of discovery, through to the end of an analysis.

Although this book is not necessarily intended for experienced forensic anthropologists, those who have not had any experience with cremated remains may wish to go through the various chapters contained in this book in order to gain a knowledge base prior to casework. Other forensic professionals will benefit from the forensic anthropological perspective by instructing them as to the reasonable goals of the recovery and subsequent analysis of cremains.

The book begins with an overview of cremains in the forensic setting. This overview is important for those new to examining cremains as it will provide them with a range of contexts and the challenges that face those of us who process these scenes and perform the analysis of the cremains. This chapter also provides the reader with an appreciation of the wide range of preservation encountered in a variety of fire contexts.

The next chapter is a basic introduction to fire. This section is not meant for training individuals such as fire investigators, but it is really geared to those who in the forensic community, such as forensic identification personnel from police services, and even some forensic anthropologists, who have not had any formal training in fire as a mechanism for altering the chemical and physical properties of materials.

The cremation process as detailed in Chapter 3 of this book is primarily concerned with the means by which human tissues burn. Knowledge in this area is of the utmost importance as it has a direct bearing on one's ability to interpret the condition of the cremains, their position, and the circumstances in which the burning event occurred. This has implications for the means by which the recovery of the cremains proceeds.

The recovery of cremated human remains will be based upon the context of the cremains. This is true of all forensic recoveries of human remains. However, one must consider that cremains may be intermixed with building materials, automobile remains, or even buried in soil or submerged in water. The emphasis in Chapter 4 is that a flexible strategy to recover remains, while documenting their context, is essential to this process. As cremains tend to be extremely fragile, some analytical work must be undertaken at the scene during the recovery. Working closely with crime scene personnel will facilitate the safe recovery and documentation of the cremains at the scene. Documenting the location and position of the cremains can yield information that may affect the charges levied in a particular case.

Although some of the analysis may have had to be conducted, to a limited degree, at the scene, the full analysis of the cremains can be a long and labor-intensive exercise. Chapter 5 examines the physical alterations of bone by fire, including shrinking, warping, cracking, and fragmenting, and how they have important implications in the analysis of the cremains. This is particularly true for discriminating between fractures that are as a result of the heat from the fire, and those that are due to a perimortem trauma. This comes back to the idea of having a thorough collection of cremains from the original scene. Nonetheless, it is possible to generate a biological profile of the person in order to assist in finding candidates for identification.

The analysis of bone tissue that has been altered by the burning process, as presented in Chapter 6, will have implications for quantifying the histological differences between heat-induced fractures, and those that are from a pre-cremation trauma such as a gunshot wound or a cut mark.

The examination dental tissue for establishing a positive identification is typical in many fire scenarios. However, the extent of damage to dental structures and dental restorative materials and appliances by fire, may greatly affect a forensic odontologist's ability to establish identity. This is particularly true when the tissues surrounding the oral cavity have been eliminated by the fire and directly affected the enamel, dentine, and cementum. Chapter 7 provides the reader with a survey of the effects of fire on these tissues and how they may still be utilized in order to contribute to rendering an identity.

The ultimate goal of an investigation of human cremains in a forensic context is to answer who the individual is, where they died, when they died, how they died and by what means. The identity of the cremains is of paramount importance to the investigation as it not only puts a name to the remains, but is also provides new investigational leads. As indicated in Chapter 8, it is without question that the most common means by which to render an identification of human remains is through DNA and dental records. In the case of forensic cremains, DNA is extremely challenging, although worthy of consideration in some instances. All positive identification is predicated on having suitably documented antemortem medical records, such as dental radiographs, or other forms of radiographic material. In many cases, when medical records are either nonexistent or of such poor quality that they are unusable, a presumptive identification may be all that can be considered on the basis of the biological profile from the forensic anthropological analysis.

As challenging as the recovery and analysis of human cremains may appear, it is far from a hopeless situation. Cremains are able to provide extremely useful information if those involved in the investigation can establish a team approach to these scenes in order to maximize the potential of the evidence.

The production of this book, although under sole authorship, is not accomplished without a team of very supportive people. This project came about several years ago due to my own involvement in recovering and analyzing forensic cremations. To that end, I wish to thank Dr. Barry McLellan, Chief Coroner for the Province of Ontario, Dr. David Legge, and Dr. Peter Clark, Regional Supervising Coroners for Northern and Eastern Ontario, respectively, for their continued support. The car and pit test fires were performed at the facilities of the Ontario Police College (OPC) in Aylmer Ontario. I would particularly like to recognize Mr. Jim Goodwin, from the Forensic Identification Training Branch of OPC for assisting with making the arrangements for fire permits and the resources to undertake these tests. Mr. Kim Adams deserves special recognition for all of his logistical support with obtaining automobiles to burn and the various fuel sources that were used in these tests. I would especially like to thank the Malahide Fire Service for providing me a house to burn down in these experiments. Mr. Rick Devine, team leader, and the other members of the Forensic Identification Training Branch of OPC, are thanked for their continued support during my stay at their facility. The pigs used in these studies were all humanely put down as a result of having an untreatable illness. No pigs were purposefully put down in order to perform this study. Other support in the field during these tests was provided by Ms. Tracy Oost, Curator, Department of Forensic Science, Laurentian University. Some preliminary library work was undertaken by Mr. Damian Fumerton. Further valuable advice and assistance with respect to finding obscure sources was graciously provided by Ms. Karen Neves of the W.K. Kellogg Health Sciences Library at Dalhousie University. Some assistance with manuscript preparation was rendered by Ms. Leeanne Croteau, departmental secretary. Finally, I would like to express my gratitude to my family for their patience and understanding during the past three years.

1 Cremains in the Forensic Setting

1.1 INTRODUCTION

The study of the effects of fire, or any means of combustion, of human tissues is one that has always had forensic implications (*The Lancet*, 1893). The idea of disposing of human remains using fire is an ancient one (Baby, 1954). Archaeologically, funerary pyres, in one form or another, have been used as a means to dispose of bodies throughout human history and prehistory. Kaczmarek and Piontek (1982) note that cremation as a means of body disposal was spread in Central Europe from Neolithic times to the Early Middle Ages. Human cremated remains that have been dated to be as old as 25,000 to 32,000 years in the Lake Mungo region of Australia attest to the early practice of cremation (Bowler et al., 1970). Yet, as much as fire has the potential to destroy soft tissue and underlying hard tissues, namely bones and teeth, it is still noteworthy that it is almost impossible to completely destroy a body by fire or some form of combustion (Bass, 1984). The fact that human remains that have been "cremated" in archaeological contexts can be examined for determining the minimum number of individuals, age, sex, and even pathology, certainly suggests that the same should be possible in more contemporary situations (see Lange et al., 1987). However, the analysis of charred or cremated human remains in forensic contexts is far different from an archaeological analysis.

Although the practice of cremation appears to have been a common feature in human history and prehistory, the use of cremation in western society as a means of funeral disposal of Christians was wrought with controversy, particularly in Great Britain (Thompson, 1891). The controversy over cremation has been noted by various authors to be a means of body disposal that can have important forensic implications in and of itself (*The Lancet*, 1893). Recent reports of possible commingling of cremated remains (henceforth referred to as "cremains") returned to a family in error or simply a family suspecting that the cremains received by them were either incomplete or altogether the wrong person have necessitated investigation by forensic anthropologists (e.g., Murray and Rose, 1993; Kennedy, 1999).

Yet, as far back as 1892, it was recognized that the cremation of human remains may be an avenue for criminals to destroy evidence (*The Lancet*, 1893). More recently, in Germany, a system was put in place to have all bodies that will be cremated examined by medical doctors in order to note external findings and to review the entries on the death certificate (Uchigaski, 2004).

In the Canadian context, the vast majority of forensic inquiries into charred remains and fire deaths are primarily related to house fires. Consider that from 1992 to 2001 there have been, on average, 377 deaths per year with 3,048 injuries in that same span of time due to fires. With an average of 60,109 fires and an annual loss of over $1.2 billion, fire is no small concern to the public at large (Council of Canadian Fire Marshals and Fire Commissioners, 2001). In 2001 alone there were a total of 55,323 fires in Canada of which 10,876 were classified as incendiary (including suspicious fires and riots).

In the Province of Ontario alone there were 996 fatal fires from 1995 to 2004 (Office of the Fire Marshal of Ontario, 2005). An overwhelming majority of these (84%) occurred in residential properties. During this same period, 721 of those fatal residential fires are considered to have been preventable. It is reported that 1% of preventable residential fires in Ontario are fatal. By virtue of the fact that these deaths must all be investigated, they are all considered to be in a forensic context. The mandate of the investigation not only includes determining the cause of the fire, but also the manner in which that fire started. A specific act, or act of omission, by a person or persons now enters the territory of homicide.

As sobering as these figures are, they do not include fires that have been set specifically to dispose of remains in open contexts, such as clandestine bonfires. Clandestine contexts typically do not only involve the burning of the body, but also the mechanical mixing and crushing of cremains with the hope of rendering them down to an unrecognizable state.

Forensic contexts of cremains include any instances in which a fire has a legal consequence. Because virtually all fires have a forensic context, until cleared through the investigation process, the search for, documentation of, and the recovery and analysis of human cremated remains must be accorded the respect due to any remains associated with an investigation.

DeHaan (2002) notes that arson is an agent of murder and a means of destroying evidence of a crime that has already been committed. These incendiary fires, that is, fires that have been deliberately set, necessitate a team of experts to properly investigate these scenes. Among those experts noted by DeHaan are the fire investigators, pathologists, toxicologists, radiologists, and even odontologists. Conspicuously absent from this list are forensic anthropologists. Forensic anthropologists specialize in the analysis of severely degraded human remains. Their goals of analysis are not mutually exclusive of those of the fire investigator. Table 1.1 lists the analytical questions posed by both forensic anthropologists and fire investigators. If we examine this list more closely it is evident that if a fire proceeds to the point that the head and appendages have been rendered down to fragmented bone, the list of questions that is more suited to the analysis of the remains clearly falls under the auspices of the forensic anthropologist. It is the forensic anthropologist who is to conduct the analysis of bone fragments that are recovered from the scene. However, it is also the forensic anthropologist who should be at the scene in the first place in order to find, document, and recover the cremains.

This sort of analysis at the scene and during the postmortem examination is, without question, a team effort. However, the types of evidence some members of the team may usually handle may have been destroyed through the burning of the body. Fingerprints, DNA, and even extant dental work may not survive the cremation process to the level or quality needed to yield a positive identification.

TABLE 1.1

A Comparison of the Analytical Questions Posed by Forensic Anthropologists and Fire Investigators with Respect to Human Remains

Forensic Anthropologist's Questions	Fire Investigator's Questions (DeHaan, 2002)
Are the remains human?	Are the remains human?
Are the remains of recent forensic interest?	Who was the victim?
How many people are represented by the remains?	What was the cause of death?
What is the age at death of the remains?	What was the manner of death?
What is the sex of these remains?	Was the person alive at the time of the fire? If so, why did he or she not escape?
What is the genetic affiliation (sometimes referred to as race) of these remains?	Was death due to the fire or only associated with it?
What is the living stature of the remains?	
Are there any identifying characteristics present on the remains?	
Is a positive identification possible based on the above?	
Is there any evidence of pathology, including trauma, that is either antemortem, perimortem, or postmortem?	
What is the manner of death?	
What is the cause of death?	

The six investigative problems listed by DeHaan (2002) have a significant overlap with those questions approached by the forensic anthropologist. Clearly, the first four of DeHaan's list have been expanded by the forensic anthropologist to address specific issues concerning identification. However, if the remains are in the condition stated above, then pathological evidence may not be as forthcoming. In such a circumstance, the best practice is to have the forensic anthropologist work with the forensic pathologist. In addition to chronicling perimortem pathology, long-healed fractures may lead to medical records that will ultimately yield a positive identification.

Question five of DeHaan's six may never be answered, particularly if soft tissue has been eliminated. With the absence of soft tissue, so goes the evidence of soot in the trachea, or toxic gases in any of the tissues or blood. This is particularly true with clandestine cremations. Should a perpetrator feel that the chosen location for the cremation is sufficiently private for him or her to tend to the fire for a prolonged period of time, then there is an opportunity to render the remains to a state consisting of bone and ash.

This is not to say that the question concerning the victim's state of consciousness or vitality are inappropriate; it is rather more practical to state that these questions are more realistic from a forensic evidence perspective when soft tissue or witness accounts are present.

It is, without question, that death due to an incendiary house fire can kill unsuspecting victims. In such a case, death being due to the fire can be difficult to ascertain if the fire is in a reasonably remote location and the fire goes unreported. Although human remains may be evident in a fire scene shortly after it has been extinguished, or the majority of the superstructure has collapsed, a persistent smoldering of material may eliminate any persisting soft tissue.

DeHaan notes, justifiably, that the fire investigator's job is to consider the body and its clothing as elements of fuel load and a potential cause or even point of origin for the fire, whereas the homicide investigator will be better able to appreciate and interpret the various elements of a violent death scene. Yet, with the omission of a forensic anthropologist there would be a considerable lack of expertise on the scene to handle questions of faunal versus human remains, as well as the recognition of skeletonized remains.

DeHaan's basic recovery recommendations include establishing a scene grid and wet-sifting debris through sieves of various sizes. Although these actions are generally recommended, there are certain details of methodology that need to be expanded upon. For example, all screening must be done away from the actual scene to prevent cross-contamination. Without someone on scene with the experience to recognize fragmented bone and dental remains, these items can be easily missed. Moreover, the position and location of cremains in a structure must be mapped so as to preserve their context. Screening of material as a sole method of recovery will destroy contextual evidence. The presence of a forensic anthropologist on the scene as part of the investigative team is clearly a much-needed resource in order to maximize the potential of the evidence related to cremains and their context.

The forensic context demands that an analysis of any human remains follow a certain set of procedures defined by law. In Ontario, such law is covered in the Coroners Act (R.S.O. 1990 c. C.37, s. 31 (1)). Specifically, any deaths not attended by a physician must be investigated in order to answer the following five questions:

1. Who the deceased was?
2. How the deceased came to his or her death?
3. When the deceased came to his or her death?
4. Where the deceased came to his or her death?
5. By what means the deceased came to his or her death?

In order to facilitate answering these questions, the coroner in charge of the case will ideally have a large team of experts upon whom to call for assistance. This team includes:

1. **Police.** Police will be involved at the scene, procure evidence at the scene, and carry out the investigation.
2. **Coroner.** The coroner will initiate the investigation and ultimately be responsible for issuing a death certificate indicating the answers to the five questions outlined above.
3. **Forensic Pathologist.** The pathologist, ideally with a forensic background, is the person responsible for the legal examination of the remains. A coro-

ner's warrant for the examination of the remains will name a pathologist to do the examination. The examination, external and internal, is performed to provide the coroner with answers to the five questions. The examination is also an opportunity to obtain samples from the remains in order to send on for further examination.

4. **Toxicologist.** Tissues may be examined chemically, for various compounds, in order to assist in determining the cause of death. For example, in fires, a common question to be asked concerns whether or not the decedent was alive at the time of the fire, and hence inhaled any smoke. Blood and tissue samples are commonly analyzed for carbon monoxide levels in the blood (COHb). As three-quarters of all fire-related deaths result from inhalation of toxic smoke (Spitz, 1993), this is an important question.

5. **Forensic Odontologist.** The use of recovered dental tissues from fire victims is a common means of establishing a positive identification. Generally, teeth are remarkably resistant to heat, due to contraction of muscles around the mandible, locking the jaws in place, and the cheeks, tongue and lips acting as insulators. However, prolonged burns can directly affect teeth by melting out dental restorations and fracturing enamel, cementum, and dentine. Even dental remains in such an advanced state of destruction have the potential to provide evidence of the location and type of dental work (Fairgrieve, 1994).

6. **Forensic Anthropologist.** Ideally, forensic anthropologists work closely with the forensic identification officers at scenes in order to assist with the recovery and documentation of human remains. The remains in such instances are typically in an advanced state of decomposition or of a fragmentary nature. In the case of cremains, the recognition of human bone material will likely be an issue with most scene officers. It is in these instances that forensic anthropologists are particularly valued for their services. Likewise, a postmortem examination of such remains usually is done as a team effort with the forensic pathologist and odontologist. However, should there not be any soft tissue remains present, then the forensic anthropologist's analysis will make up the bulk of the report on the recovered remains. A forensic anthropology analysis consists of examining the remains for age at death, sex, race (genetic affiliation), stature, presence of pathology, postmortem interval (i.e., how long since death occurred), and aspects of positive identification.

7. **Forensic Entomologist.** Forensic entomology in these contexts is usually associated with assisting in determining a postmortem interval. The succession of various insect species and their respective times of development are of particular interest. Although it is generally thought that tissues denatured by heat, in essence cooked, result in a slowing of decomposition, it has been noted that the successional waves of insects onto burned carcasses seems to occur earlier than on unburned carcasses (Avila and Goff, 1998). Yet, fire can consume soft tissues to such an extent that there is no entomological activity to speak of. To that end, a forensic entomologist is of use when there is some preserved soft tissue.

8. **Forensic Botanist.** The use of botanical remains as a source of estimating the postmortem interval is a burgeoning area of forensic science. Cremains may act as a source of nutrition for plants and promote growth in areas of scatter. Likewise, the forest floors contain evidence of any previous forest fires and can be useful in putting a limit on a possible date of deposition of remains. This is not a resource to be ignored.

9. **Fire Investigators.** Fire investigation in Ontario is under the purview of the Ontario Fire Marshal's Office. These investigators are responsible for determining the cause of a fire. They work with police and other forensic specialists who would be involved in the analysis of samples procured from the scene.

10. **Other forensic specialists.** Other specialties, from forensic chemists to explore the use of volatile ignitable liquids (VILs) (also known as accelerants) at a scene, or recovered from the body, to structural forensic engineers to comment on the collapsing of a building, are all part of the team involved in such investigations.

Although it is clear from the above list of specialists that there is a remarkable team of people behind such investigations, it is beyond the mandate of this book to examine all aspects of the interaction with these specialists. However, this book advocates the expansion of the list of experts typically used in fire investigations to include a forensic anthropologist.

This book deals with the occurrence of cremated human remains in cases of suspicious death. A suspicious death is considered to be in a forensic context until proven otherwise. Forensic contexts involving cremated remains are amongst the most vexing, as fire is an effective way of destroying evidence, or so it would seem. Although fire can effectively eliminate soft tissue from the body and also alter hard tissues, namely bones and teeth, these remains, under the right circumstances, can still yield a great deal of information. In his analysis of the cremated archaeological remains of the Ohio Hopewell, Baby (1954) was able to comment upon the age, sex, pathology and precremation treatment of these people. Baby was able to diagnose forms of arthritis, and even a case of club foot, from the Hopewell cremains. Clearly, age, sex, race, stature, pathology, manner, and cause of death need not be written off as being indeterminate just because the remains have been rendered down to a fragmentary state in a fire. Even important information, such as body position and location within a structure, sometimes critical pieces of evidence, can be determined through careful examination and recovery practices.

Although the mandate of this book is to look at the recovery, analysis, and interpretation of evidence from cremains in a forensic context, I will not ignore what can be done with human remains with varying degrees of burns. However, the focus of this book will largely involve those burns that can be classified to the fourth degree and beyond. This specifically refers to burns that have not only destroyed soft tissue, but also are directly charring the underlying bony tissue. It is very possible for a body to exhibit many degrees of burns at the same time. Bodies do not burn evenly, even if put into a situation that has a uniform temperature (a rare situation indeed).

As we will see, the body, due to its structure, reacts to fire according to muscle density, tissue depth, and even degree of exposure to a heat source.

It is obvious to most people what burnt flesh may look like. Most are familiar with the concept of skin slippage (the separation of the epidermis from the dermis) that can result from exposure to fire. Some are even familiar with the pugilistic pose that can be seen in fire victims. This pose was at one time interpreted as evidence that the victim was "fighting" for their life. Yet, when many people think about people trapped in buildings, we can often hear on the media the claim that nothing was found but ashes, so there was, *de facto*, no body to recover. Although a misconception, clearly, the idea that a body is reduced to "ashes" is perpetuated in western culture. The most famous reference is found within Christian burial rites. Some measure of understanding decomposition of the body breaking down to small components is certainly contained within the phrase, "ashes to ashes and dust to dust." This idea that remains eventually end up being nothing more than unrecognizable dust is further reinforced by western crematoria preparing remains in such a way that they can be "spread" by family members in locations of significance to the decedent. Of course, it is not realized by the general public that after the cremation process has taken place, which included a coffin and its accoutrements (metal items removed), the cremains are sent through a mill in order to grind the fragments to a size that will be appropriate for "viewing." This idea of the cremains being merely dust that is beyond analysis is far from the truth. This is not to say that forensic analysis of cremains is always going to be successful at answering all our questions; however, there is a great deal that may be done to chronicle who, what, when, where, and by what means, this person met their demise.

1.2 CREMAINS IN CRIMINAL CONTEXTS

A general survey of the forensic anthropology literature for reports concerning cremains in criminal contexts tend to speak of cases where a perpetrator attempted to dispose of remains so that they are not discovered (e.g., Fairgrieve and Molto, 1994). Hence, a missing person stays missing indefinitely. Yet, as noted above, the fact that, as Bass (1984) put it, one cannot completely eliminate a body by fire, attempts are still made by perpetrators to do just that. In my casework experience, I have found that the amount of work needed to render a human body to an "unrecognizable" state is clearly not appreciated by the perpetrator. This is particularly true when this is undertaken in an outdoor context.

Other criminally based contexts may include cremation burials. In these instances the cremains are relocated to another site and buried. A variation of this is the burial of cremains within an actual pit dug in order to facilitate the burn. Once completed, it is simply filled with soil. These burials can be particularly vexing to investigators if the original location of the pyre is thoroughly cleaned by the perpetrators. In one case, a fire pit of approximately 3 meters in diameter demonstrated a large amount of ash, and the remains of hinges, glass, nails, and carpentry staples—all indicative of burned furniture (Figure 1.1). After 5 days of going over this site using an archaeological recovery methodology (Chapter 4), the only human remains found were a middle phalanx of a hand and the distal (elbow) end of a humerus

FIGURE 1.1   An outdoor fire pit approximately 3 meters in diameter served as a crematory pit in a homicide case. (By permission of the Regional Supervising Coroner, Northern Ontario.)

(upper arm bone) in fragmentary condition. Given that an informant had described two individuals having been in the fire, the question then arises as to final location of the other remains. Moving of remains usually arises as a result of a perpetrator with time on their side. The realization that cremation of a body in order to render it down to what would appear to be unrecognizable portions is a labor-intensive exercise that seems to result in frustration on the part of the perpetrator. However, some perpetrators simply help the process by actively crushing the cremains using whatever implements are at hand. It is not atypical for the perpetrator to then mix the cremains, while actively crushing them. Finally, placing soil over the cremains is the final step.

The environment is a key player in the concealment of buried remains. Clandestine burials, in general, are usually done in such a way that they may be detected if one recognizes the characteristics of the burial. As one digs a hole, the entire matrix of the soil, and its respective layers, are disturbed. This also means that any air pockets or gaps in the soil matrix are destroyed. The soil is typically piled into a mound adjacent to the hole. With placement of the remains in the hole, the soil is then put back into the hole. However, the placement of that soil is not in the original order of the natural soil layers. The mixing of soil layers and the resulting compaction of the soil, due to the destruction of previously formed air pockets, make it difficult to fill the hole back in with a sufficient amount of soil. Additionally, the soil originally piled next to the grave will not all be recovered unless the perpetrator uses a ground sheet to keep this soil separated from the ground adjacent to the scene. A residual amount of soil originally taken from the grave usually remains next to the grave. Soil placed back in the grave will undergo a period of settling. This will result in the outline of the grave boundary being visible. In wet temperate climates, the grave outline may be visible as a large pooling of water due to the change in the drainage of the soil in the grave. In cases of a whole body being placed in the grave, there will often develop a second depression due to the decomposition of the body and the collapse of the body's chest. Graves dug in areas of vegetation, will also show signs of the excavation. Broken and dead plant life due to the severing of roots, and the breakage of shoots from moving a body, or even damage from a shovel, can act as clues to the location of a burial. However, it must be stressed that based upon the type of flora present, the rate of species recovery must be taken into consideration. Consultation with a forensic botanist is a necessity at all burial scenes involving plants.

In the burial environment, the body can act as a source of nutrients for the associated plant life. As the body may act as a highly concentrated source of nutrition for the associated plants, it is important to realize that an uncovered body may in fact promote the recovery of the plants on and around the grave. Buried bodies that have been covered by a tarp or shower curtain, and tightly wrapped, are not in a position to act as good sources of plant nutrition. Likewise, with the burial of cremated remains, the act of subjecting human remains to fire, acts as a means of advancing decomposition to a stage where the decomposition rate within the soil is slower than would be found in uncharred cases. In such a case, the cremains are not acting as a source of nutrition for the overlying plants.

Burials of a clandestine nature tend to be sloppy due to the rate at which they were undertaken. In essence, the perpetrator is usually trying to rid themselves of the body as quickly as possible. To that end, a grave is usually very shallow and only roughly conforms to the actual dimensions of the body. However, in the case of cremains, the body has been rendered down to bone fragments and the volume required to bury the cremains is not nearly that of a whole human body. To that end, smaller pits are dug and the cremains are shoveled into the burial. Likewise, the depth of the burial may be substantially more than a burial dug using a shovel for an intact victim due to the compacted nature of the cremains.

The quality of the cremains in the burial environment is typically very good. As most archaeologists have encountered, the carbonization of bone, and even plant materials, can act to preserve these materials for hundreds of years (e.g., Baby, 1954; Merbs, 1967; Gejvall, 1969). Such materials have been recovered from archaeological middens (the technical name for a type of garbage dump).

Another clandestine context for cremains out of doors includes the setting of forest fires in order to conceal a homicide. In such a scenario, the victim is either killed in a forested context, or the body of an already dead victim is transported to such a location. A fire is started in the wooded area with the intent that if the victim is found, their death will be misinterpreted as a result of the forest fire. The problem for the perpetrator is that the body usually does not burn to such an extent that internal organs and other soft tissues are completely eliminated. There is a great chance of the body being thoroughly, if not completely, recovered. If by happenstance a fire swept through an area with skeletal remains already present, the fracture pattern of such bones due to the heat may be distinguishable from charring of bones with flesh present (Stewart, 1979). However, Buikstra and Swegle (1989) do not support this position, so such an interpretation should be treated with caution.

Human cremains in outdoor contexts may be associated with some type of vehicular accident. The Hinton train disaster in Alberta, Canada in the early 1980s resulted in the charring of human remains (Stratton and Beattie, 1999). Aircraft crashes are also a source of such remains. It is important to note that the remains in such cases can range from superficial charring all the way to a thorough destruction of the soft tissue. In more remote areas, animal scavenging of remains may also be an issue. In one case, charred human bone material from an aircraft crash, found almost 30 years later, demonstrated signs of a hot, intense fire of short duration. Differential charring of the remains was evident. The cremains in this instance also demonstrated evidence of carnivore scavenging (Fairgrieve, 2000).

The most common occurrence of cremains in confined or indoor contexts would be with house fires. Most police investigators encounter their first cases of charred human remains in house fires or motor vehicle accidents. As popularly known, the cause of death in house fires is usually smoke inhalation. House materials, once set on fire, give off a variety of noxious chemicals that will result in the death of the victim. The charring of the body is often after death. The issue that surrounds these deaths is very much dependent upon how the fire proceeds and the location of the body in a house. If we consider a scenario where the superstructure of the house, including the joists that support the floors of a multilevel dwelling, are intact, a body on the upper floors will be largely intact and fully recoverable. However, if the dwelling has undergone a fire to the extent that the floors have collapsed, a body on the upper floors will also be subject to that collapse and fall through openings in the joists and other structural elements of the house. In short, the cremains may cascade down through the house and be deposited in such a way that they may very well be scattered over a wide area within the structure (Rhine, 1998). This also means that the cremains will also be deposited in such a way that they will fall upon material in the lower floors (Figure 1.2). This stratigraphic profile of remains in a house fire

FIGURE 1.2 This house was burned as an experiment to determine to what extent cremated domestic pigs carcasses fragment as they fall from the upper to the lower structure. (Photo by S. Fairgrieve.)

is important, as it will assist investigators in their interpretation of the victim's location in the house during the fire. Likewise, a victim trapped in the basement of a
dwelling will have material from the upper floors deposited on top of their remains.
Hence, a great deal of evidence concerning the victim may indeed be gleaned from
careful excavation, documentation, and collection of the cremains.

In order to document the remains in the aforementioned context, the means of
recovery is crucial. The days of going through these scenes searching for evidence
using metal grates and shovels should be a thing of the past. It is also important
to remember that these scenes must be considered crime scenes until determined
otherwise. This determination may not be made until well after the scene has been
processed. Hence, the processing of the scene can set the tone for the rest of the
investigation. Chapter 4 of this book will go into specific details on how to conduct
such a scene examination and how to go about extracting the remains in order to
maximize the potential information that the remains and the context of the remains
may provide.

1.3   CREMAINS IN CIVIL CONTEXTS

Although the aforementioned contexts for cremains may be clearly in the purview
of the criminal justice system, other contexts may certainly be in the realm of the
civil courts. A civil action is a legal action brought about by one party upon another
due to the suing party believing that they have been wronged in some way by the
other party. In other words, one person has wronged another, and the victim (the
plaintiff) is seeking restitution. Admittedly, this is a very simplistic view of civil
actions. Although this book deals primarily with forensic evidence in a criminal
context, it is true that many of our colleagues are being called upon in civil cases
to provide an expert evaluation (Murray and Rose, 1993; Kennedy, 1996, 1999).
Kennedy provides us with a fairly clear example where a family believes that a
funeral home has given them the wrong cremains. An examination of the cremains
was requested in order to ascertain any physical information, such as age, sex, and
race, about who may have been the source of the cremains in questions. Although
this may seem like one of the rare instances in which a forensic analysis of cremains
may be requested by a plaintiff, or defendant, in a civil action, the potential for other
cases cannot be ignored.

Plane crashes may be due to all sorts of reasons other than terrorist action.
Although the determination of the mechanical aspects of the wreckage of an aircraft
will be undertaken by qualified investigators from agencies such as the National
Transportation Safety Board in Canada, or the Federal Aviation Administration in
the United States, examination of the remains will also provide a source of information concerning the context of the crash. In the case of large aircraft, it is not atypical for the victims' remains to be found in a wide assortment of preserved states.
Some victims will be reasonably intact, while others may be severely charred or
cremated. The condition of the remains will be dictated by many factors, including
where they were sitting in the aircraft at the time of the incident. Questions, such as
their proximity to an onboard fire in the fuselage or an area that was subjected to an
explosive decompression, can be more intelligently approached once the condition

of the remains is documented and the original location of the victim has been ascertained. A case such as this would be a civil action if a determination was made that the plane crash was as the result of a mechanical malfunction due to, for example, a design flaw in the aircraft, or a maintenance issue. It would not be unexpected for the victims' families to file a civil action against the airline, manufacturer of the aircraft, and any other likely culpable parties deemed to be responsible by the legal team representing the families.

Civil actions can also be undertaken in cases of homicide. As most forensic scientists are aware, the prosecution of an individual under the criminal code is not meant to be a form of restitution to the victim's family. It is meant to serve the needs of the state in order to satisfy the criminal code. If a family wishes to pursue a civil action against an accused, such as in a case of homicide, the family would then be in a position to launch a wrongful death suit. One famous example of this would be the O.J. Simpson case from the early 1990s. Mr. Simpson was accused in the deaths of his estranged wife, Nicole Brown Simpson, and an acquaintance of hers, Mr. Ronald Goldman. As most readers are aware, Mr. Simpson was acquitted of the criminal charges of homicide in both cases. However, Mr. Goldman's family launched a wrongful death action in a private suit pertaining to Ronald Goldman. The Goldman family was successful in their suit; however, this resulted in a financial verdict, not a criminal one. As such, Mr. Simpson did not spend any time in jail in the case of the Goldman family action.

Civil actions pertaining specifically to cremated remains are certainly possible, particularly in the United States, which appears to be somewhat more litigious than Canada. Regardless, civil actions are becoming more common as relatives of victims are seeking some form of restitution in cases where family members have been killed due to a measured responsibility of another party. There appear to be no limits as to the type of cases in which cremation analysis is needed. My caution to other forensic scientists is that they should consider that they may not only be needed for criminal cases, but also for civil litigation.

1.4 FORENSIC ISSUES

In the handling of any set of human remains, be they in the form of a recently dead corpse with intact soft tissue, or highly fragmentary cremains, the forensic issues around these remains are consistent. One of the first problems is the actual mechanics of handling the remains in order to resolve these issues. The "forensic issues," as I have stated them, deal with the following: the detection, recording, collection, analysis, and interpretation of the remains, and the presentation of that evidence in a fashion that is suitable for court. All of these issues initially depend on the skills of those individuals involved in the detection and recovery of human remains. This area is one that police officers receive very little of in the way of training. Once the remains and related evidence are collected, the analysis falls to the forensic analysts involved in the case. A forensic anthropologist is the one who must perform the analysis, as most forensic pathologists have very little experience or training in dealing with cremains. However, that is not to say that forensic pathologists are not needed in this process. I have been involved in many cases in which the collaboration between the forensic anthropologist and the forensic pathologist is essential. As bodies burn unevenly, soft tissue analysis will be necessary more often than not.

It is important to consider that the issues surrounding the collection, analysis, and the reporting of results are all connected (Chapter 4 and Chapter 5). If any one of these areas is not rigorously pursued, evidence may be missed or misinterpreted.

1.4.1 Detection of Cremains

The detection or locating of human cremains may be one of the most vexing problems encountered in cases of this type. Remember that the body has been charred to such an extent that the soft tissue has been eliminated and the hard tissue remains are in a less than recognizable state. If the cremains have been subjected to further damage by a perpetrator, then the recognition of cremains becomes more of an issue. Even forensic anthropologists, who should be very comfortable with identifying fragmentary remains, may find that if they have not dealt with cremains in a highly fragmentary state, their skills will be put to the test.

It has often been heard that all that is left of the body is ashes and, as such, recovery is not a practical pursuit. As mentioned earlier, Bass (1984) clearly states that it is virtually impossible to completely eliminate a body by fire. To that end, he also suggests that one must recognize what cremains look like and how best to recover them. In Ontario, the people responsible for the recovery of human remains are usually the police with the assistance of a removal company that specializes in going to various sorts of scenes. However, the actual forensic documentation of the scene is left to the police who, under the Coroner's Act, are to assist the Coroner in the investigation of an unattended death. This means that the detection of remains is often left to the police. In the case of fires, police along with officers from the Office of the Fire Marshal, who are responsible for investigating fires, would both be involved in the search. As a forensic anthropologist, I have been called upon to participate in training of forensic identification officers and fire marshals in the recovery of decomposing human remains. In these specific instances, recovery of human cremains is definitely beyond their scope of expertise. The most extreme example of a crude search technique that I have witnessed is the use of a shovel and a metal grate to sift through the ash and debris in a house. Such an approach is certainly not practical, as those who are conducting the search do not have the range of experience a forensic anthropologist possesses when it comes to the recognition of human bone (fragmentary or otherwise).

Physical inspection of a scene for charred bone is the most practical approach to the detection of human bone material. The cremated material would ideally be excavated using a modified archaeological technique to facilitate the recording of the context. In the case of a structure fire, a list of people associated with the structure is obtained and that list is checked with the people who have so far been accounted for. Anyone who has not been accounted for would then become the object of a search.

The first stage of any search is to determine if any human remains are present at a scene. In my experience, an efficient means of making such a determination is through the use of specialized search dogs that have been trained to indicate the presence of remains when they detect a human decompositional scent. The dogs I have been using at scenes for the past several years have been trained not only on fresh decomposing human material, but also in cremated human bone. These dogs have been successful at detecting fragmentary human remains and cremains. In one case, the dogs had a positive indication on some rocks bounding a fire pit in a rural location, although they did not indicate on the fire pit itself. Upon examination of the fire pit, and with information from an informant, it was discovered that the cremains were removed from the fire pit and distributed in a nearby river, with the majority of the fragments being buried in another pit dug approximately 25 meters away. It is also of note that prior to this information being known, the cadaver dog team reported that the dogs made a positive indication on a low wooden bridge over a narrow (10 meters) river. Human cremains were recovered from the river below the bridge. In this case, the dogs were able to detect scent through snow. However, the dogs did have difficulty with picking up scent of cremains that had been buried to a depth of approximately 30 centimeters from the top of the cremains. Yet, when the area of the buried cremains was indicated by an accomplice, a scraping of the surface of the general area resulted in the cadaver dogs making a positive indication on a more precise location.

The use of cadaver dogs in the search for cremains will depend greatly on the experience of the dog, and the handler. If the dog has not undergone any training in cremains scent, then it is important to consider the use of another team. It is also important to use dogs that have been trained to only indicate on human decompositional scent. This is particularly true of dogs that are used by fire investigators. Many investigators have dogs that have been cross-trained for detecting VILs (fuels, such as gasoline), and human remains. This is actually quite problematic as you may have an instance that will likely have both scents present. In one instance, such a dog was used by police to investigate some intelligence that lead them to believe a body was located on a particular property. A dog owned by a fire investigator was called in to assist with the search. The dog identified many positive locations on the property. The problem was that with a cross-trained animal, you cannot know precisely what scent is present that the dog is indicating upon. In this instance, the search was being undertaken in a diesel engine repair yard. As such, the dog was of no use in this situation. Therefore, a dog trained only on decomposing human scent is best.

Beyond the actual excavation of the debris using an archaeological approach, another method has recently been suggested. The use of alternate light sources has been a growing area in forensic science for at least two decades. Bones and teeth have been found to strongly fluoresce in the presence of light in the violet–blue–green region and viewed with orange goggles (Craig and Vezaro, 1998). More recently, Mavin (2001) found that although cremated bone did not fluoresce with any combination of light frequency and barrier filter, cremains did appear dark purple when exposed to a light of 450 nanometers and viewed using a yellow filter. Although there may be other substances at a fire scene that may also react similarly to the

FIGURE 1.3 The remnants of a domestic pig (*Sus scrofa*) used in an experimental car fire. (Photo by S. Fairgrieve.)

alternate light source, this method would at least provide the recovery people at the scene an indication of likely concentrations of the bone, particularly if scattered and commingled.

The above methods presume that the cremains are in the most advanced state of modification due to fire. However, as most investigators realize, human remains in house fires, for example, can usually be recognized as a mass of tissue. The head area and the trunk are usually recognizable. However, this is due to the differential burning of a body (see Chapter 3). In fact, even in cases of extreme burn, the bones of a fire victim will be arranged in relative anatomical order unless some outside force has acted upon the remains to move them into a new position. Outside forces in this case may include the action of the structure falling on or around the remains, a perpetrator purposefully removing the cremains in order to obscure their presence, the action of fire personnel trying to put out the blaze, and finally, the actions of investigators not versed on how to proceed in cases of cremated human remains.

In my own experimental cremations, and found in various case reports, it is evident that the uneven burning of a body in a fire will result in the finding of a recognizably human tissue mass within car fires and other types of confined fires. Although the limbs may have burned away from the body, the torso will usually be preserved in order to facilitate a recovery. It should be noted that the other areas of the body will also be represented amongst the debris around the torso. As such, the other parts of the body that have fallen away should also be recovered (Figure 1.3).

The goal in recognition of the cremains is to maximize your recovery of the cremains, and hence, maximizing the potential of the evidence that is present. Part of that process is begun by accurately recording the context.

1.4.2 RECORDING THE CONTEXT

The context of the cremains refers to the location of all the fragments that are associated with a particular individual or set of individuals that are represented by the cremains. The position within a structure, or the orientation of the body, and how it is distributed within the associated burned material around it will all tell a story of what happened to the victim. More to the point, it will also tell us what a perpetrator has done in order for the cremains to be in the condition in which they are found.

The means for recording the context of the cremains will vary with the type of location. For example, a mass disaster will necessitate orienting all human remains found with respect to one another and the position of the central area of evidentiary concern. So, in a plane crash, the actual location of the various parts of the plane and the location of victims according to their seats may be of vital importance in ascertaining what happened to bring the plane down. Questions pertaining to mid-air explosions versus jet fuel fires resulting from the impact are all of concern to air investigators. The location and condition of the body, or portions thereof, will serve as indicators of what conditions prevailed at the time just prior to the crash. In these cases, depending on how large the debris field is, the means of recording the context of any charred or uncharred victims may have to deal with an area as large as several square kilometers, to a confined location within a field. In most instances, the remains will be marked with a flag and given a number. The recovery of the remains will be facilitated by use of a computerized surveying instrument, commonly referred to as a total station unit. These units are in common use by police services for purposes of vehicular accident reconstruction. They are ideal for most outdoor forensic contexts as they can map a small area (several square meters) or a large area with equal ease. Typically, a city's planning department will also have such a unit at their disposal.

In order to further facilitate the collection of cremains from confined scenes, a grid may be very useful, particularly during the search of the scene for cremains (Chapter 4). A grid is essentially a series of squares used to cover a location of interest. In our region, we tend to use squares that are one meter by one meter. The grid is oriented on a north–south axis (magnetic north) (Figure 1.4). This way, if the grid needs to be reestablished it would then be possible to do so. The grid has a permanent (or semipermanent) point of reference known as the datum. The datum can be the corner of a building or even a stake driven into the ground. It can even be a distant object that is well off the scene, yet can be used as a datum for the grid again and again should the need arise. However, as we are talking about a crime scene and not an archaeological site, it is rare for one to have to go back to a scene and reestablish a grid, simply due to the fact that the scene will likely have been released. As such, any new evidence found would be suspect. The squares are the means by which a systematic recovery can be facilitated.

1.4.3 COLLECTION OF CREMAINS AS EVIDENCE

Once the squares have been set, a clear delineation of duties for all personnel must be determined. The rule of thumb is to proceed from the outer areas (usually areas

FIGURE 1.4   A test excavation for a police training exercise demonstrates how a grid can be superimposed over a large area. (Photo by S. Fairgrieve.)

with lower concentrations of evidence, but not always) to the inner squares. The person in charge of the scene should consult with the forensic specialists on scene as to the appropriate number of people to be involved in the collection (recovery) of the cremains. This will depend on the size of the overall grid and the number of experienced personnel present.

If an actual excavation is required, then one person with the skill and training to recognize charred bone should be the one to dig. Another person should be assigned to assist that person in order to screen any soil that is removed from the square. In these types of cases, I suggest keeping the soil even after it is screened through one-quarter inch hardware cloth (mesh). Most of the relevant materials will be encountered in screening; however, there is a method for using water in order to recover further evidence from the soil (Chapter 4). In many instances, the squares will facilitate a systematic search of a confined area. This would typically involve the removal of debris. Care must be taken at this stage due to the potential fragility of the remains and associated evidence. Additionally, you must also take precautions to ensure that you are not injured as a result of going through this material. Confer with your colleagues at the scene to ensure all safety precautions have been exercised.

When cremains are found, it is important to leave them in their original context. They are then to be assigned evidence numbers, and photographed. Once documentation is complete and it is deemed appropriate to do so, the cremains may be removed. The one caveat to this stage is that cremains, as stated before, may be very fragile. To that end, simply by lifting the cremains or moving them may damage them further. An *in situ* analysis, including measurements and any notations of morphology (including pathology), may be desirable. Otherwise, repairs to fractures can be undertaken in the laboratory setting.

The packaging of cremains for transport to a laboratory for analysis will depend on the degree of charring of the bones and the friability of the cremains. Bones that are generally intact, with a great deal of soft tissue attached, are usually collected as you would a fresh body using a body bag. However, as the burn may have proceeded, the body may be in a more fragmentary state. If there is a discernible torso, it is most likely that a body bag on a hard surface, such as a backboard, would be appropriate. However, other associated cremains should be packaged in paper bags, in order to let the cremains dry. Padding, of some sort, may be necessary to cushion the cremains from further damage.

1.4.4 Analytical Goals

As with any investigation of human remains, cremains may provide a wealth of information in spite of the significant changes that fire has wrought. Ultimately, we want to know who the person was, the cause of death, the manner of death, and when they died. In order to achieve these overall goals, the forensic analysis of the cremains would seek to answer the questions listed in Table 1.1. These goals are typical of any forensic investigation involving human remains and even skeletonized human remains. Yet, the alterations of bone to the skeletal structure may be quite profound. To that end, the analyst must have experience in dealing with charred or cremated remains. Even a cut mark from a deep laceration can appear to be obscured due to the fire (Mayne, 1990). An experienced analyst will be able to investigate all markings on the skeleton. The analytical issues, as they pertain to cremains, can be quite complex (Chapter 5). The laboratory preparation of the cremains, as well as their direct analysis, must consider the extent to which fire has altered their morphology.

1.4.5 Taphonomic Considerations

By definition, fire is in itself a taphonomic process. Taphonomy is defined by Haglund and Sorg (1997) as the study of death assemblages. In essence, they refer to the reconstruction of the "life history" of the remains from the time of death to the time of recovery. This means that, in the forensic context, we must interpret the remains in order to distinguish between naturally occurring features and those that are due to the act of another person.

Even though fire is a taphonomic force for altering human remains, it is the context in which that fire takes place that will determine its forensic significance.

The importance of identifying the taphonomic forces that have acted upon the bone in a forensic context must, without doubt, result in a classification of those changes as being due to natural phenomenon, or artificially induced. This also means that alterations of the bone may be classified further as being either a form of pathology or pseudopathology. A misinterpretation of a scratch having been deposited during the recovery process as being a laceration from a perimortem interval, can have dire consequences in a forensic case (Chapter 5). Hence, careful analysis of all marks on the cremains is necessary for a successful outcome.

1.4.6 Commercial Cremation

Most of the general public has encountered cremation in the context of a lawful and commercial enterprise in the funeral industry. However, this is not to say that this industry is free of the forensic context. As mentioned earlier in this chapter, Murray and Rose (1993), and Kennedy (1996, 1999), relate instances of questionable crematorium practices. If we considered that the goal of a commercial cremation is to render the body of the decedent to a state of "viewable" ash, nonetheless, commercial cremations may also be subject to legal scrutiny.

1.5 EFFECTS OF FIRE ON BONE HISTOLOGY

The effect of the cremation process on the histological features of bone has implications for the consolidation, curation, and analysis of cremated hard tissues (Chapter 6).

Histological sections of bone are more commonly used in order to estimate the age at death through a quantification of osteon remodeling (e.g., Hummel and Schutkowski, 1993). Other uses have also included examining the histological arrangement of osteons for species identification (Harsányi, 1993). These studies have also considered the effects of heat on the microscopic structure of bone with an end to understand the contraction (or shrinkage) of bone (e.g., Grupe and Hummel, 1991; Holden et al., 1995a, 1995b; Huxley and Kósa, 1999; Nelson, 1992).

The above have implications for assessing the age at death of cremains, as well as whether or not the cremains are of human origin. Finally, contraction of the size of cremated bone has implications for the estimation of stature from reconstructed cremated skeletal elements.

1.6 CREMATED DENTAL TISSUES

One of the primary means of determining a positive identification of charred remains is through the comparison of antemortem odontological records with postmortem odontological observations of the victim. Teeth are an ideal source of information to draw upon for individuation due to the fact that they are the most indestructible component of the human body (Robinson et al., 1998). The fact is that of all the tissues of the body, dental tissues resist fire, desiccation, decomposition, and even prolonged water immersion. This is not to say that fire does not have an effect on teeth. Savio et al. (2006) have quantified the direct effects of varying temperature regimes on teeth and their associated restorative materials.

Yet, even the restorative materials can be eliminated in some contexts. In one study, the use of a scanning electron microscope of dental fragments was used to confirm the type, location and position of eliminated dental amalgams and composite fillings to confirm a positive identification of a murder victim (Fairgrieve, 1994). As resilient as teeth are to fire, it can be difficult to identify dental tissues without the aid of microscopy (Harsányi, 1975).

More recent advances in the use of DNA in the identification process have led to experiments in the extraction of genetic material from incinerated teeth (Williams et al., 2004). Prior to this, the examination of chromatin in cremated teeth had also been undertaken (Duffy et al., 1989, 1991).

As dependent as the forensic community is on the use of dental morphology and DNA analysis to achieve positive identifications, teeth exposed to fire can have a dramatic effect on these attempts at identification. Hence, an in-depth understanding of the ways in which dental tissues are altered by fire can only help to improve the analytical potential of cremated teeth (Chapter 7).

1.7 POSITIVE IDENTIFICATION

Ultimately, one of the central issues surrounding the analysis of human remains is to establish a positive identification. As mentioned above, much of the work that is done to establish a positive identification relies upon dental examination and/or DNA analysis. Having said this, it is not surprising to forensic anthropologists that when remains are discovered in a skeletonized state, particularly if unburied, or at least exposed to the elements, these remains are typically incomplete. Taphonomic forces act upon the body in order for nature to recycle its basic components. This fact, having been long recognized by forensic anthropologists, means that we have developed several different methods in order to establish a positive identification (for a review see Byers, 2005).

One of the main motivating factors for perpetrators selecting fire as a means of disposing of a body is so that as much evidence of the crime will be destroyed as possible. To that end, the attempt to consume a body using fire is actually an attempt to render the body to such a state that it is "burned beyond recognition." It is not atypical in such cases that the perpetrators tend to be surprised by the resiliency of the body and the amount of time, not to mention fuel, it takes to render that body down to bone. Much to the disappointment of the perpetrator, the body is now a plainly visible skeleton that is still fully recognizable as being human. Granted, there are cracks to the bone, and the skull has likely undergone some heat-induced structural alteration; however, the bones are still in their relative anatomical position. To remedy this situation, perpetrators tend to begin actively crushing the bones and commingling the remains so that they are no longer in any sort of anatomical order (Fairgrieve and Molto, 1994).

It is true that fire does have a profound effect on the recognition of an individual's body. However, one thing in favor of fire is that, while it is a means of destroying soft tissues, it is also a means of preserving some tissues, such as bone, albeit in an altered physical state. It is at this point in the analysis of cremated remains in which all of the issues that have been dealt with in arriving at an estimation of age at death, the sex of the individual, any antemortem injuries, stature, and even indicators of genetic heritage, all come together to provide an "osteobiography" (a life history as recorded in bone) (Saul and Saul, 1989, 1999) of the person. This biographical sketch of the person represented by the cremains is the first step in our process to arrive at a positive identification. In addition to information pertaining to the postmortem interval, police utilize this information to search through missing persons records for anyone fitting the supplied description. This would be challenging enough with fragmentary remains (e.g., Jerkic, 1999). However, with the added factor of heat-induced alterations (cracking, splitting, and shrinking of bone), and perhaps even incomplete recovery, the task is that much more challenging.

The above would seem to paint a rather gloomy picture for the positive identification of cremated human remains. However, this is not the case at all. Incomplete burned bodies, although not possessing soft tissue features that would permit visual identification, can be identified by other anatomical features (Emson, 1978; Grevin et al., 1998). The key to success in this area is having proper antemortem data. Fitzpatrick et al. (1996) found that by enhancing radiographs using optical or digital means, they were able to compare these records to postmortem radiographs of cremains in order to achieve a positive identification. Even postcremation DNA profiles may be used in some circumstances for identification purposes (Barbaro et al., 2003; Staiti et al., 2004; von Wurmb-Schwark et al., 2004).

Ultimately, establishing a positive identification from cremains, although not impossible, will nonetheless be a challenging exercise. As with all identifications, we are still heavily dependent upon the antemortem records of likely candidates.

1.8 SUMMARY OF CREMAINS IN FORENSIC SETTINGS

It is hoped that investigators are now clearly aware that the ubiquitous phrase, "burned beyond recognition," is a thing of the past. Fire scenes, clandestine or otherwise, may yield not only human remains that can be identified by a variety of means, but in themselves are valuable sources of information concerning the scene itself. The context of cremains is just as important as the cremains.

The key to the investigation of such scenes is, in the first instance, the ability to recognize human cremains. This is then followed by the recording of the context, and then utilizing the proper techniques in order to recover the cremains without causing additional trauma.

Finally, the analysis of the cremains has the potential to provide you with information concerning the temperature of the fire, the circumstances surrounding the location of the decedent, the age at death, sex, genetic ancestry, stature, and presence of pathology. A positive identification may also be forthcoming based on the foregoing.

Human cremains are an important forensic resource that must be handled using a best practice scenario; otherwise, evidence may be irretrievably lost.

2 Fire and Combustion

2.1 FIRE

In order to be able to interpret the damage done to human tissues by fire, it is imperative to have a clear understanding of what fire is and how it is physically altering these tissues.

Simply put, fire is a chemical reaction; more specifically, an oxidation reaction that generates heat and light (DeHaan, 2002). This process, known generally as combustion, involves the release of visible energy in the form of flames (Icove and DeHaan, 2004). Flaming combustion is, in fact, a gaseous combination in which both fuel and oxidizer are gases. An example of flaming fire would be the flames associated with any active fire such as those seen in a fireplace. Nearly all destructive fires involve flaming combustion (DeHaan, 2002). Glowing combustion occurs when the surface of a solid fuel combines with a gaseous oxidizer, typically the oxygen in air (DeHaan, 2002). Glowing combustion is exemplified by a smoldering fire, such as one would find in a mattress, or even a charcoal fire. The limiting factor between a flaming fire and a glowing or smoldering fire is the nature and condition of the fuel and its availability to oxygen.

Most people are aware of the three requirements in order to make a fire: fuel, heat, and air (oxygen). This so-called "fire triangle" needs to be refined and examined in greater detail if an analyst is to ultimately understand combustion of human tissues. The fuel in the triangle is simply the combustible material. The heat that is required must be of a sufficient level in order to raise the fuel to its ignition temperature and release fuel vapors. The oxidizing agent, oxygen (O_2) in air, must be present in a quantity that will sustain combustion. However, the fire triangle is actually now referred to as the fire tetrahedron. The fourth factor, given that all of the three aforementioned conditions are met, is an uninhibited exothermic chemical chain reaction. Without this last step, the combustion process cannot sustain itself (Icove and DeHaan, 2004).

In the case of fire, the uninhibited exothermic chemical chain reaction is simply a series of oxidative reactions. Atoms from the fuel are being oxidized. In essence, the atoms of the fuel are combining with oxygen in the air. Oxygen is the most critical component of all ordinary fires. If one eliminates oxygen from common combustion, nearly all fires would be extinguished (DeHaan, 2002).

Heat is an obvious factor in the fire process. The effects of a heat source on a particular fuel will dictate the type of fire that is encountered. As heat is applied to a flammable liquid fuel it will cause evaporation of that liquid. However, when heat is applied to most solid fuels there is a chemical breakdown of the molecular structure of that fuel (Icove and DeHaan, 2004). This process is known as pyrolysis. Pyrolysis results in the production of vapors, gases, and a residual solid (char). The actual flaming combustion of the gases from a liquid or a solid takes place within an area above the fuel's surface. This is due to the heat converting the mass of the fuel into a usable form that can be ignited and sustained, if the conditions are right. In the case of smoldering combustion, the oxygen contained within the air combines with the solid surface of the fuel itself.

2.2 FIRE TYPES

The professional literature recognizes four categories of combustion or fire types:

1. Diffusion flames
2. Premixed flames
3. Smoldering
4. Spontaneous combustion

2.2.1 DIFFUSION FLAMES

Diffusion flames are the most commonly recognized by the general public. These fuel-controlled flaming fires are best exemplified by the flames seen on candles, in campfires, and even log fires in fireplaces (Figure 2.1). Diffusion flames result from gases or vapors that diffuse from the surface of a fuel into the surrounding air. This process of diffusion permits the fuel gases or vapors to occur in an appropriate proportion with oxygen such that flaming combustion can occur. The initial application of heat to the wick of a candle results in a melting of the solid wax so that it is drawn up into the wick and thus can combine with oxygen in the air in the right proportion for combustion to take place.

FIGURE 2.1   The flame of a simple candle exemplifies a fuel-controlled flame, also known as a diffusion flame. (Photo by S. Fairgrieve.)

2.2.2 Premixed Flames

Premixed flames are a result of the combination of fuel and oxygen prior to ignition. In this instance, fuels are either vaporized liquid fuels or gases. The ignition of fuels or gas mixtures is only possible within clearly defined concentrations of the fuel and oxygen. An example of such a system occurs in any sort of internal combustion engine. Gasoline is converted into vapors that are combined with oxygen in a cylinder and then ignited by a sparkplug. If the premix has too little oxygen and too much gasoline, the ignition will fail and the engine is said to be "flooded." The proportion of the fuel and the oxygen are critical to successful combustion.

2.2.3 Smoldering

Smoldering is a slow exothermic process where oxygen combines directly with the surface of the fuel, or within the fuel if it is highly porous. Smoldering produces charring, yet without flames (Figure 2.2). The surface may glow with incandescent reaction zones if there is enough heat being produced (Icove and DeHaan, 2004). A good example of a smoldering fire is seen with a cigarette on a mattress.

2.2.4 Spontaneous Combustion

Although it may seem counterintuitive, spontaneous combustion is actually a slow chemical process. For a fuel to undergo spontaneous combustion it must be self-heating (hence, spontaneous) to the point that the heat produced is of sufficient

FIGURE 2.2 The glowing embers of this nonflaming or smoldering fire is an example of oxygen combining directly with the surface of the fuel (wood). (Photo by S. Fairgrieve.)

magnitude that flaming combustion results. The point at which this occurs is known as thermal runaway. Typically, spontaneous combustion is found to occur in natural fuels, such as peanut and linseed oils.

2.3   HEAT TRANSFER

The means by which substances, such as tissues, ignite in a fire is generally through the transfer of heat from one object to another. As heat is one of the factors in the fire tetrahedron, understanding the means by which heat is transferred to a body in order to ignite its tissues can help in the interpretation of cremated remains.

As with fire types, there are four methods by which heat transfer commences:

1. Conduction
2. Convection
3. Radiation
4. Superimposition

2.3.1   CONDUCTION

Conduction is a process by which heat, in the form of thermal energy, passes from a warmer area of a solid material to a cooler area. This process requires direct physical contact between the warmer source and the cooler target material. In house fires, heat may be conducted through walls or other adjacent objects. As the target material heats up, that same process of conduction acts to spread that heat within the same object as long as it is in contact with the source material.

2.3.2   CONVECTION

Convection is a means by which heat transfer is the result of the movement of liquids or gases from a warmer to a cooler location. As heat rises, so does the plume of hot gas produced in that fire. Fire investigators look for evidence of this on the surfaces of objects that have been in contact with a fire plume that contains these hot gases, as well as soot, ash, and even burning embers. As a general rule, the farther an object is from the fire plume, the less damage it will exhibit (Figure 2.3).

2.3.3   RADIATION

Radiation, or electromagnetic waves, transmits heat energy from a warmer to a cooler surface. Any surfaces that are facing the plume, but are not in contact with it, may be damaged by radiation. When sitting near a campfire or a fireplace, the transfer of heat to you is a result of radiation. If a gust of wind shifts the heat in your direction, the intensity of the heat transfer to you increases. Tissue burns from fires are usually the result of a combination of convection and radiation. It is the rate of that heat transfer that will dictate how quickly damage is inflicted upon animal tissues.

FIGURE 2.3 The signature of a plume inside a house fire demonstrates that items further away from the hot plume demonstrate less damage. In this case the wall of this house is only charred in the area of the flame. (Photo by S. Fairgrieve.)

2.3.4 SUPERIMPOSITION

Finally, superimposition, as the name suggests, is a combination of the effects of two or more of the aforementioned methods of heat transfer. This type of situation may cause some confusion to the fire investigator, as there will be multiple fire damage indicators.

2.4 CHEMICAL REACTIONS OF FIRE

There are many types of chemical reactions taking place in any flame. These reactions will be examined in greater detail with respect to the burning of bone tissue. However, oxidations are of the greatest interest in most fire investigations. If a simple oxidative reaction is considered, the oxidation of hydrogen (H), a fuel, would be depicted by the following chemical equation:

$$2H_2 + O_2 \Longrightarrow 2H_2O$$

In this example, the reaction proceeds in such a way that these two gases are combining to produce a more stable molecule, namely, water. Because the reaction is proceeding from two relatively unstable gases to produce a stable compound, the reaction is described as intense and exothermic (producing great heat). This basic reaction is an important one for fire investigators, as hydrogen is found in almost all fuels. Even complex molecules found in wood, plastic, and oil contain hydrogen that will combine with oxygen to produce water vapor. The burning of these compounds produces less heat than the burning of pure hydrogen. The hydrogen is bound up into more complex molecules that require more energy to break the chemical bonds holding them in place. Therefore, the energy content of complex fuels is less than that of pure hydrogen.

Carbon compounds seem to be ubiquitous in fuels. As a major component, carbon is the element around which most flammable compounds are built. The oxidation of carbon can be demonstrated by the following chemical equation:

$$C \text{ (solid)} + O_2 \Rightarrow CO_2$$

Carbon dioxide is always produced in fires of carbonaceous material. It is the end product of nearly all combustions, including those that occur in the animal body. Carbon monoxide is also produced in all fires. In this case, the oxidation of carbon to carbon monoxide is represented by the following chemical equation:

$$2C \text{ (solid)} + O_2 \Rightarrow 2CO$$

The carbon monoxide gas can achieve relatively high concentrations in structural fires (DeHaan, 2002). It is this gas that is responsible for asphyxiating fire victims.

These three reactions constitute the most basic combustion reactions of a fire. Other elements are also found in most fuels, such as sulfur. It, too, is oxidized in the fire, producing sulfur dioxide:

$$S \text{ (solid)} + O_2 \Rightarrow SO_2$$

Other elements, in addition to sulfur, that are encountered include sodium, silicon, aluminum, calcium, and magnesium. These elements are all found in wood, and when oxidized, form the white or gray ash that is seen in most fire scenes (DeHaan, 2002).

Nitrogen, an element also present in some abundance, does not burn producing an exothermic reaction. More commonly, nitrogen may be part of a nitrate that is supplying extra oxygen to the combustion reaction (DeHaan, 2002).

2.4.1 COMBUSTION OF ORGANIC COMPOUNDS

The combustion of compounds containing carbon has already been discussed, in a limited way, above. However, organic molecules require special consideration as they make up the most important fuels found to be involved in structural fires, and more germane to this book, the human body.

Hydrocarbons, compounds composed solely of carbon and hydrogen, deserve special mention because of their combustion properties. For example, methane (CH_4) is the chief component of natural gas. Although the chemical reaction of oxidizing methane seems a simple matter, it actually goes through about 100 elementary reactions in order to finally produce carbon dioxide and water vapor, as seen below:

$$CH_4 + 2O_2 \Rightarrow CO_2 + 2H_2O$$

The intermediate steps result in producing ethane and acetylene within the flame as well as unstable molecular species such as $-OH$, $-CH_2O$, and $-CHO$. These free radicals will undergo further reactions before finally producing carbon monoxide and water. The free radicals produced can only exist at relatively high temperatures. As these free radicals cool, they can condense to form pyrolysis products that are found on various surfaces after a fire. It is important to consider that this is just for the combustion of the simplest hydrocarbon, methane. With more complex hydrocarbons there are more intermediate reactions and pathways to generate a greater variety of free radicals (DeHaan, 2002).

As anyone who has taken basic organic chemistry knows, carbon atoms have a remarkable capacity for combining with one another to form chains, rings, and various other complex structures. The number of possible compounds is staggering. The petroleum industry is responsible for producing fuels that are made up of a relatively large number of compounds. As interesting and relevant as these fuels are to fire investigators, there are compounds that have greater relevance to the combustion of a human body.

2.4.1.1 Carbohydrates

The most common fuel in a structural fire is wood. Wood, in turn, is largely composed of carbohydrates. These complex molecules contain a large proportion of oxygen atoms, *de facto* being partially oxidized. So, the process of burning wood is simply a means of completing the oxidation process that was originally begun by the plant itself when that molecule was originally formed. Chemically, these carbohydrates contain carbon, hydrogen, and oxygen (essentially, carbon with water $-CH_2O$).

If the burning of a simple carbohydrate is considered, glucose for example, then the reaction would be as follows:

$$C_6H_{12}O_6 + 6O_2 \Longrightarrow 6CO_2 + 6H_2O$$

However, it is important to note that oxygen may not be as readily available to oxidize all of the carbon present. As a result, some CO will be produced as opposed to CO_2. Additionally, as hydrogen in the carbohydrate is already partially oxidized, the burning of carbohydrates, such as that in wood fires, will not generate the same amount of heat as would be found using other fuels (DeHaan, 2002).

The combustion of fats is of greater relevance to the burning of a body. Fats are composed of carbohydrates and fatty acids. Fatty acids contain a long hydrocarbon chain and a terminal carboxyl group. As fats burn, they generate significant amounts of heat and will readily burn. This should not be surprising as *triacyglycerols* are the body's chemical means of storing fuel. In fact, the yield from the complete oxidation of fatty acids is about 9 kcal/g in contrast with about 4 kcal/g for carbohydrates and proteins.

Triacyglycerols are regarded as highly concentrated stores of metabolic energy because they are reduced and anhydrous. Because triacyglycerols are highly nonpolar, they are stored in a nearly anhydrous form, whereas proteins and carbonhydrates are much more polar and, hence, more highly hydrated (Stryer, 1988). If a comparison of energy storage were made between a gram of nearly anhydrous fat and a gram of hydrated glycogen (a carbohydrate), the fat would be found to store six times as much energy. This fact alone suggests that the fats stores of a body would indeed be the greatest source of fuel, and energy, during the burning of a body. For example, a typical 70 kg male has fuel reserves of 100,000 kcal in triacyglycerols, 25,000 kcal in protein (mostly muscle), 600 kcal in glycogen, and 40 kcal in glucose (Stryer, 1988). Therefore, of all of these components, the triacyglycerols will generate the most heat and play a significant role in the combustion of the body. Further details regarding the mechanisms involved in the burning of animal tissues follow this chapter.

2.4.2 HEAT RELEASE RATE (HRR)

The heat release rate (HRR) is a measure of the amount of heat released per unit time by a heat source. The measurement of the HRR is expressed in watts (W), kilowatts (kW), megawatts (MW), kilojoules per second (KJ/s), or British Thermal Units per second (BTU/s). The general annotation for the HRR is a dot over Q.

The HRR is a good measure of the size or power of the fire (Icove and DeHaan, 2004). Babrauskas (1996) suggests that the three most important influences of the HRR are:

1. Creation of more heat.
2. Correlation with other variables.
3. Survivability of occupants.

As heat is released by a fire, the heat also feeds the fire by producing more fuel through the process of evaporation or pyrolysis. This process continues until there is no longer any adequate supply of fuel and/or oxygen to keep it going.

The rate at which heat is released is directly correlated with the production of smoke, the production of toxic by-products, the temperature of the room (if in an enclosed space), mass, heat flux, and flame height impingement. All of these variables are important for a fire investigator to evaluate the dynamics of a fire scene. Likewise, these variables all come to bear on the dynamics involved in the burning of human tissues.

As part of a fire investigation, particularly where victims are involved, the question of survivability is particularly pressing. As discussed above, the HRR correlates with many other factors. These factors can directly relate to the survivability of a fire. For example, a high HRR will produce high mass loss rates of the material being burned, which in turn, may produce toxic gases. Occupants of a structure may become overwhelmed by the resulting high heat fluxes. High heat fluxes are a measure of the rate at which heat energy is transferred to a surface per unit time per unit area (Icove and DeHaan, 2004). In this instance, large amounts of smoke at high temperatures, and toxic gases, may have a devastating effect on any occupants in a structural fire.

The heat release rate is a means by which investigators, and those interested in the analysis of human cremains, can approach a variety of questions relevant to the circumstances, that is, the manner and cause of death of victims. Icove and DeHaan (2004) list four of the questions that are commonly approached in a fire investigation. First, how hot was the fire, and could that HRR result in igniting nearby combustible materials including thermal injuries to a body? Secondly, was an ignitable liquid of sufficient quantity used in the fire, and what height did the resulting flames reach? Third, were the conditions right for flashover to occur? Fourth, when did the smoke detector(s) and/or sprinklers activate, if at all? It is clear that all of these questions are germane to not only the investigation of the cause of the fire, but also to the heat-induced trauma exhibited by human remains.

2.5   FIRE DYNAMICS

At this point, it should be clear that anyone conducting an analysis of human remains found in fires must not only have a clear grasp of fire investigation, but also be involved in the fire investigation process. The reason for this is to determine if the damage exhibited in fire debris is consistent with the injuries seen on the remains. Further, this is essential to being able to distinguish trauma that has a heat-induced origin from other trauma that does not. To that end, the following concepts involved in evaluating the dynamics of a fire are required knowledge.

The mass loss rate is, in essence, a "burning rate" (Icove and DeHaan, 2004). It is the amount of mass consumed by a fire and is expressed as the mass lost per unit time. For example, a mass loss rate may be expressed as kg/s or g/s. Experimentally, the loss of mass may be measured by weighing a fuel while it burns and observing any change in mass within a prescribed period of time. Three factors are involved in the mass loss rate: the type of fuel, the configuration of the fuel, and the area that is involved in the fire. It should be obvious that the greater the area involved, the higher the amount of energy produced by a fuel, and the position or orientation of the fuel will all have a profound effect on the HRR.

The mass flux of a burning object is also known as the mass burning rate per unit area, expressed as $kg/(m^2)$. This concept is related to the heat of vaporization in which the amount of heat that is generated results when a solid or liquid fuel is being converted to a combustible vapor.

Heat flux is the rate at which heat is striking a surface or passing through a specified area, and is expressed as kilowatts per square meter (kW/m^2). This concept is important to the interpretation of ignition, flame spread, and burn injuries. It follows that the heat flux from a source is directly related to the temperature of that source. This factor, combined with the duration, can help in determining the extent of thermal injuries if a victim is exposed to the fire.

Table 2.1 lists the minimum heat flux needed to produce thermal injuries and to ignite some common fuels. It is interesting to note that second-degree burns to the skin at 5 seconds have a radiant heat flux of 16 kW/m^2, whereas wood ignites after "prolonged exposure" at almost double that radiant heat flux (29 km/m^2). This certainly demonstrates that human tissues are much more vulnerable to thermal

TABLE 2.1
Radiant Heat Flux Rates and Their Observed Effect on Human and Selected Wooden Surfaces (drawn from Icove and DeHaan, 2004: 48, Table 2.5)

Radiant Heat Flux (kW/m^2)	Observed Effect on Humans and Wooden Surfaces
170	Maximum heat flux measured in postflashover fires.
29	Wood ignites after prolonged exposure.
20	Floor of residential family room at flashover.
16	Pain, blisters, second-degree burns to skin at 5 seconds.
10.4	Pain, blisters, second-degree burns to skin at 9 seconds.
6.4	Pain, blisters, second-degree burns to skin at 18 seconds.
4.5	Blisters, second-degree burns to skin at 30 seconds.
<1.4	Exposure to sun.

injuries than wood. This fact should be inherently obvious as sun exposure can cause a first-degree burn at $<1.4 \ kW/m^2$.

2.5.1 Fire Development

So far, the discussion of fire dynamics has concentrated on the conditions for a fire to start and to spread beyond its origins. The fact is that fire, particularly in enclosed environments, will progress in a predictable manner until it is finally extinguished due to an exhausted fuel supply. Fire reconstructionists separate the development of a fire into four separate fire phases. Each of the phases is based on specific characteristics, that are largely based on the HRR, and the timeframe in which it occurs. As a result, a fire development curve can be plotted. Such a plot can be constructed in a variety of circumstances and would thus constitute a fire signature. The phases are as follows:

1. Phase 1—Incipient ignition
2. Phase 2—Growth
3. Phase 3—Fully developed
4. Phase 4—Decay

The fire signature is used by fire investigators as a means of predicting the growth of a fire as well as determining if automated sprinkler systems, smoke, and heat detectors will activate in these conditions (Icove and DeHaan, 2004). The risk of heat exposure to a building's occupants, and even estimating evacuation times and scenarios are key considerations when utilizing the fire signature as both an investigative and research tool.

Each of the four phases, listed above, exhibit certain characteristics that can be recognized by investigators and used to evaluate a fire scene.

2.5.1.1   Phase 1: Incipient Ignition

Phase 1, or incipient ignition, is characterized by low heat, the presence of some smoke, and *no* detectable flame. The ignitability of an object depends on its density (p), its heat capacity (c_p), and thermal conductivity (k). The heat capacity is a measure of the amount of heat that must be added to an object to increase its temperature (Icove and DeHaan, 2004). By taking the product of these three factors, this will provide a measure of an object's thermal inertia (kpc_p), whereas, the thermal diffusivity is a value that results from kp/c_p. In the case of thermal inertia, the term refers to a measure of the difficulty of igniting an object. The higher this value is, the more resistant it is to ignition. This means that the ignition of an object with a high thermal inertia value will require a larger amount of heat or a longer duration of exposure to the heat.

It should not be surprising then that three levels of ignitability—easy, normally resistant, and difficult—have been established (Babrauskas, 1982 as cited by Icove and DeHaan, 2004). Fire investigators would examine a scene and note the materials present, and evaluate the dynamics of the fire in that context using ignitability.

2.5.1.2   Phase 2: Fire Growth

Phase 2, or fire growth, refers to the lateral spread of a flame, exemplified by the growth of a flame front across a horizontal surface (Icove and DeHaan, 2004). The rate of fire growth is, of course, an integral aspect of how a fire spreads. The literature refers to a common assumption that the initial growth rate geometrically approximates the square of the time that the fire has burned (i.e., a t-squared [t^2] fire). If a fire had unlimited fuel and ventilation there would likely be an exponential growth rate (Icove and DeHaan, 2004).

2.5.1.3   Phase 3: Fully Developed Fire

Phase 3, the fully developed fire, is also known as the "steady-state" phase. This phase is reached after growth has occurred and the maximum rate of burning has been reached, or there is insufficient oxygen to continue the fire. In the latter case, the fire is controlled by the ventilation properties of the fire's context. This is typically the case with fires in an enclosed structure. Under these ventilation characteristics the temperature may be greatly increased, such as seen when using a forge with a bellows to increase the oxygen and, hence, the temperature. A room in a building can reach this stage of postflashover (see below) in which case the fire is consuming all of the fuel in the room.

2.5.1.4   Phase 4: Decay

Phase 4, the decay phase, is typically initiated when approximately 20% of the original fuel is remaining (Bukowski, 1995b as cited by Icove and DeHaan, 2004). This phase is of particular relevance not only to fire service personnel, but to any fire scene specialists, including those that are concerned with any human remains. Residual amounts of toxic by-products of combustion are of great concern in this context. Likewise, high concentrations of carbon monoxide and other toxic gases produced by the smoldering remains of the structure can be extremely dangerous. It is for these reasons that it is strongly recommended that *all* smoldering fires be thoroughly extinguished prior to the recovery of human remains, particularly when the body is still in a relatively enclosed space within a building.

2.5.2 ENCLOSURE FIRES

Enclosure fires require special attention here due to the difference in fire dynamics when compared to open fires. Fires in this context should really be thought of as constrained rather than enclosed (Icove and DeHaan, 2004). The flow of air, smoke, hot gases, and even the fire growth will all be constrained within a structure.

As rooms vary in size and shape, the effects of the following variables come into play:

1. Ceiling height
2. Ventilation openings
3. Room volume
4. Location of the fire

These factors are all relevant to the effects they may have on the burning of human remains found in enclosed spaces. It has been the author's experience that perpetrators who are trying to conceal/destroy a body by fire will choose to do so within a structure rather than an outdoor context. The hope of the perpetrator is that if the body is found it will be concluded to have been the victim of a structural fire for reasons other than homicide/arson.

2.5.3 FLASHOVER

The term flashover is commonly heard in the context of enclosed structural fires. However, it bears particular importance to the burning of human remains found in structures, more specifically, fires within rooms or compartments.

Recall that Phase 2 of the development of a fire deals with the growth of the fire. This phase begins with the ignition of an object and then spreading to other objects in the room. The mechanisms through which fires spread include direct contact by a flame, radiant heat, convection, or even the immersion of the object in the hot gas layer within the room (Icove and DeHaan, 2004). The flashover occurs when all the fuel in a room or compartment is ignited and is burning as fast as possible, and is only limited by the available oxygen. Hence, flashover is really a transition from a spreading fire to a fully developed fire.

Flashover is characterized by the emission of flames from openings of the room, such as a window or a door. The upper layer of gas produced in a flashover will have a temperature that meets or exceeds 600°C. The heat flux at the floor level of the room reaches at least $20kW/m^2$ and may exceed this value (Icove and DeHaan, 2004). To bring this figure into context, upholstered furniture would certainly ignite under such conditions. Certainly, human tissue would char and begin combusting to produce burns in excess of the second degree.

The ignition of smoke in the room is referred to as flameover or rollover. The concept of a room that has a hot gas layer above no longer applies in this context. The volume of the room now consists of what is termed a mixed combustion zone (Icove and DeHaan, 2004). This means that the previously layered quality of the gases and flame found in a room is replaced by fire throughout the room. The oxygen concentration in this environment drops to below 3%, and high temperatures, commonly 1000°C, are achieved. Areas that once had some protection, such as under chairs or tables, will now be ignited.

As a crematorium will have temperatures that exceed 900°C, the finding of cremains in a room that has undergone flashover should not be unexpected. The real issue will be to assess to what extent the remains are damaged, and does this fit with the scene? Fires of longer duration will, logically, affect a larger proportion of the body.

2.6 SUMMARY

Understanding the nature of fire, or more specifically, combustion, is a necessary prerequisite to the documentation of cremains at a fire scene and their subsequent analysis. The discovery of human remains in forensic contexts, and for that matter, all death scenes associated with fires, should be considered as suspicious until proven otherwise. To that end, the analysis and interpretation of the remains must always begin at the scene. The interpretation of the cremains is best done in their original context. It is through attending the scene that the forensic anthropologist can best direct any aspects of *in situ* documentation that is usually undertaken by forensic identification officers.

The extent of the damage done by fire can be extremely confusing to the non-specialist. It is for this reason that the investigation be a collaborative effort between the fire investigator, police, coroner, and any other forensic specialists, including the forensic anthropologist.

As the above has chronicled the details of how fires work and their overall dynamics, the forensic expert must be able to recognize all manner of heat-induced alterations to a human body. As mentioned above, the course of a fire is predictable. However, the caveat associated with that statement is that the context of the fire dictates how that fire has begun, undergoes growth, and eventually, decays. It is within this same paradigm that the assessment of human remains must be approached.

.

3 The Cremation Process

3.1 INTRODUCTION

The layman is clearly under the mistaken impression that a body can be easily reduced down to ashes and thus not be recovered from a fire scene. On occasion, forensic anthropologists are asked to recover and analyze human remains from a fire scene. This concept of completely eliminating a body by fire has crept into everything from religious doctrine that refers to decomposition (i.e., "…ashes to ashes and dust to dust.") to popular culture as evidenced by countless movie scripts and books where fire is used by a perpetrator to destroy evidence. Yet, it is clearly understood by any of us in the field that this is not the case.

As with any area of forensic recovery, if you do not know what you are looking for, you will not recognize it when you encounter it. Therefore, it is crucial that, in an endeavor to recover human remains from any fire scene, a team include someone with training in human cremains recovery and analysis. In addition to expertise in fragmentary bone recovery and documentation, the forensic anthropologist must have an explicit understanding of how a body burns, and the effects this will have on the various tissues of the body.

The burning of a body is not simply the combustion of the tissues resulting in a pile of ash to be lamented over. The burning of a body proceeds in a regular fashion under a particular set of circumstances. The tissues will pass through the various degrees of burning, as seen in clinical contexts on living individuals. These different degrees have well-defined diagnostic parameters. However, as a body does not burn evenly, it is possible to see remains with all four degrees present. This fact may aid an analyst in evaluating the temperature, location, and duration of a fire.

The position of the body in the context of the fire is also an important consideration. Again, if the recovery team is not able to recognize charred bone fragments and the skeletal elements to which they belong, it will not be possible to say anything regarding the body position.

Finally, fire can have a profound effect on the area where there is suspected trauma. The heat of a fire may mimic trauma on the remains, creating a pseudo pathology (false pathology), or the pathology may be obscured by the action of the fire.

The burning of human tissues will clearly cause macroscopic and microscopic changes. Yet, these changes may affect our ability to conduct any kind of analysis. Fortunately, there is a literature base to help resolve these problems; however, one's ability to do so is predicated on a firm understanding of the cremation process.

As indicated in Chapter 2, the severity of the burn is dependent upon the intensity of the heat and the time of exposure (Bohnert et al., 1998). Intuitively, most of us know from day-to-day experience that meat in an oven may be burned if left for too long. To speed up the cooking process, increasing the temperature may help in cooking meat, but if the temperature is too high the outer layers of the meat will burn before the inside is cooked, depending on the thickness of the meat. Prolonged exposure will eventually lead to charring over the entire surface of the meat. With further exposure, the heat will affect the deeper portions of the meat and eventually dry it out, and it may even reach a critical temperature to sustain its own flame. The same can be said of bodies exposed to a heat source.

The temperature of a fire is linked to the type of material being burned. Different types of wood are known to be hot and fast burning, while others provide a long, steady burn at a consistent temperature. If we consider the potential fuel sources, there is a wide array of temperatures possible in any given fire situation. However, a fire in a house will not generate temperatures that we would see in some chemical fires.

A confined space in which the heat of a fire may be concentrated will result in an increased temperature. The most extreme example of this is a crematorium using natural gas as its fuel source. The body of an adult can be reduced to bone and ash at about 1500°F in 1–1.5 hours (Spitz, 1993). The body of a child (5 years of age or less) will be reduced faster due to the size difference, and lower level of mineralization of the bones. Spitz (1993), in fact, relates that a body of a newborn infant can be incinerated in an ordinary oven in less than 2 hours. There are, of course, other factors that can influence how a body will burn (see below). However, these factors cause minor variations that will be seen on the body as differential preservation.

The effects of fire on human tissue will vary according to the proximity of the body to the fire, the temperature reached by the fire (which is a function of the type of fuel), and the duration of exposure to the fire. Regardless of these factors, a body will undergo heat-induced damage in a regular and predictable fashion. A full appreciation of this process is a necessary first step in the analysis of cremated human remains.

3.2   DEGREE OF BURNS

The clinically defined degrees of tissue burns are based on the intensity and duration of exposure to the heat source. Therefore, the degrees listed below also act as an indicator of the process of burning.

3.2.1   FIRST-DEGREE BURNS

Burns of the first degree are the most superficial. The outer layer of skin is damaged in such a way that peeling of the upper layer of the epidermis of the skin may follow the incident. It is usually characterized by a redness and swelling of the site of the burn. Redness is due to the increase in blood to this area as a result of vasodilatation. The accompanying swelling is due to an edema also found in the area. A mild sunburn is a good example of a first-degree burn.

3.2.2   SECOND-DEGREE BURNS

The next step in the burn process is the destruction of the superficial layers of the skin. In these cases, the hallmark of second-degree burns is the formation of blisters over the affected area. The base of the blistering does not go deeper than the epidermal layer of the skin. This category can be further subdivided into two other levels, namely, 2a and 2b. The first of these sublevels deals with burns in the upper layers of the epidermis, whereas the second deals with necrosis of the entire thickness of the epidermis down to, but not including, the dermis itself.

3.2.3 THIRD-DEGREE BURNS

Once the heat passes beyond the superficial layers, the heat would then act directly on the entire thickness of the dermis and proceed into the hypodermis. The depth of these third-degree burns will result in the destruction of nerve endings, so the pain that was experienced with the first two degrees would not be present in these cases. It is in cases such as this that skin grafts are required for a patient's recovery.

3.2.4 FOURTH-DEGREE BURNS

Finally, fourth-degree burns are characterized by the destruction of all the layers of the skin and the underlying tissues, including muscle, tendon, and ultimately, bone (Spitz, 1993). Some authors, such as DeHaan (2002) list a fifth-degree categorization of burns that include underlying muscle and bone. However, it is certainly clear that fourth-degree burns involve the charring of underlying (i.e., beneath the skin) tissue. It is equally clear that once charring of bone occurs there will not be any subsequent viability of that tissue. That having been said, the burning of bone is a different process than the burning of soft tissues, due to its hard inorganic matrix.

As with all other tissues, bone does not burn easily. Bone has a tough inorganic matrix of salts that provides bone with its rigid structure, but there is also a softer organic portion, largely composed of collagen and noncollagenous proteins that provide structural flexibility. Among the organic portions of bone is bone marrow, found in a marrow cavity running the length of the long bone, and also in a network of spongy bone found in flat, short, and irregular bones. Once the soft tissue around bone is eliminated, the fire then acts on the bone and all its components. However, there are many other tissue effects to consider before the direct exposure to bone can be discussed. The burning of soft tissues, such as muscle, can affect the position of the body as well as the differential states of preservation of the remains.

3.3 THE CROW–GLASSMAN SCALE (CGS) OF BURNED REMAINS

The Crow–Glassman Scale for describing the extent of burns to the remains of a fire victim follows the premise that bodies decompose generally following a systematic pattern based on increased exposure to fire temperature and duration (Glassman and Crow, 1996).

The inspiration to develop such a system arose from the degree scale described above for fire survivors. Further, Glassman and Crow (1996) note that by having such a scale in place, first responders are able to describe the conditions of remains to the medical examiner/coroner to better assess the types of consultants that should be at the scene. The other intent of this scale (as described in Table 3.1) is to standardize the description of these remains for reporting purposes by professionals associated with recovery and analysis of these scenes, and their associated remains. Glassman and Crow (1996) also include in their levels recommendations on personnel that should be considered in the recovery and identification process (Figure 3.1).

Traditionally, reference to the cremation of human remains in the forensic literature has separated the burning of soft tissue from hard tissue (Thompson, 2005). This seemingly logical separation is due to the inherent differences in these matrices. However, Thompson (2005) argues that these two tissue types are intrinsically connected as a unified system. To that end, the nature of the burning of these tissues should be considered jointly. As the literature base does tend to treat the combustion

---

TABLE 3.1
The Crow–Glassman Scale for Burn Injury to Human Remains (compiled from Glassman and Crow, 1996)

CGS Level	Description
1	Burn injuries characteristic of typical smoke death. The body may exhibit blistering of the epidermis and singeing of the head and facial hair. Recovery of the body is similar to that for other victims not involving burn injury. The body is recognizable for identification at this level.
2	The body may be recognizable, but most often it exhibits varying degrees of charring. Further destruction of the body is limited to the absence of elements of the hands and/or feet, and possibly, the genitalia and ears. Additional searching near the body is warranted for recovery of disarticulated elements. Identification is made, most often, by the collaboration of the medical examiner and a forensic odontologist.
3	Further destruction of the body is demonstrated by missing major portions of the arms and/or legs. The head is present at this level although identity is not evident. The search area for associated disarticulated remains should be widened. A forensic anthropologist should be included to facilitate successful search and recovery procedures at the death scene. Identification is coordinated by a medical examiner who may require the aid of a forensic odontologist. If needed, a forensic anthropologist may be called on to determine sex, age, race, etc. from the skeleton.
4	The skull has fragmented and is absent from the body. Some portions of the arms and/or legs may still remain articulated to the charred body. Search and recovery should be aided by a forensic anthropologist using systematic bioarcheological methods including screening procedures to locate small body fragments and dental elements. Identification is coordinated by a medical examiner using a forensic anthropologist and an odontologist as consultants as needed.
5	The body has been cremated and little or no tissue is present. The remains are highly fragmentary, scattered, and incomplete. A forensic anthropologist should be an on-site consultant for the identification and recovery of cremains. Personal identification is most difficult at this level and a forensic anthropologist may be best trained to interpret cremains for identifying physical attributes of the deceased. Recovery of dental elements will require the expertise of a forensic odontologist. As with all fire deaths, a medical examiner is, most likely, designated to coordinate consultant activities.

FIGURE 3.1   The Crow–Glassman Scale level #5 is exhibited by these remains. (By permission, Regional Supervising Coroner, Northern Ontario.)

of these two tissue types separately, the subsequent sections of this chapter will deal with the effects of fire on these tissues in a similar format. Regardless of the arguments posed by Thompson (2005), the fact remains that the burning of these tissues is going to commence with the most superficial layers first and continue, with time, to the deeper tissues.

3.4   SOFT TISSUE

Initially, soft tissue burns proceed as indicated in the descriptions found in Section 3.2. As outlined in the CGS above, postmortem burns do have a characteristically different appearance than burns found on a live victim. Postmortem burns are never reddened by the natural inflammation reaction exhibited in living tissue. Postmortem burns exhibit a characteristically hard consistency with a yellowish appearance (Spitz, 1993).

For the purposes of this book, the alterations of tissues due to smoke inhalation will not be dealt with here. Although it is important for investigators to consider that in cases of bodies found with intact soft tissue, CO levels in hemoglobin are key to the investigation of the vitality of the person at the time of the fire. The assessment of CO levels in hemoglobin, and the deposition of soot in the trachea are undertaken by the pathologist and the toxicologist.

Given the degrees of burns that have been documented on living fire victims, and those levels used in the CGS assessment of burned bodies found at the scene, the broad spectrum of morphological manifestations of burns on any one set of remains should be anticipated.

Soft tissue heat-induced damage can range from small foci of superficial burns to areas demonstrating calcination of bone tissue. Table 3.2 summarizes the related external and internal findings on bodies exposed to heat (Bohnert et al., 1998).

TABLE 3.2

The Effects of Heat on the Body and Related External and Internal Findings (drawn from Bohnert et al., 1998)

Effects of Heat	External Findings	Internal Findings
Burns	Burns of skin Singing of hair Consumption by fire	Burns and consumption of internal organs and bone Edema, mucosal bleeding, and detachment of the mucosa of airways
Changes of content and distribution of tissue fluid	Skin blisters	Vaporization of body fluids Rupture of abdominal wall with prolapse of intestinal loops Leakage of fluid from mouth and nose Heat hematoma Accumulation of fat in body cavities, vessels, or heart
Heat fixation	Leather-like brownish fixation of skin	Induration of internal organs and muscles Fragmentation of erythrocytes
Shrinking of tissue	Tightening of skin Splitting of skin Protrusion of tongue Petechial hemorrhages of neck and head Pugilistic attitude	Shrinking of organs "Puppet organs"

The kind of heat a body is exposed to in a fire scene will have an influence on the burning of the body. For example, the loss of body mass is more pronounced from a direct fire than radiant heat (Bohnert et al., 1998). This difference is a result of the body itself acting as a fuel source for the fire, whereas radiant heat acts to reduce body mass by eliminating tissue fluids.

In general, as heat progresses, the epidermis and its appendages (i.e., hair and nails) are also profoundly affected. The process of burning tissue is very much a process of the tissues acting as either a direct fuel source or undergoing dehydration.

The initial reaction of skin to heat is a dilating of the dermal and epidermal blood vessels. As heat exposure and/or an increase in temperature continues, the circulation to this area ceases. As indicated by the description of degrees of fire injury, burns then tend to proceed to blistering of the skin, which can include the slippage and gloving of the epidermis from the dermis.

At the same time, hair is undergoing heat-dependent alterations. When a temperature in excess of 300°C is attained, the hair is charred. The keratin of hair begins to melt at 240°C. Finally, as the heat of the fire increases, the hair is consumed in the fire.

A commonly encountered reaction to fire exposure is a *heat rupture*. Heat ruptures can occur before or after death. These ruptures, also referred to as splitting of soft tissue, superficially resemble lacerations or incised wounds. However, unlike lacerations, there is no bleeding due to the coagulation of blood vessels by the heat. In fact, blood vessels and nerves in the deepest portion of the rupture are intact. The margins of ruptures are irregular and lack any signs of vital reaction. There is also a lack of bruising around the ruptures. These ruptures can be found anywhere on the body, including the scalp (Spitz, 1993; DeHaan, 2002).

As the burning of soft tissue proceeds, the contraction of the epidermis and the underlying dermis, due to the fire's dehydrating effects, exposes the hypodermis and the underlying subcutaneous fat. In this situation, the fat can act as a source of fuel for the fire (DeHaan and Nurbakhsh, 2001). The presence of clothing, assuming it has survived the fire up to this point, can act as a wick for any adjacent fat (Spitz, 1993; DeHaan et al., 1999). The net effect is an increase in the rate of cremation as well as the completeness of the burn. It should also be noted that tight clothing, such as shoes, socks, clothing with an elastic, and even belts, may act to exclude air, and hence hinder the progress of the fire on a victim.

Cremated bodies are most commonly encountered in house fires. It has been purported that a body exposed to temperatures between 670° and 810°C will show the "pugilistic attitude" or "pose" after approximately 10 minutes (Bohnert et al., 1998). After 20 minutes of exposure, the vault of the skull would be free of soft tissue and even the outer table would exhibit fissures. If the body continues to be exposed for another 10 minutes, the body cavities (i.e., internal organs) are visible. At the 40 minute mark the internal organs have shrunk and demonstrate a "net-like or sponge-like structure" (Bohnert et al., 1998). Fifty minutes into this process the extremities "are destroyed" (meaning no longer in a complete state), leaving the torso. From 1–1.5 hours the torso is broken down. In total, the incineration of the body, in this temperature range, takes about 2–3 hours.

Bohnert et al. (1998) have not been the only ones to qualitatively assess the effects of fire on human remains. Günther and Schmidt (1953) and Richards (1977) have all examined the destruction of the body as a unit. These studies are very much complements of one another. To that end, Table 3.3 and Table 3.4, adapted from Bohnert et al. (1998), deal with the findings of these three studies on the skull and the remainder of the body, respectively. If we compare the condition of a body to the surrounding structure, in the same amount of time, a timber would be charred to a depth of half an inch or so (DeHaan, 2002).

Differential charring of tissues is a fact in cremation contexts. One study suggests that exposures of the bones of the arms, rib cage, and face would occur at 1200°F in about 20 minutes. This presumably means those areas that are closest to the surface of the skin, as opposed to those areas that are deeper to associated muscle. The anterior tibial margin is also reported to be exposed after 25 minutes at the same temperature, with the femur and the rest of the tibia and fibula (i.e., lateral side of the lower leg) not being exposed before 35 minutes (Spitz, 1993).

All of these studies presuppose a uniform temperature and an even exposure to that temperature. Yet, the reality is that heat tends not to be uniform, especially if the fire is not in a confined area, or there are various types of fuel present. In fact, the flame temperatures and durations reached in a frame house fire will not be sufficient to destroy skeletal remains of an adult or even all of the soft tissues of the

TABLE 3.3

The Effects of Fire on the Skull (drawn from Bohnert et al., 1998)

Time	Günther and Schmidt (1953) 1000°–1100°C	Richards (1977) 680°C	Bohnert et al. (1998) 670°–810°C
8–10 min	Soft tissues of the face charred		Skull-cap free of soft tissue, soft tissue of the face charred
13–16 min	Forehead and vertex free of soft tissue, protruding facial bones calcined	Bones of the face showing	
20 min		Skull showing	Sparse soft tissue remains in the face, heat fractures of the skull-cap
20–25 min	Severe shrinkage of soft tissues at the skull, calvaria breaks, brain superficially charred, destruction of prominent parts of the facial skull		
30 min			Tabula externa of the calvaria crumbling
40 min			Brain showing, bones of face begin to disintegrate
50 min			Bones of face largely destroyed, base of skull showing
45–75 min	Base of skull still intact, head sometimes severed from trunk		

torso because of the significant percentage of water found in those tissues (DeHaan, 2002). Yet, there will be significant alterations to those bones due to their exposure to the fire.

Accelerants are materials that literally accelerate or enhance the burning process. They tend to be highly inflammable substances that have been designed to act as fuels in internal combustion engines of all sorts. In the forensic context, kerosene and gasoline are the most readily available, and hence most commonly encountered. Burns as a result of kerosene or gasoline result in a patchy distribution of charring of variable degrees of burning. Readily recognizable aspects of the face and anterior dentition may be severely damaged, while the chest and abdomen are not nearly as severely burned (Spitz, 1993). Any ignited adipose tissue may undergo prolonged smoldering in a defined area. As accelerants tend not to combust completely, residual accelerants may be detected in clothing and even underlying soil.

As the skin chars and heat ruptures appear, the heat will also have an effect on muscle tissue. All of the muscles of the body contract due to the heat. Heat contractures proceed in such a way that the dominant muscles, the major flexor muscles of the body, overpower the contractions of the extensor muscles, producing the characteristic "boxer's" or "pugilistic" attitude or pose. The actual rigidity of the

TABLE 3.4
Effects of the Fire on the Trunk and Extremities (drawn from Bohnert et al., 1998)

Body Region	Time	Richards (1977) 680°C	Bohnert et al. (1998) 670°–810°C
Thorax/abdomen	20 min	Ribs showing	Thorax muscles charred, ribs and sternum showing
	30 min		Thoracic and abdominal cavity exposed, organs blackened and shrunken
	40 min		Shrunken, charred organs with bumpy surface
	50 min		Organs largely consumed by fire
Arms	10 min	Arms badly charred	Pugilistic attitude
	15 min	Arm bones showing	
	20 min		Hands are largely destroyed, ulna and radius partially showing
	30 min		Hands and distal forearms burned away
	40 min		Forearms completely consumed, upper arms largely free of soft tissue
	50 min		Arms burned away
Legs	14 min	Legs badly charred	
	20 min		Carbonization of muscles
	25 min	Shin bones showing	
	30 min		Tibia and distal femur free of soft tissue
	35 min	Thighs and shins completely bone	
	50 min		Calcined stumps of the thighs

body, which develops during the cooling process, is due to the denaturation of the muscle proteins (Spitz, 1993). In this context, the arms tend to be raised above the shoulders, with the elbows flexed, and the fingers curled almost into a fist. The head is often extended (looking superiorly) as a result of the contraction of the massive muscle mass at the back of the neck. The masticatory muscles will contract, acting to close the mouth unless the tongue was previously protruding out of the mouth. The back may exhibit hyperextension. The thighs will likely be flexed relative to the torso, with a marked flexion of the knees. The feet will be plantar flexed with the toes curled. This position is not to be confused with postmortem rigidity or rigor mortis. If a body is burned with fixed rigor mortis or has already passed through that stage, a pugilistic pose will *not* be in evidence. This reaction of muscles to the heat of a fire would account for the observation in outdoor funerary cremation pyres, such as in the Hindu culture in India, of the body appearing to move, and even sit up during the cremation process.

The pugilistic position of a body must be considered in the search for remains. Different areas of the body, such as the arms and legs, will fall away from the rest of the body as the cremation progresses. However, if the intensity of the heat is maintained or increases, a pugilistic pose may not occur due to the pose generally being assumed as the fire, and the body, cools.

As the skin and muscles undergo direct charring, the increase in heat to deeper portions of the body starts to affect the internal organs. With increased heat inside the skull, the formation of a heat hematoma may occur (Polson and Gee, 1973). A heat hematoma may be originally interpreted as an extra-dural hematoma. The clot has a light chocolate color or even a slight pink appearance due to blood saturated with carbon monoxide (CO). This soft, and friable clot is not solid throughout. It has more of a honeycombed appearance due to bubble formation from the heat. This is not to be confused with an intracerebral hemorrhage as the cause of death (e.g., Chiba et al., 2003).

With the destruction of the skin and the progressive burning of muscle tissue, the area of highest concentration of soft tissue, the trunk of the body (thoracic, abdomen, and pelvic regions) will tend to be the last to go. Although fire may have ignited subcutaneous fat, the heat will have the effect of cooking the internal organs from the surface. Again, uniform burning would be the exception rather than the rule. As a result, even though the limbs and head may be significantly damaged, the internal organs may be well-preserved. This preservational state will often yield the recovery of tissue samples and other fluids that may be subjected to toxicological analysis, and in some cases, histological analysis.

By now it should be clear that the elimination of soft tissue by fire is not a simple task. Yet, there are many forensic cases in which the circumstances have resulted in the complete elimination of soft tissues and significant damage to the underlying hard tissue.

3.5 HARD TISSUE DAMAGE

3.5.1 INTRODUCTION

Hard tissues usually refer to bones and teeth. However, cartilage is a precursor to the development of bone, so in some instances it may also be included in this category. Yet, cartilage will burn in much the same fashion as any of the soft tissues.

As a tissue, bone is a vascularized, living, and constantly changing mineralized connective tissue. Bone consists of cells and an intercellular matrix. This matrix is composed of organic materials, primarily collagen (~20%), and inorganic salts composed largely of calcium and phosphate in the form of hydroxyapatite.

Bone tissue occurs in two forms: dense, compact lamellar bone, and spongy or cancellous bone. The location and proportionality of these two types of bone tissue will dictate how bone tissue is altered in a fire.

Teeth also have a hard matrix of inorganic salts; however, enamel does not regenerate once formed. Cementum, the tissue covering the roots, can have appositional layers of cementum added over time. Dentin, deep to both enamel and cementum, does not so much regenerate as, like cementum, it adds a layer from inside the pulp chamber of the tooth, called secondary dentin.

The process of burning bone is essentially a process of dehydration and recrystallization. Once muscle is eliminated, the next tissue to undergo heat stress is the periosteum, a thin epithelial tissue covering the bone, providing it with a blood and nervous tissue supply. However, the heat easily disperses within the periosteum by charring it directly and flaking off easily.

The direct burning of the bone is going to occur in the areas that are closest to the surface of the body. These areas include the knuckles, elbows, the acromion of the scapula, the neurocranium, the chin, the bridge of the nose, the knees, ankles, and the phalanges of the hands and toes. Areas with a greater density of soft tissue will be charred later in the process. Areas that are insulated from the fire, such as the back and buttocks (if the body is in a supine position), will be the last to burn. In other words, points of contact the body may have with an object or the ground can result in delayed exposure. This differential burning will continue with the direct charring of bone.

With the elimination of macroscopic soft tissue (i.e., the epidermis, dermis, hypodermis, adipose, muscle, and other soft connective tissues) the bone will undergo heat-induced alterations. As in diseases that leave a pathological finding on bone, hard tissues have a limited repertoire of response to heat. Bone will undergo dehydration and be subjected to the corresponding changes. Specifically, the elimination of water, and the subsequent consumption of the organic portion of bone and the microstructural alterations to the hard matrix of bone resulting in a color change, as well as splitting and warping.

3.5.2 HEAT-INDUCED COLOR CHANGES TO BONE

The most persistent remains encountered at cremation scenes are the remnants of bones and teeth. The macroscopic appearance of the varying colors encountered on these specimens has been of great interest to cremation researchers (e.g., Lisowski, 1968; Bonucci and Graziani, 1975; Gejvall, 1969; Heglar, 1984; Shipman et al., 1984; Mayne, 1990; Mayne Correia, 1997). It is considered as fact that the color of bone can provide information pertaining to the physical condition of the bone and the context of the burn. Table 3.5 provides a summary of the interpretations of the various colors encountered on cremated bone.

Although the colors exhibited on cremated bone may be indicators of fire temperature, duration, and combustion circumstances, these colors may all be present on the same bone at the same time. Variation in fuel load, oxygen availability, and even bone contact with metals may account for the range of colors encountered on bones from a fire scene.

Some sense of this process is best considered by examining the process of bone being exposed to heat in relation to its relative anatomical position. This factor alone can explain much of the variation in color encountered on the same bone and/or adjacent bones.

The direct charring of bone on the extremities proceeds first. The extremities, namely the arms, legs, and head, will have bone directly charred in the regions previously mentioned. The evidence of exposure to fire is indicated by a characteristic color change to the bone. The bone will first exhibit a surface that appears to be light amber. At this stage the organic components of the bone have not been completely eliminated. In fact, the periosteum may still be intact in these areas. However, as

TABLE 3.5
Interpretation of Color Change to Cremated Bone

Color	Interpretation	References
Brown	Hemoglobin and/or soil discoloration	Gejvall, 1969; Lisowski, 1968
Black	Carbonized bone due to burning in O_2 starved context	Herrmann, 1970
Gray-blue, gray	Pyrolized organic components	Dokládal, 1969, 1970
White	Calcination; complete loss of organic portion and fusion of bone salts	Mayne Correia, 1997
Other Colors: green, yellow, pink, and red	Burning in the presence of metals, including copper, bronze, or iron	Dunlop, 1978; Gejvall, 1969; Lisowski, 1968

the process continues, the bone begins to blacken. At this stage the periosteum has been eliminated and the inorganic components of the bone, along with any leaching bone marrow, are combusted. The bone itself is now feeding the fire. Researchers studying the microstructure of burnt bone have found that the lamellar bone structure is intact (Holden et al., 1995a). This is important, as histological aging may be a means of contributing to an age at death estimation. The black color indicates that the bone, in this case cortical bone, has attained a temperature of approximately 300°C (Holden et al., 1995a). This is the temperature of the bone itself and not the air surrounding it.

In the temperature range of 200–400°C the ultrastructural orientation of collagen fibers is well preserved in older individuals who have well-mineralized bone, such as that found in older adults.

Bone that has turned gray has reached a temperature of at least 600°C. This gray color is further evidence that the organic portion of the bone has leached out even further. In this case, the bone exhibits the development of small spherical-type crystals. These spherical-type crystals, as described by Holden et al. (1995a), measure approximately 0.06 ± 0.007 μm in diameter. As the heat intensifies, these crystals will alter their shape and size. The lamellar bone pattern is less well organized. As an age effect, the size of the crystals exhibits a decreasing trend with age. This is, once again, due to the degree of mineralization of the bone.

As the heat rises, the bone can take on a blue–gray appearance that will eventually yield to become white. The white color of bone is found to occur in bone that has attained a temperature of at least 800°C. Of course, the bone could attain temperatures in excess of 800°C, but the white color is an endpoint color in this process. At this point the crystals are now a hexagonal-type, measuring from 0.25 ± 0.07 μm to 0.41 ± 0.09 μm in size, and there is no discernable lamellar pattern to the bone (Holden et al., 1995a). As such, histological examination would be a fruitless exercise. In older individuals the overall quality of the hexagonal-like crystal mor-

TABLE 3.6

Bone Temperature and Resulting Bone Color (compiled from Holden et al., 1995a)

Temperature (°C)	Color Effects
300	Black color of cortical bone
200–400	Ultrastructural orientation of collagen fibers is well preserved
600	Gray color indicates a leaching out of the organic portion
800	White color of bone

phology improved with the age of the deceased. Again, an age effect on the crystal morphology is once again demonstrated.

It has been postulated by Holden et al. (1995a) that based on an examination of the color, the degree of fraying of individual collagen fibers, the lamellar bone orientation, and the formation of crystals, a bone may be placed into an age group. Holden et al. (1995a) admit that this would only serve as a rough estimate of the age, but it may assist in the sorting of commingled cremains in a highly fragmented condition (Table 3.6).

Recently, the relationship of cremated bone color to organic content and oxygen availability has been explored by Walker and Miller (2005). In this study, black bone and white (or calcined) bones were produced in the same temperature scenarios. Yet, with an increase in the exposure time, the influence of oxygen availability on bone color was found to gradually diminish. As it was also found that bone collagen persisted in specimens exposed to temperatures as high as 600°C, bone color was found to actually be an indicator of collagen content. Indeed, in a pilot study by Marsh and Klem (2002) it was found that the depletion of collagen yield from bone did decrease with the increased temperature and time of exposure. However, their study did not attempt to correlate the collagen yield with cremation color.

The color change is associated with the elimination of the organic constituents of the bone. The progression of color change is roughly from black to gray to white. Some studies have indicated that some other colors occur, such as browns, and even shades of red (e.g., Shipman et al., 1984). However, Holden et al. (1995b) found that when bone has reached 600°C it has consistently turned a gray color. The elimination of collagen fibers, proteins, and fats in the bone tissue was found to be complete at 600°C. Beyond this temperature the aforementioned production of spherical-type and then hexagonal-type crystals proceeds at the ultrastructural level. In addition to this, the color eventually changes to white. This white stage is also known as the complete, "calcined," or "calcinated" stage. This is the extreme outcome of bone recrystallization.

3.5.3   HEAT-INDUCED MORPHOLOGICAL CHANGES TO BONE

The ultrastructural changes are all associated with the dehydration process, or drying, of the bone as the cremation progresses. A change in color is not the only macroscopic alteration associated with heat. A structural breakdown of bone, as suggested by the changes noted above, is also going to occur.

The dehydration process involved with burning bone is actually the combustion of organic materials; this process then continues with a recrystallization of the hard matrix and will result in a contraction (shrinkage) in the bone's normal dimensions. Further, there is also a warping effect on the bone. At the same time, cooling of the bone also results in the development of cracks or fractures. All of these changes will impact the metrical analysis necessary for the osteobiographical characterization of the cremains.

3.5.3.1   Heat-Induced Fractures

On long bones there are several different types of fractures (Stewart, 1979; Hermann and Bennett, 1999). *Patina* fractures are a type of fracture that is observed on the surface of the bone, typically on flat bones, and even on the surfaces of long bones (Figure 3.2). These fine cracks do not penetrate through to the medullary cavity of the bone. *Longitudinal fractures* follow the long axis of a long bone and may penetrate to the marrow cavity of the bone (Figure 3.3). The longitudinal direction follows the orientation of collagen fibers along the cylindrically oriented osteons. *Curvilinear (or curved transverse) fractures* circumscribe the long bone shaft proceeding around from one side of the bone to the other (Figure 3.4). They may be extensions of longitudinal fractures and even exhibit an oblique orientation. *Transverse (or straight transverse) fractures* are perpendicular to the longitudinal axis of a long bone. Transverse fractures tend to penetrate through to the medullary cavity and may even result in a complete transection of the bone (Figure 3.5). Finally, *delamination fractures* appear as peeling or flaking of bone layers, particu-

FIGURE 3.2   The patina fractures on the surface of this bone are typically seen on the surfaces of long bones or flat bones. (Photo by S. Fairgrieve.)

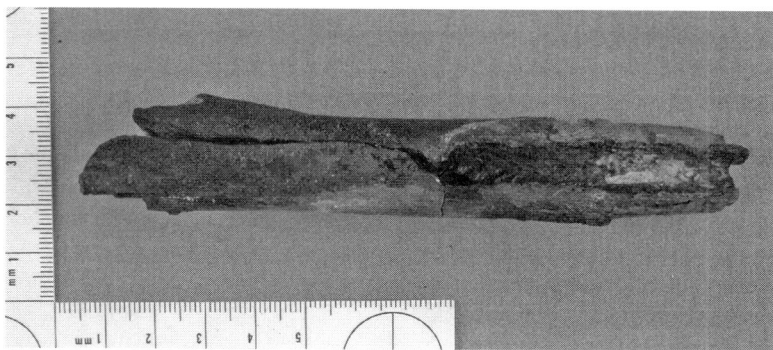

FIGURE 3.3   The longitudinal fracture on this specimen has penetrated to the marrow cavity in this case. (Photo by S. Fairgrieve.)

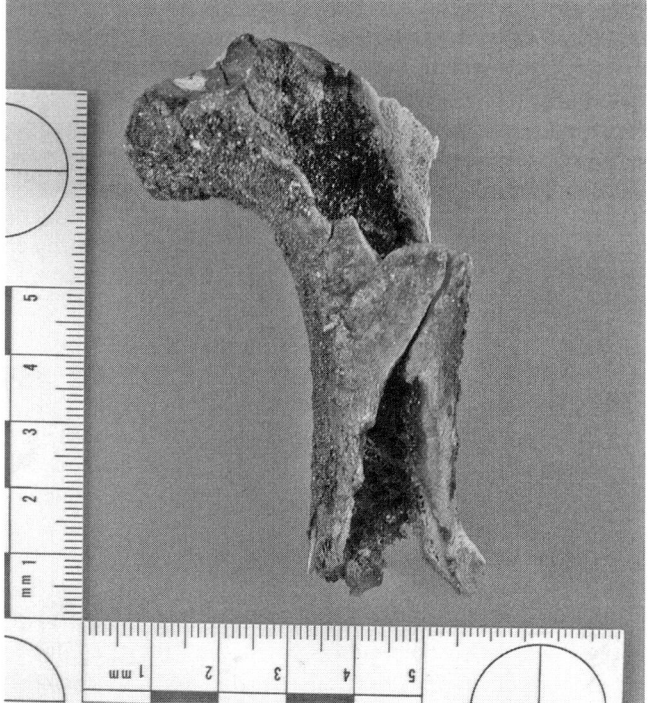

FIGURE 3.4   As the name describes, curvilinear fractures, as seen here, circumscribe the long bone shaft. (Photo by S. Fairgrieve.)

larly with the separation of cortical from cancellous bone in the epiphyseal region of a long bone.

Krogman (1943) claimed that a burned bone demonstrating sharp and "clear-cut" heat fractures of the patina variety, as well as charring, calcinations, and splintering is indicative of bone having a scant or thin covering of soft tissue. He further

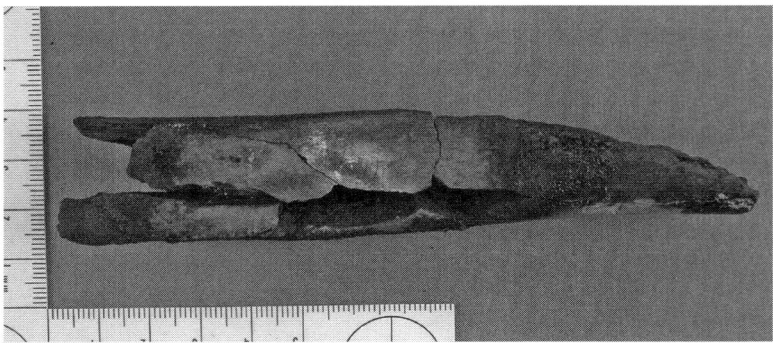

FIGURE 3.5   This completely transected long bone demonstrates a transverse fracture. (Photo by S. Fairgrieve.)

characterizes bone that is deeply embedded in the muscle as eventually undergoing fusion due to the heat in a "molten condition." Krogman's comments clearly indicate the need to be able to distinguish bones that have been recently defleshed (referred to as "dry bone") from those that have been burnt with soft tissue present (referred to as "green bone").

The problem with distinguishing dry bone from green bone has been examined by several authors (Baby, 1954; Binford, 1963; Stewart, 1979; Buikstra and Swegle, 1989). Baby (1954) noted that dry bone does not demonstrate the warping found on green bone. Additionally, dry bone is claimed to show "superficial checking" (likely referring to patina fracturing), longitudinal fractures, and transverse splintering. Binford (1963) reported dry bones as having straight transverse cracking. Green bone, on the other hand, has curved, transverse cracking. Stewart (1979) summarized his findings on defleshed and dried specimens as having a similar appearance to that reported by Binford. Yet, Buikstra and Swegle (1989) do not support either Baby or Binford based on their own study of bovid, human, and canine bone. They report warping in both green and dry bones. Deep transverse cracks were not felt to provide sufficient evidence of fleshed bone. However, they did conclude that it was easier to interpret a bone as being either green or dry at the time of burning based on the color rather than the fracture pattern.

In any event, the point to being able to identify heat-induced fractures is so that they are not interpreted as being due to another origin, such as direct trauma. Ultimately, the best way of chronicling fractures as either being due to the cremation process or a mechanically induced trauma is to reassemble the broken portions. Fractures due to trauma are generally found to exhibit characteristic patterns as seen in unburned remains. This fact permits analysts to provide an explanation of the origin of all fractures. Mayne (1990) conducted a study on precremation trauma and the identification of trauma on cremated faunal bones. She was able to distinguish heat-induced fractures from those caused by tension, compression, and shear dynamic forces. However, she cautions that in order to do so, the analyst must adhere to a six-step procedure (see Chapter 5).

Fractures to the cranial bones will also occur in a similar pattern (Bohnert, et al., 1997). However, fractures to the cranial bones are also caused by increased intracranial pressure as a result of the heat. Fractures penetrating both the inner and outer table are largely due to this pressure and the weakness that may be inherent in the various regions of the neurocranium. The release of pressure along the cranial sutures is reported by most researchers to be a rare occurrence due to the ossification process and the interdigitating osteophytes that make up the sutures. The structure of the cranial vault often results in fractures separating the inner and outer tables of bone exposing the diploë (Figure 3.6). The bones of the facial skeleton are not as readily charred as those of the vault due to the greater thickness of soft tissue. Nonetheless, once exposed, the facial bones, which are less dense than the bones of the cranial vault, will undergo the same process of shrinkage and cracking as any other area of the skull. Areas closer to the surface will, of course, be subjected to a more prolonged period of heat stress.

The exception to the aforementioned pattern of cranial heat-induced fractures is said to be in situations where the cranial vault has been breeched due to a cranial trauma (Rhine, 1998). For example, a traumatic perimortem cranial fracture that penetrates the neurocranium would allow a means of escape for any increased pressure inside the skull as a result of the heat. Hence, the fractures will not be associated with a sudden release of pressure. As Rhine (1998) points out, in such a case, the cranium and its components will be in much better condition as a result of the pressure being released through the breech. In this instance, Rhine would be referring to temperatures akin to those found in a house fire. At this temperature range, cremains are typically identifiable as to their location and position in the house. However, the head is not usually intact for the above reasons. If the head were in a

FIGURE 3.6 This cranial fragment from a victim of an aircraft crash demonstrates the separation of inner and outer tables of bone. (Photo by S. Fairgrieve.)

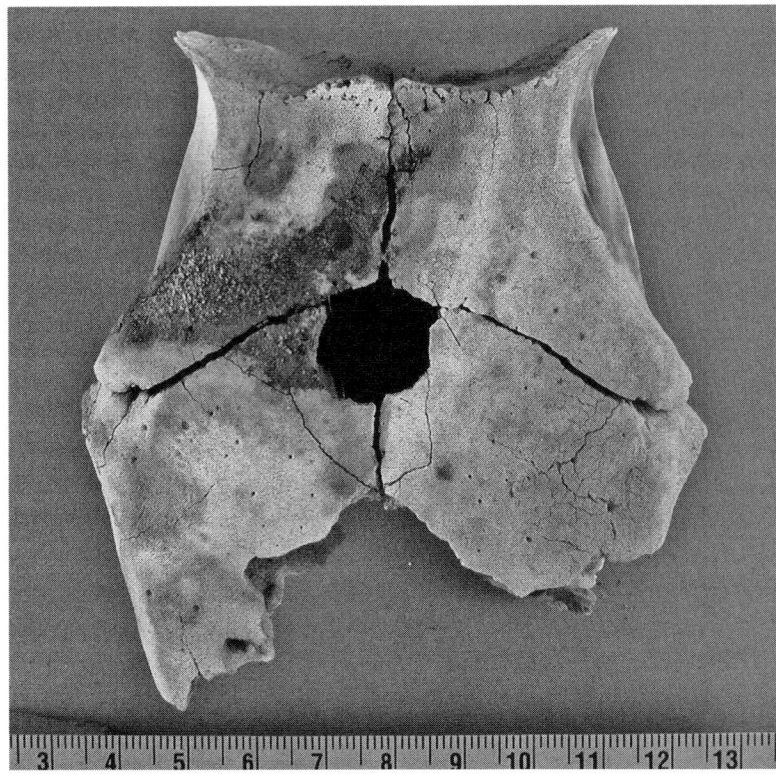

FIGURE 3.7   This cremated pig (*Sus scrofa*) skull from inside a car fire clearly demonstrates the evidence of a gunshot wound. Note the sharp edges of the external aspect of the wound. (Photo by S. Fairgrieve.)

reasonable state of completeness one would certainly be suspicious of a perimortem trauma. It is important to remember that, even if the skull were in minute pieces, the skull should always be reconstructed to examine the fracture patterns for any type of trauma.

In experiments using fresh pig carcasses in automobiles with accelerants, such as gasoline, the head is typically rendered down to small fragments even with a postmortem gunshot wound to the neurocranium (Figure 3.7). As the temperature of these fires exceeded 1200°C, according to an infrared temperature monitoring system, this well exceeds the temperatures reached in typical house fires. Therefore, it would appear that in spite of a gunshot wound to the head, a high degree of fragmentation of the skull is certainly possible.

3.5.3.2   Heat-Induced Dimensional Changes

The burning of human tissues will often result in something being left to recover and analyze. It is up to those individuals performing the recovery to recognize those altered remains and document them for analysis and interpretation.

The investigation of skeletal remains, cremated or not, depends on the use of multivariate statistical methods, including discriminatory analysis. This fact is particularly important in light of the additional standards required by U.S. and Canadian courts pertaining to the admissibility of scientific evidence (i.e., Daubert vs. Merrill–Dow; Regina vs. Mohan; and Regina vs. JLJ, respectively). This is a particularly acute problem should the remains in question not yield a positive identification, but a presumptive identification based on analytically derived information, such as the sex, age at death estimation, stature estimate, and the location and types of documented pathologies (e.g., antemortem fractures). Van Vark (1974) concluded that the two main causes of difficulties in the application of multivariate statistical analyses are the changes in the size and shape of the bone in the cremation process, and the fact that small and fragmentary remains are recovered. Although these factors are a function of the temperature and duration of exposure to the fire, the fragmentary nature of the cremains may be due to the action taken by a perpetrator to conceal the cremation. The skill of these undertaking the recovery of the cremains may also be a limiting factor in the completeness of recovery (see Chapter 4). However, the changes in size and shape should be ascertainable through experimentation.

So far, the discussion of heat-induced alterations to bone has treated these topics as mutually exclusive events. The same cremation process that has changed the color of the bone and produced fractures will also result in shrinking the bone and warping its dimensions. Table 3.7 summarizes the stage of heat-induced transformation in bone based on some revised temperature ranges (Thompson, 2004). According to this information, it is in the fusion stage, that is, the melting and coalescence of the crystal matrix of bone, that dimensional changes are observed.

Thompson (2005) has conducted the most recent research into heat-induced dimensional changes in bone. The two key and most widely accepted precepts that explain why warping occurs, specifically the claim that warping is more apparent in bone that is fleshed at the time of burning (Binford, 1963 and Kennedy, 1996), and that the burning process causes expansion of air in the medullary cavity (Spennemann and Colley, 1989), are speculative and not substantiated by quantitative data (Thompson, 2005). Further to this, nothing is mentioned about the actual

TABLE 3.7
The Four Stages of Heat-Induced Transformation of Bone (Thompson, 2004)

Stage of Transformation	Evidence	Revised Temperature Range (°C)
Dehydration	Fracture patterns; weight loss	100–600
Decomposition	Color change; weight loss; reduction in mechanical strength; changes in porosity	300–800
Inversion	Increase in crystal size	500–1100
Fusion	Increase in mechanical strength; reduction in dimensions; increase in crystal size; changes in porosity	700+

structure of the bone contributing to the manner in which it predisposes the bone to distort in a particular fashion.

Bone shrinkage in fire has been documented to affect both the length and width. Malinowski and Porawski (1969) conducted a study of pre- and postcremation metrics of bone specimens. In their study, they found that the radial head diameter decreased by 0.7 mm. Dokládal (1971) cremated one half of each of five cadavers in a study to examine bone shrinkage. A comparison of the unburned side with the cremated side yielded a 5 to 12% shrinkage. However, this study does not consider the fact of asymmetry of intrapersonal dimensions. Herrmann, in a series of studies (1976, 1977), based his experimentation on compact bone segments measuring 20 millimeters by 5 millimeters. This resulted in the formulation of three phases with the following corresponding temperatures:

    I. 150°C–300°C = 1–2% shrinkage
   II. 750°C–800°C = 1–2% shrinkage
  III. 1000°C–1200°C = 14–18% shrinkage

These studies by Herrmann led to the conclusion that there are four criteria for considering the shrinkage of bone in fire:

1. Distribution of bone types in the bone (i.e., compact, spongy, and lamellar)
2. Temperature of exposure
3. Mineral content of bone
4. Aspects of the mineral content of bone tissue

It seems reasonable to assume that different types of bone tissue will respond differently to heat. The mineral content is referring to the level of mineralization. This can also refer to the relative amounts of the organic portions of bone (i.e., the collagen), and the hard matrix. Finally, aspects of mineralization seem to relate to the inherent variation of mineral content within the bone. Upon closer examination, Herrmann found that the higher percentage of bone mineral results in a greater amount of shrinkage. Grupe and Herrmann (1983) found that there is a 12% reduction in measurements for spongy bone. In the case of compact bone, Bradtmiller and Buikstra (1984) found a 5% shrinkage when subjected to temperatures not exceeding 600°C. In a subsequent study, Buikstra and Swegle (1989) recommended the use of a correction factor for measurements from 0 to 10%.

Changes in bone dimensions were not found to be consistent within the same bone. Hummel and Schutkowski (1989) measured the length of compact bone and found a 5% shrinkage up to a temperature of 1000°C. However, they also found a 27% reduction in the cross-sectional diameter of the same bone. This indicates that the orientation of the collagen fibrils has a significant influence on the manner of shrinkage. Essentially, the fibrils arranged in a parallel and longitudinal axis relative to the length of the long bone will undergo a smaller relative amount of shortening than will be observed in the transverse reduction. If this is borne out, then it would be expected that other bones that have a less regular arrangement would also differ in their amount of shrinkage. Holland's (1989) anticipation of a 1–2.25% decrease in the size of the cranial base exposed to fire would reflect the kind of orientation of collagen in bone with an intramembranous ossification. With temperatures of up to 800°C it was concluded that shrinkage in the cranial base was not significant.

Thompson (2005) recognized a contradiction in the literature as to whether spongy bone or compact bone shrinks more readily with exposure to heat. Gejvall's (1969) work suggests that spongy bone shrinks only slightly and retains its original shape. Gejvall (1969) and Gilchrist and Mytum (1986) suggest that compact bone will shrink more than spongy bone. Conversely, McKinley (1994) and van Vark (1974) argue that spongy bone shrinks the greater amount. Thompson's analysis of this split in the literature may be due to the interpretation of relative versus absolute size. Additionally, Thompson (2005) also notes that Holden et al. (1995a) suggest that older bone, with greater intermolecular cross-linkage of collagen, resists shrinkage. But this is only to a point where the heat is so intense that collagen is being destroyed.

Thompson's (2005) study of heat-induced dimensional changes on 60 complete sheep long bones is an attempt to address many of the questions raised above. The strength of this study lies in its adherence to the methodology. However, it would have been better for Thompson to utilize long bones of the same type and side (e.g., a left humerus) in an attempt to control as many variables as possible. The methodology involved the heating of these long bones for differing periods of time at particular temperatures. It is important to note that the methodology involved removing soft tissue and then drying each bone on a rack. The unfortunate aspect of this is that it does not simulate an actual fire situation with a fleshed victim. However, this simple study is valuable as it is the actual property of heat-induced bone shrinkage that is being studied.

Thompson (2005) reports that, with increasingly intense burns, there were more long bones that fragmented and, hence could not be remeasured with cooling. This indicates that a postcremation repair of the bones and measurement was not attempted. This is a shame, as recording such measurements would have recorded interesting data of importance to forensic anthropologists who are often faced with fragmentary material from cremation scenes.

It is clear from Thompson's study, and others, that the variation in the destruction of a bone by heat is dependent upon the architecture and constituents of the bone itself.

One result that seemed to surprise Thompson was the fact that as the bone specimen cooled, the dimension of the bone changed. In Thompson's words, "...this temporal influence means that heat-induced shrinkage is more dynamic than has been previously realized." This conclusion was reached by taking repeated measurements at 5-, 15- and 25-minute intervals after removal from the oven. Although the amount of difference between the recorded dimensions at these time intervals may have been surprising to Thompson, the laws of thermodynamics would certainly lead one to expect that with the cooling, there would be a contraction of the bone's dimensions until it reaches an equilibrium with the room temperature at which the original pre-cremation measures were taken. Of equal interest is the fact that, in some instances, there was an increase in the dimensions over the original measurement with the heating of the bone. A gradual contraction of the bone followed with cooling, how-ever, in a few instances after 25 minutes of cooling, there was still a net increase in the dimension. Again, this can be explained by the fact that 25 minutes may not have been a sufficient amount of time to cool. However, given that this effect was seen to occur in the epiphyseal width, the architecture of this area is certainly amenable to dynamic forces on a regular basis, such as compression, shearing, and torsion. Con-trary to Thompson's statement that collagen in the epiphyseal region is "randomly arranged" and thus has less structural support, collagen is actually arranged as the structural proteinaceous basis for the intersecting bone spicules, or trabeculae, that form a multiple arched support structure for the articular ends of long bones. It is known that the arch is an extremely efficient architectural structure that provides strength and stability with a minimal amount of mass. The intersecting arches of the trabeculae that composes spongy (or trabecular) bone produce an extremely strong and light framework. The trabeculae are surrounded in the intervening space by marrow that can act to insulate the trabeculae. However, this type of structure does expose a greater surface area of bone to the heat. Hence, trabecular bone is more readily expanded by the heat, relative to the compact bone found in the diaphysis. Therefore, a longer period of cooling will be required prior to taking measurements to account for cooling of trabeculae at a greater depth. Likewise, if the temperature and duration are increased, as done in Thompson's study, the trabecular bone will contract more than compact bone. This explanation, and Thompson's findings, are consistent with McKinley (1994) and van Vark (1974). The "nonwarping origin" of increased dimension is nothing more than the expansion seen in a heated substance according to the laws of thermodynamics. Thompson's study certainly confirms the finding of an increase in temperature producing an increase in the percentage the bone tissue contracts.

The ultimate goal of studying the dynamics of bone contraction is to account for the amount of contraction when undertaking an osteometric analysis. Thompson has generated predictive equations utilizing step-wise regression for various recorded dimensions. The recrystallization of the organic phase of bone is an important factor in the changing dimension of the bone. Temperature was not found to be an accurate predictor of the amount of contraction. Temperature, in combination with the dura-tion of the exposure, will have a greater effect on bone contraction than temperature alone. Logically, a bone may reach a specific temperature, but it is the duration at that temperature that will directly influence the contraction of hard tissues. Further, a principal components analysis indicates that the removal of the organic phase from the bone has the greatest influence on the following variables: duration of heating, weight loss, alterations in mechanical strength, changes in crystal size, and microscopic porosity. A strong association between temperature, skeletal density and microporosity (pores with diameters between $0.01–0.1\ \mu$) implies the involve-ment of the inorganic phase (Thompson, 2005).

3.6   CREMATION SLAG AND "CLINKERS"

The appearance of a somewhat porous material directly associated with cremated remains is often referred to as cremation slag or "clinkers." A "clinker" is defined by the *Oxford English Dictionary* (1989) as:

> ... a hard mass formed by the fusion of the earthy impurities of coal, limestone, iron ore, or the like, in a furnace or forge; a mass of slag.

Wells (1960) described crystalline lumps of material found in direct association with cremains. Wells theorized that these clinkers were formed from the keratin contained in hair, and in combination with fat and tissue burned at the same time. Wells' conclusions were challenged almost 30 years later by Henderson et al. (1987). In a search of the literature, they found a citation by Brandt (1960) referring to a study by Von Stoker of "urn resin" or *"urnenharz"* from cremation burials from northern German archaeological sites dating from the Stone Age to the Migration Period. Von Stoker found that this resin was soluble in acetic acid and chloroform and produced an aromatic smell. Von Stoker's conclusion was that the resin was derived from Scots pine (Henderson et al., 1987).

Analysis of cremation slag from Illington, in England, was found to be composed of Si, Ca, Al, P, Mg, and Fe with smaller quantities of K, Mn, Ti, Zn, Na, B, Zr, Cu, Ba, Sr, Ni, and Pb. There was a complete lack of organic material. Further, when the slag was heated for two hours at 450°C it lost only 2% of its original mass (Henderson et al., 1987).

In 1962, the British Museum analyzed the same slag and found that it was chiefly composed of sintered grains of silica (SiO_2) mixed with small amounts of other materials, such as a bead of iron/iron oxide, and fragments of bone (Henderson et al., 1987). X-ray diffraction analysis of the quartz form of silica had been almost completely converted in fused areas into the high temperature form of cristobalite. The conversion of pure silica to cristobalite takes place at 1470°C. In the presence of impurities, the conversion temperature would be lower.

Henderson et al. (1987) conducted a study of cremation slag or "clinkers" in order to investigate Wells' claims and to provide macroscopic, microscopic, and chemical analyses. Such an undertaking provided an opportunity to characterize cremation slag and determine its likely origin. They determined that the raw materials needed to produce cremation slag include silica, alkali (such as K or Na) and Ca from the cadaver or wood ash, with sufficient fuel to raise the temperature of the pyre to a level that would result in fusing these components into the slag. The sources for silica include the human body, wood, and plant ash.

The amount of energy it takes to burn a body has been previously discussed. However, the body itself should also be considered a fuel. Consider that a body weighing 140 pounds, placed inside an elm coffin weighing 90 pounds, will yield over 800,000 BTUs as along as there is sufficient oxygen to complete the combustion process (Polson et al., 1962 as cited by Henderson et al., 1987). If there is a lack of a critical level of oxygen, the body will char rather than burn to ash. In this scenario, the body and the coffin act as fuel and raise the temperature of the crematory chamber higher than the flame generated by the supplied gas alone. Hence, achieving the requisite levels of heat may not be a problem for this context, but in other contexts, such as house fires, this may not be the case. Open cremation pyres of a clandestine nature may reach such temperatures if the fire is tended by a perpetrator through the addition of fuel.

Regardless of the mechanism by which cremation slag is produced, the slag is derived from silica-bearing sandy soils fusing with material at a high-temperature (Henderson et al., 1987). Its importance for forensic casework would serve to act as a rough indicator of combustion temperature.

3.7 SUMMARY

This chapter has dealt with reviewing the combustion of human remains from a forensic perspective. It is clear from the literature that it is impossible to completely eliminate all evidence of a body through the act of burning it. Perpetrators obviously encounter this fact if they are actively tending to the cremation pyre. Hence, their attempts to further render the remains to an "unrecognizable state."

Understanding the mechanisms of body immolation will serve the investigator well at fire scenes. Of course, recognizing the fact that there are remains worth recovering from fire scenes of various types is the first step to a successful recovery. The next step is to assemble a team that will competently undertake the documentation and recovery of the cremains.

4 Scene Recovery

4.1 INTRODUCTION

As most investigators are aware, the first stage of processing any secured crime scene is the search for evidence. This necessitates having people with the training and experience to recognize this evidence and take steps to preserve its context. It can be argued that this stage is the most critical in any investigation. Without personnel who can recognize the evidence and subsequently preserve, document, and recover it without contamination or damage, an investigation at a scene would be severely compromised.

Although there are general references on scene recovery utilizing forensic archaeological technique (e.g., Skinner and Lazenby, 1983; Morse et al., 1983; Bass, 1987; Ubelaker, 1989), none of these volumes deals with the specific recovery of cremated human remains in a forensic context. It is true that basic forensic archaeological technique can be learned by most police forensic identification officers; however, the lack of experience with recognizing fragmentary, and certainly, charred human remains, emphasizes the essential partnership that must exist between a forensic anthropologist and the forensic identification team. It is this team approach, and those who constitute the team, that will make all the difference to processing the scene.

The context in which cremated remains are found may be quite variable. To that end, cremains may be found on the surface, buried, partially buried, in water, within structures, inside burned automobiles or trains, and of course, aircraft in postcrash/fire contexts. Each of these situations requires a different search strategy and set of documentation and recovery protocols. In short, there is no "one size fits all" solution to processing scenes with cremated remains. However, the strategies outlined in this chapter will certainly be transferable and/or adaptable to any of the contexts outlined above. In order for any scene processing to work, any means that facilitates maximizing the potential of the recovery of the remains and associated evidence will serve the goals of the investigation.

This chapter first details the strategies that may be utilized in order to find cremains in various scenarios. Presuming that the recognition of the actual scene is not an issue, it is the responsibility of the investigating agency to preserve the scene. Subsequently, a more thorough examination of the scene by personnel with expertise in this area should be conducted. This more detailed search of the scene is done in cases of scattered cremains. Once the areas of concern have been delineated, the process of recovery can commence. During this phase of the operation, the process of documenting the scene is also undertaken by the identification officers. The methods of documentation will be dictated by the scene conditions and the context. For example, use of computer-based surveying equipment for sites of varying sizes is now a standard practice. Additionally, a combination of video and digital still images will also be used, although there may be some issues or police service policies that may dictate the means of documentation. Finally, documentation and recovery considerations demonstrate the necessity of a trained team to successfully process scenes with human cremains.

4.2 SEARCH METHODOLOGIES

Searching for noncharred human remains can be quite challenging, particularly with remains that have undergone significant decomposition and in some contexts, scavenging. Likewise, cremated remains also present a further challenge because the remains have been subjected to an accelerated means of decomposition, namely combustion.

Primarily, police services will traditionally undertake a search based on visual inspection. In outdoor contexts, it is not atypical for a large area to require a search. To that end a grid search pattern using varying numbers of personnel with equally varying experience and expertise. As such, a visual inspection is highly dependent upon the ability of the searcher to recognize human remains. Additionally, if the cremains are scattered in an outdoor context, and hence significantly altered, there is a high probability that the remains may be overlooked. Therefore, a search strategy is particularly important when remains are likely to be in a disarticulated state, or even if suspected to be in small fragments due to a process such as combustion.

As mentioned above, in cases of cremated remains, it is essential to have experienced personnel with a background in human anatomy and, particularly, in cremated human bone; otherwise, the likelihood of overlooking some of the remains is increased.

The search for cremated human remains follows many of the same basic strategies outlined by Killam (1990). However, Killam also explores the use of everything from cadaver dogs to instruments for measuring the production of methane by decomposing tissue in order to find burials. Such methodologies do have some merit in the search for cremains. Yet, as with any search and recovery strategy, the key here is to be flexible in that strategy. There is, once again, no ubiquitous solution that will suit all contexts.

4.2.1 Outdoor Grid Search

The traditional grid search of an area is based on the premise that a line of individuals approximately 1 meter apart will walk over an area at approximately the same rate, examining the ground and surface foliage for evidence (Figure 4.1). The merit of such a system is that the close proximity of searchers results in overlapping fields of vision to the right or left of a particular searcher. This "two pairs of eyes are better than one" approach is sound, and has had great success in the past.

Once an area has been covered in one direction, the line then moves from one side of this theoretical square, to an adjacent side. The line would then walk over the same area using the same methodology as before; however, its path is perpendicular to the previous route taken. Under this system the entire area has been visually examined four times and from two difference angles, and hence two different lighting angles (Figure 4.2).

FIGURE 4.1   A grid-search line of police officers looking for bone fragments. The overlapping fields of vision increase the chances of detecting evidence. (Photo by S. Fairgrieve.)

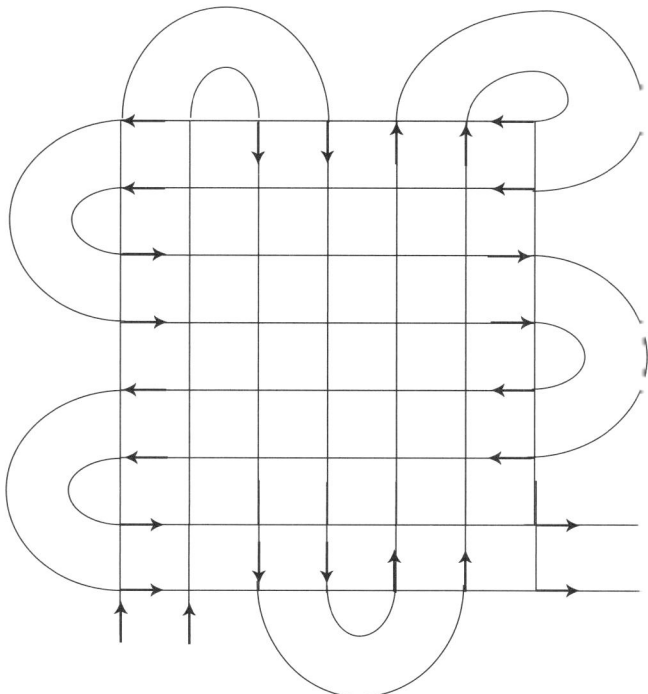

FIGURE 4.2   This schematic representation of a grid search demonstrates how an area is walked through twice and at different approaches by two searchers. Arrows indicate the direction of travel by each searcher in their respective tract.(Drawn by S. Fairgrieve.)

This methodology is predicated on the assumption that the searchers will actually recognize what they are looking for if they see it. In my experience, training forensic identification officers in the appearance of uncharred bone, and letting them become familiar with the, size, shape, and color of human bone, will certainly add to their success. However, the success rate for these officers has been found to be variable. To be fair, it does depend on the amount of foliage covering the ground and any other items that may obscure the evidence being sought. Likewise, the size of the fragment is also a factor in any successful search. Again, this is highly dependent on the context of the search. A search being conducted within the remains of a house that has been razed to the ground or searching for remains in a context that has been reported by an informant as having been buried subsequent to a cremation require very different search strategies.

Bass (1984) cited the example of a house fire in which the owner was missing. The complete nature of the fire necessitated the use of a team of people to search the charred remains of the house starting at one end and proceeding to the other. This yielded the remains of a victim who was found in direct contact with the basement floor, but the upper and lower portions of the body were separated by several feet. This careful examination by people with expertise in human skeletal anatomy, and training in the application of simple archaeological principles, yielded a wealth of information from the scene. In this case it was proven that the victim was bifurcated by an explosive device prior to the fire and all the debris subsequently accumulated on the body. Clearly, a search using a shovel to scoop up material and metal grates to sieve out the bone from other materials would not have yielded such important results.

In my own experience, dogs trained specifically in the recognition of human decomposition scent can detect human cremated bone. Surprisingly, even cremated bone that is largely calcined (i.e., most organic components eliminated), can also be detected by properly trained canines (Figure 4.3). The key to using cadaver dogs in any search, including those on cremation scenes, is scent availability. The scent needs to have an opportunity to be exposed to the air currents so that they can be distributed, and hence detected, by the search dog. Cremated remains are no different in this respect; however, if the cremains are buried within the soil, as in the case of a cremation homicide in which the cremains were later interred in a small burial pit (Figure 4.4), and there is no opportunity for the fire degraded scent to be exposed to the air and circulated by a breeze, the dog will not detect the scent. To that end, any and all soil disturbances need to be probed in order to make that scent available. A 1-inch diameter soil auger is sufficient to this task as it is also used in deep burial detection using search dogs. In this case, the burial site was indicated by an informant and the surface was scraped using a trowel and the dog gave a positive indication on the site. By means of confirmation, a second dog was brought to the area and also provided a positive indication.

The use of the dog on a cremation scene may also be of service to the investigation by tracking where human remains have been. The fire pit in one case was indicated by an informant as being the location of missing individuals. During the initial excavation of this roughly circular fire pit with an approximate diameter of 3 meters (approximately 10 feet), two cadaver dogs independently indicated on a

FIGURE 4.3 This cadaver dog, a Belgian Mallinois, has been trained to distinguish human decomposition scent from that of other mammalian species. Dogs tested and certified by professional external agencies that specialize in this area should be used. (Photo by S. Fairgrieve.)

FIGURE 4.4 The pit in this figure was dug after the cremation of multiple victims and one used to inter their cremains. (By permission, Regional Supervising Coroner, Northern Ontario.)

series of large stones used as part of the boundary of the pit. Additionally, charred material on these stones, later determined to be human flesh, was the source of the scent detected by the dogs. As the actual excavation of the fire pit only yielded a middle phalanx from a human hand, and a portion of a distal humerus (Figure 4.5), both calcined. The question remained as to the location of the rest of the victims. A further search of the surrounding area using the cadaver dog team yielded positive indications on a small wooden bridge over a flowing creek (Figure 4.6). Subsequent examination of the creek floor (approximately 3.5 feet in depth) yielded the recovery of a limited amount of human cremated bone. Hence after burning, some cremains were dumped in the creek from the bridge. The cadaver dogs were picking up the scent from some material that had bone lodged in the joists of the bridge. This scenario was later confirmed by an accomplice. Subsequently, the remainder of the cremains were buried in a shallow pit on the property (as shown in Figure 4.4).

In this instance the use of a cadaver dog team provided investigative leads and assistance in the interpretation of events and corroborated the information provided by an informant, and subsequently an accomplice.

In some instances the search for cremains may be very easy. A simple visual inspection in most house fire scenarios will yield a mound of material usually covered in ash, that may be suspiciously shaped like that of a human body (Figure 4.7). In fact, depending on the location of the body in the structure, it may be very well-preserved and even provide blood and other biological samples at autopsy. However, because a body does not burn evenly, the completed recovery of the cremains should be left to a professional in this field as this will help to mitigate any investigative difficulties should a scene that initially appeared to be an accident is later determined to be a homicide. A grid search of these scenes should still be undertaken,

FIGURE 4.5   This *in situ* photograph of an adult human's humerus from within an outdoor fire pit was the largest surviving bone fragment from this scene. (By permission, Regional Supervising Coroner, Northern Ontario.)

FIGURE 4.6 The search of this wooden bridge, covered in snow, using cadaver dogs yielded a positive indication from the joists. Human cremains were recovered from the river below. (By permission, Regional Supervising Coroner, Northern Ontario.)

FIGURE 4.7 The remains of a pig carcass used in an experimental house fire. Note the presence of a discernable mound and black charred appearance. The fire and remains are still in a smoldering state. (Photo by S. Fairgrieve.)

but only when the structure has been determined to be safe for an examination (see Section 4.2.2).

The examination of remains found *in situ* is of the utmost importance. Not only does such an examination indicate the position and location of the body in the structure and any associated evidence, it may also indicate inconsistencies with the condition of the remains and the condition of associated items. An investigation of the fire scene by fire investigators, police, and a forensic specialist with knowledge of fire dynamics and human remains must be undertaken to address any inconsistencies.

As mentioned before, it is virtually impossible to eliminate a body by fire. Even in confined, intense fires, such as in a vehicle, the remains will still be present. Recent experiments of automobile fires using domestic pigs of varying size as victims, demonstrated that those ranging in size from that of a young human child to an adult were always observable. In the experiment depicted in Figure 4.8, the car had used tires filled with diesel fuel to create an active and extremely hot fire. Even under these conditions, the remains of the pig were still identifiable and recoverable in spite of severe fragmentation of the skull and the distal elements of the fore and hind limbs (Figure 4.9) at temperatures over 1200°C and over a course of 40 minutes. In spite of this temperature and this elapsed time, the torso is still present and soft tissue still remained (Figure 4.10). Clearly, a familiarity with the process by which a body burns is essential to successfully detecting, documenting, and recovering the cremains.

Charred bone may be encountered in a variety of contexts that may be seemingly innocent, or at least without any suspicion of foul play. Charred bone in dumpsters or other refuse may certainly be burned food debris. However, if a search for remains and/or evidence has yielded such a find it is incumbent upon the investigator to assume that it is human unless otherwise proven. In such instances an on-scene assessment is the most desirable. However, failing this, digital images may

FIGURE 4.8   An automobile burning with the silhouette of a domestic pig (weighing approximately 75 pounds) is clearly visible in the driver's seat. (Photo by S. Fairgrieve.)

FIGURE 4.9 The cremains of the pig depicted in Figure 4.8, 40 minutes after ignition.
(Photo by S. Fairgrieve.)

be taken in the field and e-mailed directly to someone with experience in identifying cremains. This method has been used in my own lab in northern Ontario for
the past decade due to the large area (approximately the size of western Europe)
it covers. The caveat with such a system is that if diagnostic features are not visible or sufficiently preserved, the actual specimens must be brought in for a direct
examination.

FIGURE 4.10 The margin and position of the liver are easily distinguished in the torso of
the cremated pig in Figures 4.8 and 4.9. (Photo by S. Fairgrieve.)

Confined contexts, such as enclosures and dumpsters, do not necessarily require a grid to be superimposed for the recovery and documentation, although photography and mapping will need to follow the same procedures as in other recovery contexts.

It is clear that the search for cremated remains is an in-depth process that requires a team consisting of not only police searchers, but individuals with experience in the recognition of human cremains. The use of a qualified cadaver dog team should not be overlooked as they can cover a vast area in a short amount of time. The caveat here is to be sure that the team utilized has trained on cremated human material.

4.2.2   BUILDING AND CONFINED SEARCH

The search for human remains inside fire-damaged structures can be a very dangerous pursuit. In all instances a search of any structure for remains must initially be done under the supervision of the fire service responsible for that scene. Additionally, as the recovery of remains by forensic identification personnel/forensic anthropologist and the investigation of the fire by a fire investigator have a common purpose, it would be ideal to work as a team in order to ensure that neither destroys nor alters evidence pertinent to the other's investigation.

Once an active fire has been extinguished, the structure will likely not be safe for a detailed examination. Prolonged smoldering of materials is still dangerous to those conducting the search (Figure 4.11). It is recommended that a fogging spray be used to douse any smoldering areas. It is often the practice that such areas are turned over by fire personnel or pierced with a specialized nozzle in order to extinguish

FIGURE 4.11   The smoldering remains of an experimental house fire. Fuel, including human remains, continue to be consumed in a smoldering fire. (Photo by S. Fairgrieve.)

.the smoldering mass. This procedure does have the potential to disturb the original context of any cremains and other evidence. Therefore, any search and subsequent analysis must take this into consideration when examining the context of cremated remains or related evidence.

As a forensic specialist will likely attend the scene well after the fire service has left, it is prudent to request that someone from that service attend the scene to describe the circumstances of the fire and the means used to extinguish all active and smoldering areas. If this step is not taken then the disturbance of cremated remains due to the process of putting out the fire may be misinterpreted as having another origin.

The detailed examination of the scene by forensic specialists must be done under the safest possible conditions. Hard hat, safety boots, coveralls/bunny suits, lung and eye protection must be worn in any examination of these scenes.

Once the search has revealed cremains, the area can be bounded using survey flags. This will permit a general plotting of the cremains on a floor plan. The location and position of specific skeletal elements will be added to any detailed mapping as the recovery process proceeds.

During the initial search for cremains, it is important to consider that other charred material may mimic the appearance of charred bone. Some forms of plaster can appear to have a porous structure and even appear to have inner and outer tables similar to human cranial material (Figure 4.12).

During this process it is important, as in all scenes, not to ignore associated items. Fire victims that have been burned while in bed, even if on an upper floor that has collapsed, will be found in association with mattress springs (Figure 4.13). In fact, in a recent house fire experiment, it was found that cremains from an upper

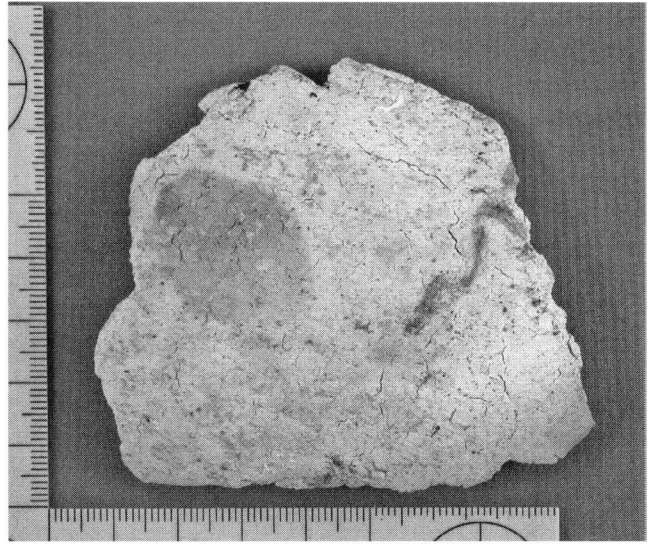

FIGURE 4.12 This segment of plaster from a house fire has a form and consistency that is reminiscent of a neurocranium fragment of a skull. (Photo by S. Fairgrieve.)

FIGURE 4.13   The cremains of a pig sandwiched between two mattresses after the collapse of a second-floor room into the main floor of a house. (Photo by S. Fairgrieve.)

floor did not cascade through the superstructure of the house as it collapsed and subsequently become scattered as suggested by Rhine (1998). The remains were concentrated in the same relative area as originally placed in an upstairs bedroom (Figure 4.14). This is not meant to negate the statement by Rhine, but it does underscore the need to be cautious when examining the context of cremains during the search of a collapsed structure. It is prudent to remember that a body will burn in such a way that the skeletal elements will remain in relative anatomical order unless acted upon by another force during or after the burn. Such a force may include gravity, fire extinguishing/suppression equipment and techniques, or actions taken by an individual before, during or after the cremation process.

Suffice it to say that examination of a burned structure for human remains requires a systematic plan to ultimately recover the cremains and any associated evidence.

4.2.3 AUTOMOBILE SEARCH

Automobile fires can result from collisions, spontaneous ignition of engine components due to faulty electrical systems, and even leaking fuel systems. Some vehicle fires are due to the actions of individuals who intentionally ignite a vehicle in order to destroy evidence. In these instances the perpetrator is typically undertaking such an action in a clandestine context. In short, the fire is done in an isolated area in order to facilitate the escape of the perpetrator, and the hope that there is enough time for the burn to render down any evidence, or human remains for that matter, to ash.

As with all other contexts, vehicle fires need to be handled in such a way as to preserve the context of the cremains as well as any associated evidence. Vehicle fires may be more challenging to process. The confined nature of the interior of the vehicle will act to intensify the heat and the rate of combustion. Yet, cremains in vehicle fires, regardless of the type of fuel being burned, are highly recoverable.

The confined space of the vehicle's passenger compartment, or trunk area, can make the use of a grid impractical. However, the actual structure of these areas of a vehicle can be used as reference points for documentation. Detailed photography and video recording of these scenes are essential to the recovery process. Cremains in this context are particularly friable and can easily break during the recovery process.

Part of the recovery kit should include a small geological sieve with 1mm mesh. Additionally, a soft brush is required to aid in collecting ash and other debris with minimal damage. Larger skeletal elements are usually visible amongst the burnt debris of the vehicle's interior. The position of the body can be discerned from the orientation of these elements; however, it should be considered that the combustion of the seat, likely supporting the body prior to the fire, will result in bones falling through springs and come to rest in a new position. In Figure 4.15 the starting position of a pig carcass prior to a test burn of a compact automobile is represented. In Figure 4.16 the postfire cremains of the pig are shown. It is interesting to note that

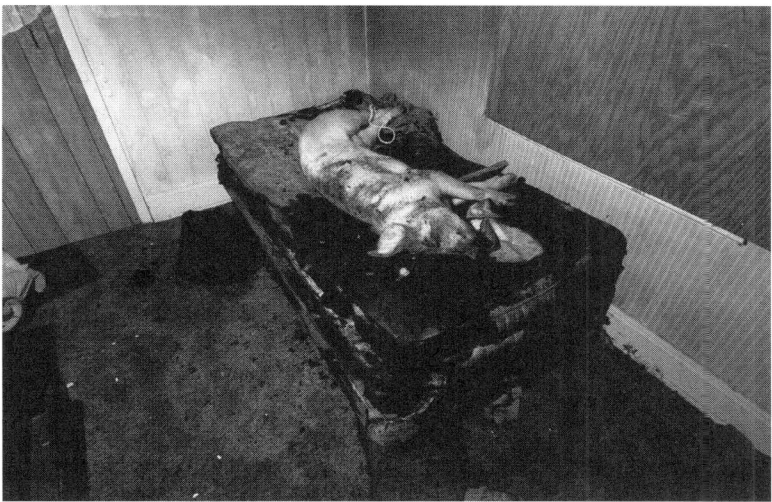

FIGURE 4.14 The original position of the pig from Figure 4.13 in a second-floor room on two mattresses and a box spring prior to ignition. (Photo by S. Fairgrieve.)

FIGURE 4.15   This pig carcass is positioned behind the steering wheel prior to ignition of the test fire pictured in Figures 4.8 and 4.9. (Photo by S. Fairgrieve.)

because of the thoroughness of the burn, components from the interior of the automobile are on top of and beneath the cremains. However, in Figure 4.17 the right knee joint of the pig is clearly visible.

The body of the pig in the aforementioned figures was not entirely rendered down to calcined bone. Figure 4.10 demonstrates the abdominal region of the pig as having preserved internal organs. Note that the liver and even portions of the small

FIGURE 4.16   A detailed view of the calcined remains of the head of the cremated pig seen in Figure 4.15. Note that the upper dentition, maxillae, and a portion of the orbit are visible. (Photo by S. Fairgrieve.)

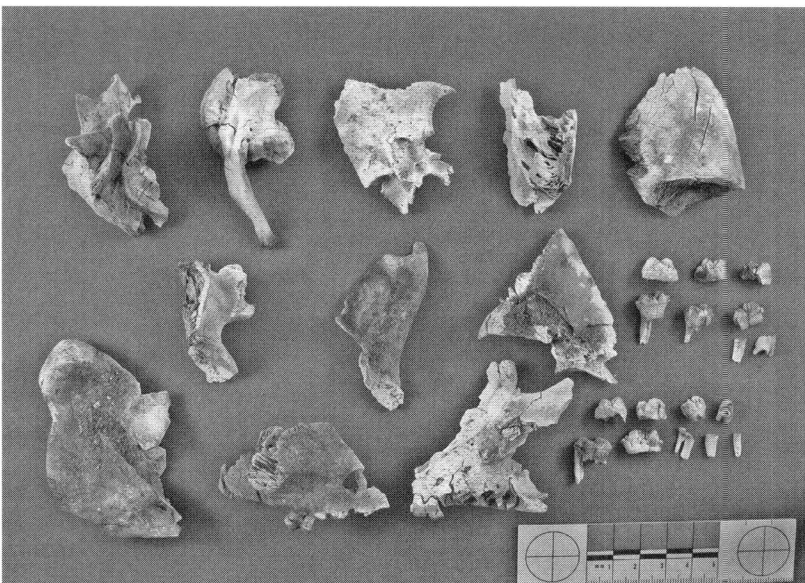

FIGURE 4.17   The scattered fragments in this photograph are those of the skull of the cremated pig in Figure 4.16. (Photo by S. Fairgrieve.)

intestine are preserved. Intact units of a body should be preserved and removed en masse. The preserved portion of the body should then be wrapped in plastic and placed in a suitable container, such as a metal transfer casket used by body removal services, due to the fragile nature of the remains. Likewise, all other cremains should be transported in the same container if possible. Cremated bone that has been collected prior to the body should always be placed in brown paper bags as this will allow any moisture to gradually escape and resist mildew growth.

The possibility of commingled remains in these contexts should always be considered. Stratton and Beattie (1999) encountered this situation with the train disaster in Hinton, Alberta, Canada during the mid-1980s. In that instance temperatures were reached that not only incinerated the bodies of victims, but also resulted in the melting of metal around those remains. As in this context, automobiles may also have multiple occupants. To that end, the commingling of remains is possible; however, particular attention to the location of different skeletal elements will assist in sorting out the individuation of particular bones and bone fragments. Lighting in this context is important, as a well-lit area will permit one to see the elements more clearly. Likewise, gentle removal (read brushing) of the debris from on top of the cremains will assist in visualizing the elements.

If the vehicle is in a suitably remote area and undiscovered for a period of time, it has been my experience that fly larvae (maggots) will be feeding off of the remaining soft tissue. In fact, in one study, our group found that maggot activity acted to completely skeletonize the remaining portions of the body not already rendered down to bone by the fire within a faster timeframe than observed on fresh uncharred remains. The fire has already eliminated the dermal layers and subcutaneous fat; this allows insects to have direct access to the internal organs. Such insect activity in a vehicle can certainly assist in locating the presence of a body, even with debris. However, it has been my experience that a burned body in a vehicle can be skeletonized in midsummer in as little as 5 days after the burn has finished. Hence, using insects as an indicator of the location of remains will only have a brief window of opportunity.

In general, the fact that bodies burn unevenly means that there will likely be some soft tissue mass left in the abdomino-pelvic region of the body. This can create a perceptible mound within the vehicle. This obvious mass may be easily recognizable; however, depending on the amount of material and fuel burned within the vehicle, recognition of any mass as being human may be more challenging than expected. One must remember that a perpetrator is burning a vehicle in order to dispose of human remains. In order to accomplish this goal the use of accelerants and other materials (such as old tires, diesel fuel, gasoline cans) will enhance the combustion of the body by reaching a higher sustained temperature and for a greater duration of time.

Although the abdomino-pelvic region of the body is most likely to have preserved soft tissue, the extremities and head will likely be rendered down to bone and be severely fragmented. Figure 4.16 demonstrates the head region of the same pig shown in Figure 4.15. Note that some areas, such as the dentition and alveolus, are clearly evident in this instance. The level of fragmentation is severe due to the intensity of the heat. As this animal was put down prior to the fire (due to a medical condition) by a gunshot wound to the head, it would be anticipated that the bones would not be subjected to any explosive release of pressure normally encountered in crania without an intact cranial cavity. Hence, such an orifice forms a *de facto* pressure release valve to accommodate the expanding cerebrospinal fluid (CSF). Yet, in spite of the gunshot wound in this particular test case, the elements of the neurocranium were severely fragmented due to heat-induced damage (Figure 4.17).

The search for cremains in burned-out vehicles can be a reasonably complex undertaking. Although the original context of the cremains is generally preserved, shifting of the cremains due to the combustion of other objects within the vehicle will undoubtedly affect its final position. Caution must be exercised during a search of the vehicle as persistent hot spots may be lingering. Additionally, the potential commingling of multiple occupants and even commingling of cremains with the materials within the vehicle is always possible.

4.2.4 Water Search

The idea that cremains may be found in a water search may seem antithetical. However, from my own experience, perpetrators, on occasion, discover that the burning of a body does not render it down to unrecognizable ash. If the perpetrator still feels the need to dispose of these remains further, disposal in a body of water is not farfetched.

A water search should be initiated by the police service involved in the investigation of the scene. In general, water searches are conducted in a systematic method, just as land searches are undertaken (Becker, 1995). In this instance, the search for cremains presents a whole new set of considerations for the divers.

Divers accustomed to undertaking body recovery are usually responding to drownings or some sort of body disposal scenario. The familiar shape of a human body, clothed, unclothed, wrapped in plastic, or even being scavenged by sea lice, makes the recognition of the body less problematic. In fact, the actual recovery process follows the same general procedures in each of the aforementioned scenarios (Teather, 1994).

The difference from these other aquatic scenarios is that, in this instance, human cremains (friable, fragmentary bone) are being disposed of in water. Depending on the size of these fragmentary cremains, it is certainly possible for a diver who lacks the training in recognizing such remains to overlook them. Hence, finding the remains is an important issue in itself.

In my own work with the Ontario Provincial Police Dive Unit, we have successfully used a strategy where the diver is on a surface-supplied air system with full video and audio communication ability. This allows an expert to communicate with the diver and provide direction as to where to look, and if any items need to be seen in detail on the video.

In Northern Ontario this type of system is very important as cremated bone may look like other types of debris found on the bottom of a lake or river. In Figure 4.18 a diver is underwater in a shallow stream (approximately 5 feet deep) with a support diver there to receive items that have been recovered.

FIGURE 4.18   Two divers from the Ontario Provincial Police Dive Unit recovering human cremains from a river bottom . One diver (right of frame) is breathing using surface supplied air while the second diver (standing) receives recovered material for transfer to the surface. (By permission, Regional Supervising Coroner, Northern Ontario.)

Figure 4.19 is a detailed view of human cremains recovered from the stream depicted in Figure 4.18. Note that the differential degrees of burning of the bone are preserved even after being submerged for several months. However, if the interval of time had been greater we would have also had the added difficulty of silt and other debris covering the cremains. In this particular case, the cremains would not be as prone to silting in this stream due to the rate of flow.

Ideally, divers undertaking this type of search will have training on how to minimize disturbing the silt on the bottom. Training that is similar to that undertaken by cave divers is ideal for this type of recovery work.

Once the search of the area has been completed by the diver(s), the documentation of the cremains will commence in much the same fashion as any other cremation scene. It is generally known in the police diving community that the technology exists to process scenes underwater much the same as you would on land.

The direction of current and turbidity of water are serious considerations in a water context. The current is of significance because bone fragments that have trapped air will be positively buoyant and may be carried by the current to a location other than the original deposit. If the cremains are negatively buoyant they will sink directly to the bottom without much displacement in location. As with drowning victims, the best place to begin a search is in the location where the body first went beneath the surface. The same applies to cremains. However, in this case, the easiest place from shore to dump cremains in the water will likely be the place to begin.

The search for cremains in turbid (low visibility water) conditions is particularly challenging. Imagine searching a crime scene on land that can only be observed

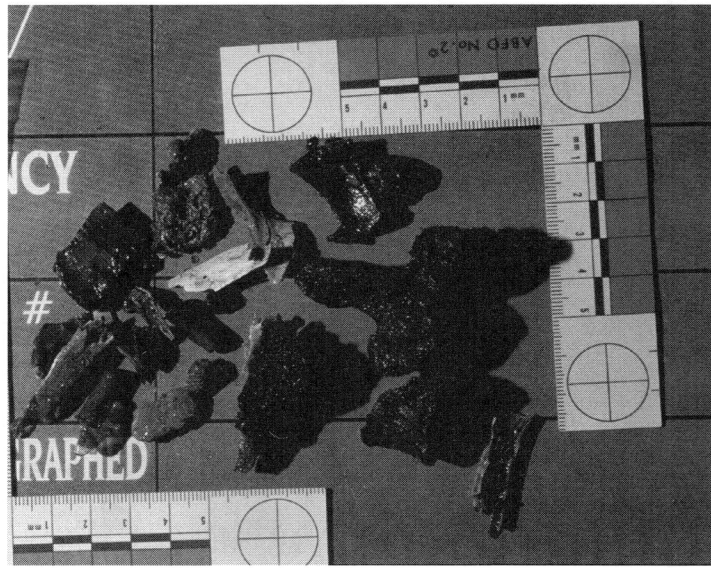

FIGURE 4.19 Human cremains recovered at the scene pictured in Figure 4.18. Note the variety of shades and sizes of fragments. The upper left fragment is carbonized wood. (By permission, Regional Supervising Coroner, Northern Ontario.)

through a small window in front of your face and being able to see items less than 1 foot away from that window. This should provide you with a good idea of what a search diver must contend with during an underwater search.

In order to enhance visibility, lights usually accompany a diver; however, the lights may very well further obscure vision due to the reflection of light off the particles suspended in the water. The use of a remotely operated vehicle (ROV) with a camera system may help in particularly deep searches. Side scan sonar is another search option; however, as we are looking for cremains that may have been rendered down to fragments that, on average, are the size of a 25-cent piece, the practicality of such a device would be called into question.

Ultimately, the best search for cremains in water is to use a diver, and have a system of communication with the surface for direction. A systematic examination of the bottom of the lake/river/stream is the best method to find cremains in the water.

4.2.5 CREMAINS IN MASS DISASTER CONTEXTS

So far, the previous contexts have considered cremains in isolated or small-scale occurrences. Yet, we have become more acutely aware of mass fatalities after the terrorist attacks of September 11, 2001. Likewise, mass fatalities involving aircraft crashes, passenger and cargo trains, and even large traffic incidents can result in charred and cremated remains. The search for cremains in these contexts will require a coordinated strategy with many searchers and agencies.

Generally, searching for remains in mass disaster scenarios is usually done with many of the same considerations mentioned in previous sections. Searcher safety and the ability to recognize remains become even more of an issue due to the emotional stress involved in the processing of these scenes. Hence, resources from across a region, or even across borders, may be necessary.

In these instances, the use of a canine search unit will be essential. Likewise, a GPS (global positioning system) mapping system will facilitate the organization and mapping of all phases of a search.

It is strongly recommended that the reader refer to local, city, state/province, and emergency response plans in order to clearly understand who is involved in the search for, and recovery of victims, both living and dead.

A more detailed discussion of cremains in mass disasters is covered in aspects of the analytical procedures in Chapter 5, and as it pertains to establishing a positive identification of cremains in Chapter 8.

The search for cremains in mass disasters is entirely dependent upon the team approach. In Ontario, for example, the Office of the Chief Coroner is mandated to investigate all unattended deaths. An investigation of such a magnitude would draw upon a team whose composition would include coroners, forensic pathologists, forensic odontologists, forensic anthropologists, forensic engineers, police, ambulance, and fire personnel, to name a few. Such a search team would have well-defined roles and procedures for the location, documentation, and ultimate recovery of remains, cremated or not.

In summary, mass disaster scenarios will require a search methodology similar to the aforementioned contexts, although, the scale will be a new and important factor.

4.3 FIELD RECOVERY EQUIPMENT

Human remains, as demonstrated, may be found in a wide variety of contexts and differing states of preservation. A plan on how best to document and recover the remains must take the context and conditions of the remains into account. The goal of this process is to accurately record the context of the remains as found and any other associated evidence. This means the horizontal context (surface location) as well as the vertical context (relative depth) of the cremains are both required. This, in essence, demands an approach that is based on the same procedures and practices used by archaeologists in the excavation, documentation, and recovery of artifacts from ancient sites.

The recovery of cremated remains may be from extremely confined contexts ($< 1m^2$) and the opposite extreme (several hectares). The common difficulty in these cases is being able to distinguish human skeletal material from other material that was charred in the same event. Building materials and household objects can be altered by fire to such an extent that they may closely resemble bone. Additionally, the presence of pets, or even animal hunting trophies, may also act as a source of confusion. Therefore, it is not enough to have basic familiarity with human bone, but also knowledge of the potential for other objects to be misinterpreted as human bone.

Assuming that the recognition factor has been overcome, the actual recovery of the cremains, in addition to the documentation, need not be overly complex as long as it is systematic. It cannot be stressed enough that simply going into the remains of a house with a shovel and grate or some other screen in order to sieve ashes is actually destroying evidence rather than recovering it. This is not to say that there is not a time and a place for the use of a shovel. However, as with all equipment, the applications of that equipment will depend on the needs of the scene and the material to be recovered.

Let us assume that the recovery team includes forensic personnel from a police service who are responsible for the processing and documentation of crime scenes. Based on this assumption, basic equipment, such as crime scene tape, and still and video cameras (likely digital) will usually be at all scenes. Additionally, the use of some form of mapping technology, perhaps a laser-based surveying system, such as a Total Station®, will be used to document the location and depth of objects (typically used by traffic accident reconstructionists in Canadian Police Services).

It should be obvious that clearly photographing the scene, starting with the approach photos, and overall exterior and interior views, is standard procedure when examining structural fires. This should be undertaken in consultation with whatever authority is responsible for the investigation of fires (in Ontario, this is the Office of the Fire Marshal). Detailed views of suspected areas of remains must be photographed prior to the actual movement of any debris. Notes pertaining to the time the photographs were taken, who took them, and at what stage of recovery in that location, all need to be noted.

Prior to entering any fire scene for the purpose of evidence recovery, including that of human remains, the scene must be assessed for all safety concerns.

Once safety issues have been addressed, a systematic plan for conducting a search of the debris, along with the recovery, should be initiated. These two plans are not mutually exclusive of one another. Specifically, the establishment of a grid over the scene will not only facilitate a search of the scene, but also act as a control for recording the context of any remains or items of interest to the investigator.

The superimposition of a grid must first take the size of the area into consideration. If a house that has been razed to the ground is of concern, a grid composed of a series of 1-meter squares is ideal. This size of square is particularly useful in cases of explosions or any context in which small fragmentary evidence is to be collected. Regardless of size, the grid must have a boundary. The use of wooden stakes or some other means of establishing the boundaries of the grid should be used. Running string from the top of each stake in such a way that grid squares are formed by the intersection of these strings will provide an excellent visual aid (see below for details on establishing a grid) (Figure 4.20). Wooden stakes, such as 1-inch by 1-inch, will serve the purpose of establishing the grid.

In addition to string and stakes, a mallet will be required to pound the stakes into the ground. In some instances, particularly scenes within structures, the use of the actual architectural features of the structure can be used to facilitate the collection of remains and other evidence. Flagging tape is useful in most situations, as this will help with making the grid visible. Measuring tapes of varying lengths will be needed to assist in sighting-in the stakes with a surveyor's transit, or theodolite.

FIGURE 4.20 Cremains and debris being collected at a scene within the confines of a grid system. (By permission, Regional Supervising Coroner, Eastern Ontario.)

Once the grid has been established, some basic equipment for the examination of each square will be needed. In the first instance, once photography has recorded the square prior to excavation, large debris may be removed by hand (wearing nitrile or latex gloves) or other means as necessary. The clearing of smaller items of debris is usually done by hand. Once the size of debris makes hand removal impractical, a standard mason's trowel, such as the type used by archaeologists, can help to move material directly into a receptacle (i.e., a dust pan), and collected for later screening. The screening of material is done using a mesh of, at most, one-quarter of an inch square. The standard is to use a one-eighth inch mesh. All screening from areas where human cremains are found should be saved in a sealed container and re-screened in the laboratory setting. All screening needs to be done on a new plastic sheet or tarp to prevent contamination of the scene (Figure 4.21).

Standard photographic equipment to document significant finds are fairly standard pieces of equipment for crime scene personnel. A north arrow and scale should always be present in all photos. It is standard practice to photograph the scene and items in their original context both with and without the scale. A means of identifying each photographed grid square, either by an annotated photo record sheet or a sign directly in the photograph, must be done for purposes of continuity, particularly in these typically complex scenes.

Recovered material must be placed in appropriate containers for transportation to the laboratory for analysis. In general, the most appropriate container for the preservation and safe transportation of cremains is a paper bag. This will promote

FIGURE 4.21   The screening at this scene is done away from the area being examined and all screening is done over a new plastic ground sheet. (By permission, Regional Supervising Coroner, Northern Ontario.)

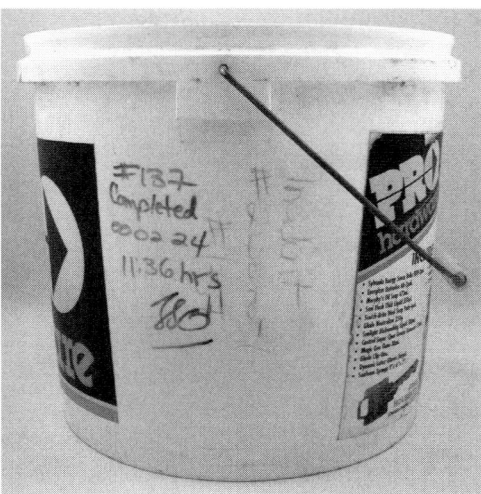

FIGURE 4.22 Cleaned containers with sealable lids are ideal for transporting large amounts of mixed soil and cremains for separation in the laboratory. (Photo by S. Fairgrieve.)

a gradual drying of the remains if they are moist, and also prevent the growth of mildew.

For the transport and storage of large amounts of ash and/or fire debris that will be sorted later, large pails with sealable lids will work well (Figure 4.22).

Finally, other small friable items, such as dental remains, will require medicine bottles with cotton, or some other sterile and soft medium for storage. This will keep dental remains from rattling inside a container, causing further damage.

In all cases, the items are all evidence, and will require evidence seals and larger cardboard containers for transportation and storage in an evidence lockup.

4.4   THE RECOVERY PROCESS

Although the various contexts in which cremains may be encountered have been previously covered, consideration must be given to the most efficient means of recovery. Some scenes will require a confined excavation grid of only a few meters. Other scenes, with a larger distribution of cremains, will require extensive surveying for documentation and recovery. Likewise, cremains located in structures, motor vehicles, trains, aircraft, water, or any combination of the above, will, by necessity, require different recovery strategies.

The recovery process is an inherently destructive undertaking. In essence, in any crime scene, once an object is moved from its original location, it can never be placed back in precisely the same location and orientation. As any forensic identification officer or criminalist will tell you, the documentation of the original context of any item to be recovered from a crime scene must include photographs of the overall area of the scene, and detailed photographs both with and without a scale. However, ultimately the item will be seized and given an evidence number, and logged as part of an overall evidence/exhibit list. This act of controlled destruction of the scene is even more dramatic when cremains and associated evidence are involved.

Cremation scenes tend to have a great deal of debris in addition to the cremains. In fact, just recognizing the cremains among the debris, as mentioned earlier, may be an issue. Debris in such scenes may be layered in such a way that the cremains are not in plain view. Hence, the search that was dealt with earlier may be destructive itself. So, the documentation of the scene should have been considered at that point. Debris is, therefore, adding the dimension of depth to the scene.

Depth is a consideration in most scenes involving cremains. In addition to general debris from the fire, cremains may have been clandestinely buried. This will necessitate an excavation of a scene, and documentation in both the horizontal and vertical axes. This will also be true for aquatic scenes.

The documentation of the scene is a continuous process that is considered during all phases of the field recovery. The recovery of the cremains will also include the best means by which to protect these items during the recovery process. Many of the techniques utilized in this process have been adapted from standard archaeological procedures. In fact, the dependence on these techniques has spawned the term "forensic archaeology." Yet, it is important to consider that although the techniques have been adapted from those used on archaeological sites, the needs of a crime scene are quite different from those of an archaeological excavation. Specifically, the recovery must not only permit the scene to be reconstructed on paper, as in an archaeological report, but also stand the rigors and requirements of the legal system and the laws of admissibility of evidence. This difference is dramatically demonstrated in the types of reports that are produced.

The recovery process must also be done in such a way so as to maximize the potential of the evidence. This simply means that the recovery process must consider that any item, including cremains, may be subjected to a series of tests by various experts/analysts. As such, the recovery process must consider all possible needs of any tests and take precautions to prevent the destruction or contamination of that evidence. Hence, the removal, transportation, and storage of the evidence, in the case of human cremains, must be done in such a way that the friable nature of the cremains is considered. An intact specimen without additional fractures will be important to a morphological analysis. Likewise, the cremains may be subjected to a DNA analysis and thus must be stored in such a way to prevent any further degradation or contamination.

4.4.1 THE COLLECTION/EXCAVATION GRID

For the purposes of this section, I will use a scenario that will encompass a terrestrial scene requiring the recovery of cremains using both horizontal and vertical controls. In this scenario, there is information provided by an accomplice in a missing person's case that the victim was taken out to a wooded area and shot in a shallow pit. Wood and accelerants were ignited over the body as it lay in the pit, and as a result, cremated over a period of several hours. The remains were subsequently crushed using a shovel and then covered with soil. The deed was done at the height of summer (July) and the informant came forward in September. Hence, two full months had passed from the time of the cremation and burial to the time of discovery.

The aforementioned scenario is actually based on elements from my involvement in several actual recoveries. This scenario will be referred to throughout the remaining portion of this section, however, in order to make each stage of the recovery relevant to the other potential contexts, exceptions or adjustments to any of the following procedures will be noted in light of other contexts.

The concept of an excavation grid is an old one. It is based on a simple Cartesian grid that assigns a series of coordinates to points where the lines intersect (Figure 4.23). All grids need a starting point. In archaeological contexts, a point with the coordinates of (0, 0) are given to a location off the site and usually to a fixed object. This is done so that the grid may be reestablished in subsequent field seasons without the loss of this fixed permanent reference point known as a datum.

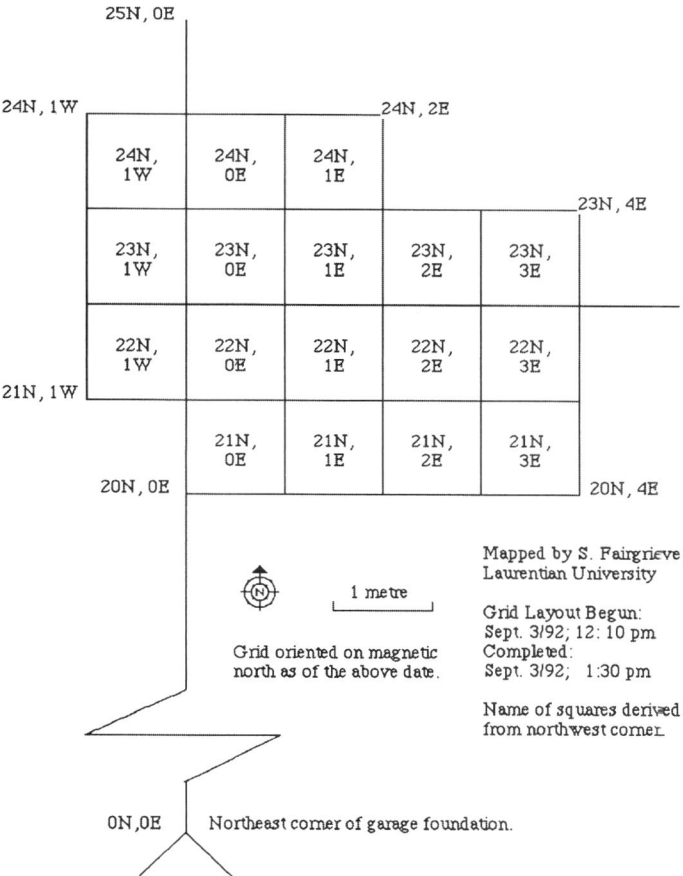

FIGURE 4.23   This grid schematic highlights the means by which items may be documented according to their coordinates. (Drawn by S. Fairgrieve.)

The archaeological grid is something that is anticipated to be reestablished field season after field season. In contrast to the archaeological grid, the forensic recovery grid is only meant to be used once. This is due to the fact that a scene will be entered and processed under a search warrant. This document gives the police the power to limit access and control an area, as in our example, during the search, documentation, and seizing of evidence. However, access to this area is not granted in perpetuity. Hence, there is a finite amount of time that a scene may be under police supervision. So, the onus is on the authorities to have requested, with justification, a reasonable amount of time for that warrant to be valid. It is possible in some cases to indicate to a judge that they need to be able to come back and request that the time for the warrant be expanded should the scene be sufficiently complex to process. As a forensic scientist, you may be asked for an opinion of the time needed to process a scene given your area of expertise. This will be handled by the police in their warrant application and any subsequent requests for an extension.

A forensic scene will also require a grid to have a reference point, or datum. However, I recommend that whatever point is used as a datum should be mapped in relation to two other reasonably fixed objects. Although it is unlikely you will have to reestablish a grid at a scene some time after it has been released, it has happened (e.g., Melbye and Jimenez, 1997).

The issue with setting up a grid is selecting the scale of the grid. The size of the grid squares can be as large or as small as you need. In our scenario, the preliminary examination of the scene exhibited a shallow depression about 2 meters in length with one end of the depression uncovered with cremains evident and scattered over an area of approximately 6 square meters adjacent to the depression. In this case, a grid using a series of 1-meter squares will be superimposed over the entire area that has been deemed necessary for investigation. It is always best to make the grid larger than the area in question, rather than just fitting it to the area in which you "know" evidence is located.

The actual grid itself will use a series of surveying stakes to demarcate the external boundaries of the grid. It is essential that you never pound stakes into the ground inside a scene. This is not only generally true of all scenes, but this is particularly true of scenes with friable cremains. Additionally, you never know what is buried, and as such, you would not want to put a stake into a burial location and destroy or alter evidence.

The grid orientation must be on a north–south axis. Therefore, all boundaries of the squares are either north–south or east–west, depending on the side. Most grids use magnetic north as a means of orienting the grid. However, as magnetic north is transient, you must record the date on which you set your grid according to the position of magnetic north.

With a fixed reference point, the datum, and a size selected for the grid, the boundary stakes are placed around the scene in 1-meter intervals. There are several ways to do this, including the use of a surveyor's transit, or theodolite (referred to earlier), or in remote locations by means of a compass and some tape measures. These methods are generally well-known to most forensic anthropologists, as this would have been a part of their original training. However, I would refer the reader to a new book on forensic recovery edited by Dupras et al. (2005).

Once the stakes are in the ground, and a nail has been placed on the top of each stake, the position of which has been measured in, the stringing of the scene may commence. The string provides a visible reference for all photography of the overall scene and assists with the systematic documentation of the evidence within individual squares. Additionally, the points of intersection of the string will also correspond to particular grid coordinates relative to the datum. Hence, a point of intersection that is 3 meters north and 5 meters east of the datum will have coordinates of 3N, 5E. If these coordinates corresponded to the northwest corner of the square the other corners would have the following coordinates: 3N, 6E; 2N, 5E; and 2N, 6E.

Traditionally, archaeologists label each square according to the coordinates of one square. It does not matter which corner is used as long as it is consistent for that scene. Therefore, in the case of the square with the coordinates mentioned above, and the convention for naming the square is the northwest corner coordinates, the square would be designated as 3N, 5W. This system will allow you to not only keep track of where you are working, but also the square from which the evidence originated.

4.4.2   DOCUMENTATION AND RECOVERY WITH THE GRID

The establishment of a collection grid now provides you with the ability to document and recover the cremains from a scene in a systematic fashion. Part of that systematic methodology is to work from the outside of a scene, that is, the area with the least dense concentration of evidence and/or cremains, to the area with the highest concentration. Proceeding in such a way will ensure that evidence will not be trampled/destroyed or potentially missed. The clearing of peripheral areas will also allow scene personnel a greater range of movement if the grid has been established in a confined space, such as a tent, as in winter recoveries.

As evidence in the square is identified, it must be photographed *in situ* with and without a scale. An ABFO (American Board of Forensic Odontology) No. 22 scale is typically used in these instances. A photograph record sheet of all photos taken, either on film or digital, must include a brief description of the object and an indication if the photo is a detailed or overall view. When taking the photograph, it is important to include some indicator of the evidence number assigned by the forensic identification officer, and to orient the photograph so that the north boundary of the square is at the top of the frame. If it is not possible to have north at the top of the frame, you can mitigate this by having a north-pointing arrow included in the photograph (always recommended).

The photo record sheet and the evidence list made at the scene will act to corroborate one another. The evidence list must contain the assigned number, the location found (i.e., grid coordinate), a description of the item (such as "bone fragment" if there is no one on scene who is able to provide a more specific identification), and the date and time located and recovered.

A measurement of the location of the item found may be done in several ways. In some instances, measurements may be consistently taken from the north and west boundaries, or even measured using a laser-based surveying unit and sightedin directly. If it is a large item, such as a long bone, this can be done by recording a series of points that serve to outline the bone or bone fragment. With fine fragments (2 centimeters or less in size) a single point to demonstrate the position will be sufficient. A rough sketch plotting all of these points can then be produced (see Figure 4.24). The importance of such a map is that it will enable the analyst, and subsequently a jury, to examine the distribution of the cremains. This will also lead to information pertaining to the treatment of the cremains by a perpetrator or taphonomic (natural) forces.

So far, the above scenario has dealt with surface cremains. However, there are many more contexts to consider. In the partially buried scenario, we must excavate the remains in order to uncover them *in situ*. The excavation of individual squares is typically done using a small mason's trowel with a diamond shape. The trowel is scraped across the surface of the soil from the opposite edge of the square from that of the excavator. In doing so, the excavator gently removes a thin layer of soil so as to result in a smooth, even surface. This is done in such a way that the highest point of the soil surface in the square is removed first and then other lower areas are undertaken once the higher areas are scraped down to these lower levels. This ensures a clean surface with each scrape and a consistent means of removing the soil in a uniform manner.

The soil scrapings are removed from the square by means of a clean dustpan. The soil is placed in a bucket that is designated for that square. The soil is subsequently screened by another person at the scene. Should any item of evidence be detected using the one-quarter inch mesh (also known as hardware cloth) it will be placed in a bag indicating the square and the level of the screened material. It will

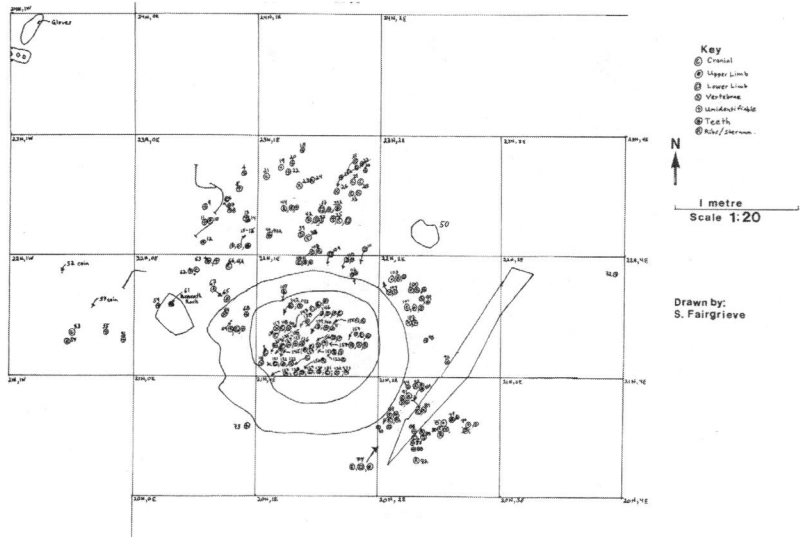

FIGURE 4.24 A rough distribution map from a cremation homicide case in which cremains were scattered across nine squares of the grid. This map also served to demonstrate that cremains were not in relative anatomical position to one another. (Drawn by S. Fairgrieve.)

be noted as one evidence number for the bag and indicated as being from screened soil for that particular square and level.

The removal of soil in this fashion allows the excavator to note the changes in the color, texture, and density of the soil. It is possible to see the outline of an excavated burial pit by using this method (Figure 2.25). This contextual evidence permits confirmation of a pit being dug and likely the method used.

As items are found during an excavation, particularly cremated bone, the item will be left *in situ* while other areas around the item are excavated, hence a pedestal of the item. It also permits the excavator to determine the extent of an item (see Figure 4.5). This will mitigate further damage to the item if it has been damaged by the fire.

The excavation around a bone fragment is usually done using a wooden implement, such as a sterile tongue depressor. Wood is roughly less dense than bone and is less likely to cause damage to the bone if contact is made. However, careful excavation technique can remove soil from around a bone without any physical contact. Depending upon the degree of fire damage to the bone, it may be too friable to remove directly. In these cases the entire pedestal may be undermined and removed *en masse*, and put in a suitable container and dealt with in a laboratory setting. As noted in a recent paper by Rossi et al. (2004), consolidation of bone may be required for microstructural or histological analysis. However, even some form of consolidation in the field will assist in preserving the morphology of the charred bone. Simply applying diluted water soluble white glue to the specimen and allowing it to dry will enhance its strength, and can always be removed in the lab using water.

The excavation of a specimen that clearly crosses the boundary into another excavation square is not a problem. If the specimen has been pedestalled, as recom-

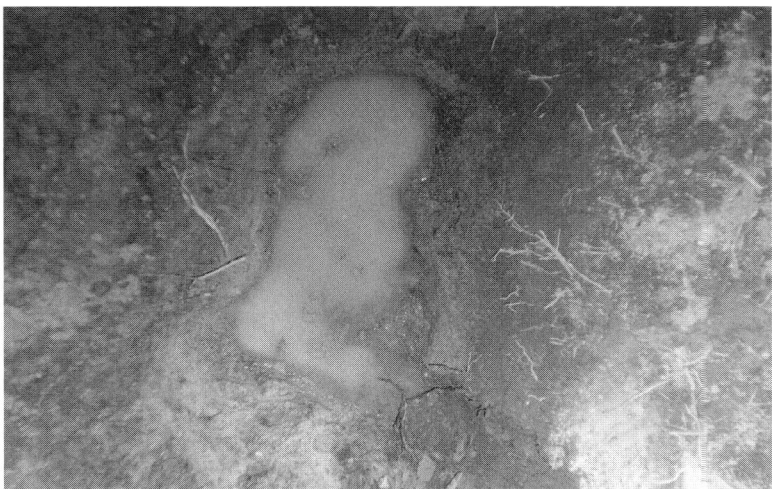

FIGURE 4.25   The outline of a small pit dug to dispose of human cremains. Careful excavation permits the visualization to the pit's outline. Water accumulated in the pit due to the melting of moisture-laden frozen soil. (By permission, Regional Supervising Coroner, Northern Ontario.)

mended above, then it is supported by the soil and not sticking out of a wall ready to fall out, or worse, break free of the embedded portion. The excavation of the adjacent square can proceed in a similar fashion as any other square with the added advantage of knowing that there is an item that is at a particular level. Mapping of the specimen in each square and in a composite diagram can also be done. The rule here is not to be bound by the boundaries of the squares, but to utilize them as a means of assisting with the documentation of the scene.

4.5 SUMMARY

The recovery at the fire scene is one that must be undertaken utilizing a team approach. By having a coordinated effort of fire investigators, police, forensic identification scene personnel, coroner/medical examiner, forensic anthropologist, and in some instances, a forensic odontologist, a plan can be executed to maximize the potential of the evidence at the scene.

The actual recovery and documentation of the cremains is best left to a small group at the scene so as not to cause confusion. The forensic anthropologist is directly responsible for the identification of cremated skeletal material, and its documentation and recovery. The complexity of the evidence at these scenes requires us all to be mindful of the potential testing that associated evidence may be subjected to in the laboratory. Familiarization with the recovery and testing protocols to prevent contamination are incumbent on all members of the recovery team.

Finally, a discussion with the personnel responsible for attending and suppressing the fire at the scene will provide the forensic anthropologist with invaluable contextual information that will play a role both at the scene and in the laboratory.

5 Laboratory Analysis

5.1 INTRODUCTION

Once the cremains have been properly documented and recovered in the field, the question of analysis comes into play. To that end, the nature of cremated remains requires that the laboratory processing, cataloguing, repairing, and analyzing be undertaken considering the friable nature of these remains. Typically, consolidation is undertaken in the field prior to, or during, removal from the originating context. This is done, obviously, to facilitate the subsequent analysis using cremains that are in the best condition possible. The key here is to consider in the field and in the laboratory the areas of the skeleton that are crucial to generating an osteobiography that will enable an identification of some quality, either positive or presumptive.

Recall that our basic questions to arrive at an osteobiography include assessing the skeleton for the sex, age at death, ancestry, stature, and any other physical attributes in life that would assist in establishing an identification (ideally positive). Even at the best of times, the analysis of the human skeleton for the aforementioned characteristics can be problematic, as they are subject to the availability of intact remains, or at least portions thereof, that conform to those required by the analytical methodology being utilized. Cremains have the added complication of thermally generated alterations that can not only obscure traits, but also influence measurements and alter morphological traits to such a degree as to render them useless.

The analysis of the remains is entirely dependent on their condition at the time of analysis. It is rare for cremains, or even uncharred remains, for that matter, to be ready for analysis as soon as they enter the lab. A process of washing, sorting, and cataloguing must be done so that all fragments may be accounted for and ready for mending fractures. The mending of fractures is crucial to the analysis of cremains. This technique allows the analyst to note the pattern of the fractures, and the level of color changes associated with the fire (Pope and Smith, 2004). The importance of these observations is that they will enable the analyst to distinguish between fractures/trauma that occurred prior to the cremation episode from those that were heat-induced, or incidentally produced due to external forces acting on the bone, such as the impact from parts of a collapsing structure, or the use of a cold water hose during fire suppression.

The analysis is also geared to answer questions concerning the context of the cremains. Are the location and position of the remains consistent with the injuries sustained? This question is a key consideration due to the nature of all forensic investigations. To accomplish this goal, the analysis of the cremains is very much dependent upon the visual analysis as to the condition of the bone. Bone color, change in morphology, and as noted above, the presence of fractures will very much influence the conclusions reached in other aspects of the analysis. Age, sex, stature, and ancestry are derived by direct morphological analysis through taking measurements or noting bone developmental features. Ultimately, the condition of the cremains, including the organic content, reflecting the degree of thermal alteration, will affect the accuracy of our results. Unfortunately, there is a great deal more that needs to be done in order to examine the question of how thermal alterations affect morphology and, hence, the accuracy of one's analysis.

5.2   CATALOGUING

Once in the laboratory, it is necessary to make a complete inventory of all of the evidence containers that have been signed over to you. This is usually done with someone from the agency that has delivered the evidence to your laboratory. There should be an evidence number list that was maintained by the forensic identification officer in the field.

I have found it good policy to maintain the evidence numbers that have been assigned to specimens in the field. This way there is always parity with the catalog of specimens you will eventually build for your inventory of the cremated elements and the recorded context. Even if the number assigned is in reference to a concentration of bone fragments that were recovered en masse, the evidence number can be maintained as a root designation and then another number added to provide a subclassification. For example, if a grouping of cremated bone fragments is assigned an evidence number of 128, and the field notes indicate that 128 was found in grid square 28N, 15E at a specified location and depth, we can maintain that information by adding a secondary digit to 128 for each additional fragment. If there were five additional fragments we would then label each (or its respective container) as 128-1, 128-2, 128-3, 128-4, and 128-5. We can then complete the other portions of the catalog and record the other information specifically for each fragment. I would caution against the use of alphabetical designations, as it has been my experience that the number of fragments that may be recovered from a specific recorded location may exceed the number of letters in the alphabet. The use of numbers resolves any problems with cataloguing.

The catalog itself is best done on a spreadsheet with the headings listed in Table 5.1. The purpose of these headings is to keep a running record of your analysis of the cremains. This document will prove to be very useful as a reference for all aspects of the analysis. This is particularly important given the vast numbers of specimens that are likely in a cremation scenario.

The actual numbering of specimens may be done in several ways. Firstly, the traditional archaeological method of actually writing the number with ink has a place. However, this should only be done if one is sure that the bone will not be subjected to other chemical tests, and is of a size that such writing will not interfere with the visibility of features. Due to the friable nature of cremains, and their propensity to disintegrate into smaller pieces, it is not practical to write on cremated fragments. It is usually suggested that all numbering be done on containers that will hold the remains. Containers may be bags of some sort, or more commonly, pill bottles or any other type of container that can be conveniently stored.

By way of a final word on the catalog, this document may be subject to subpoena and hence become a document for the court. I have found that a jury's examination

TABLE 5.1
Cremation Analysis Laboratory Catalogue with Definitions

Column Heading	Definition
Catalog Number	This is the same as that used in the field; however, there may be subdivisions added to this number if there are several fragments recovered under the original evidence number.
Square Number (if applicable)	This is the actual grid square number that was the origin of the material described under evidence number. A total station set of coordinates will be entered here if such a system was used on the scene.
Coordinates in Square (if applicable)	This is used in cases that have the location of a bone or concentration of bone fragments measured within a specific grid square if the recording of the context is being done with a total station unit.
Recovered Description	This is the original description that was given to the object in the field. The fragment of bone recovered may not have been readily ascribed to a particular type of skeletal element and, hence, may only be known as "bone fragment."
Skeletal Element	If the analysis permits the skeletal element to be subsequently identified, or a confirmation of the identification in the "Recovered Description," the most precise description of that element is used, e.g., medial epicondyle of a left humerus. If, by chance, the bone fragment is not from a human source, this would be the place to note this.
Weight (grams)	The weight of the item under this number is particularly important when handling cremains. Due to the friable nature of cremains, number of cremains fragments may actually increase inasmuch as subsequent fragmentation may occur due to handling. By having a recorded weight you will be able to ascertain if any of the material is missing. Additionally, there are some studies that suggest that cremation weights may be of assistance in determining the minimum number of individuals.
Color of Specimen	This is noted in specimens that have been cleaned and there is no adherent material obscuring the bone. If there are several colors, these should be noted. It is best to use Munsell Soil color charts as the standard to describe the color.
Category of Fractures	There may be many fractures present on a specimen. To that end, note the general category of fractures present, i.e., patina, longitudinal, curvilinear, transverse, delamination, or indeterminate.
Sequencing of Fractures	This refers to the timing of the fracture formation. Specifically, antemortem, perimortem, or postmortem.
Fracture Aetiology	This refers to the mechanical origin of the fracture. It is either traumatic (prior to heat exposure), heat-induced, or incidental.
Repairs and Matches	The catalog number of any specimens that were found to mend with this specimen should be noted here.
Disposition	In this cell, one would note if the item has been retained by the laboratory, or transferred to another specialist for another type of analysis.
Date of Transfer	The date of the transfer of remains, either released for burial, or to another forensic scientist for further analysis, would be placed here. If retained, enter N/A.

of such a document lends a great deal of credibility to your statements as a witness. It also attests to the careful nature of the examination. It can be a very impressive document reassuring your professionalism to a jury. However, it is, first and foremost, a tool for you to use in the investigation of the recovered cremains.

5.3   MINIMUM NUMBER OF INDIVIDUALS

5.3.1   BASIC INVENTORY METHOD

The minimum number of individuals (MNI) is a concept that has been long known by physical anthropologists, osteologists, and forensic anthropologists. The concept is that when we come across commingled remains, cremated or not, the only true way to tell how many people are represented by the remains is to do an inventory and count up the number of repeated elements. For example, should we examine the number of patellae recovered from a scene, we may find that there are four right patellae and three left patellae. As it is clearly impossible to have an individual with more than one right patella, the number of possible individuals represented by the patellae is four. However, you will note that I stated above that we only have three left patellae. The fact of the matter is that there may be some good reason that we did not collect all the elements from a scene, such as carnivore scavenging. This fact alone dictates that we must use the phrase, "minimum number of individuals."

In addition to the raw count of elements recovered, we must also consider size differences, variation in ages, the sex, pathology, and any other traits or physical variables that may indicate that some elements come from a completely different person. For example, if we were to recover three right humeri and three left humeri we would, logically, conclude that there are at least three individuals represented by these remains. Yet, if we were to examine these recovered humeri more closely, and saw that one of the right humeri was from a juvenile, that is, a humeral diaphysis (or shaft) with intact epiphyseal surfaces, and there was no other left humerus that was of a similar level of development, we would have to refine our MNI to at least four individuals rather than three.

The above are rather crude examples of determining an MNI; however, the situation may be even more complex with cremains. The large degree of fragmentation of cremains necessitates that we make our estimates using any, and all, anatomical indicators. Given the resiliency of dental tissues, it may be more practical to base the MNI on particular types of teeth. However, the problem here is that antemortem tooth loss may not be known and hence confound an estimate. The best way to resolve this problem is to use an area of the skeleton that is particularly dense and less likely to be eradicated by a perpetrator. The region of the first molar (M1) socket in the mandible can be a reliable region to examine. The advantages to this include the fact that the mandible is very dense in this area with a bone thickness in adults that approaches 1 to 2 centimeters. Further, even if there is no M1 socket, the body of the mandible in this area is dense enough that it typically survives a fire. Although the same can be said of any robust area of the body, one of the best options to consider would be the petrous portion of the temporal bone. Regardless of the area being considered in this context, the point is to examine the recovered elements and consult the inventory to account for the minimum number of individuals represented by the recovered remains.

The MNI can be refined once there is information provided by the investigators as to the numbers and characteristics of those individuals who have not been accounted for. As forensic scientists, we usually prefer to render our own analytical conclusions without being told by the authorities who we are supposed to find. However, in fires, there is a great deal of pressure exerted by the community and authorities to render conclusions. I have found that providing me with the medical records of missing persons unaccounted for can at least reassure me as to how a recovery and subsequent cataloguing is progressing. Nonetheless, one must always be cognitive to not try to fit the data to the information provided by the authorities.

5.3.2 CREMATION WEIGHTS, ESTIMATION OF MNI, AND ORIGIN OF CREMAINS

On the surface, the concept of weighing cremains as a means of determining how many individuals are represented by these cremains seems to make some sense. However, in practice, the application of cremation weights to MNI is fraught with problems. Warren (1996) proposed that variables including sex, age, stature, cadaver weight, skeletal weight, and four anthropometric measures would have an influence on the final mass of commercially produced cremains. This study of 91 commercially produced cremains (with an original sample consisting of 55 males and 42 females) found that all weights above 2750 grams were male and all those above 1887 grams were female. Yet, a more recent study conducted by Bass and Jantz (2004) compared the cremation weights found in various other geographic locations in the United States. Cremation weights were obtained from the cremains of 151 males and 155 females produced by the East Tennessee Crematorium and compared to cremation weights reported from Florida (Warren and Maples, 1997) and Southern California (Sonek, 1992). Bass and Jantz (2004) also considered ash weights of anatomical human skeletons reported by Trotter and Hixon (1973). The central question being asked by Bass and Jantz was to see if the cremation weights reported by Warren and Maples (1997), or anyone else for that matter, can be extrapolated to other situations? This question has direct forensic implications as it goes directly to cases involving commercially produced cremains. Table 5.2 is a comparison of the East Tennessee sample to the other sources of cremation weights.

The result of this study by Bass and Jantz (2004) is that cremation weights are variable, and perhaps even regionally so according to the population under study. Bone mass is certainly thought to be an important variable in ultimately dictating the cremation weight. As with any area of analysis in forensic anthropology, human variation is the root of the difficulty in applying cremation weights to determining an MNI. However, in cases of cremains with a noncommercial origin, these cremation weights may only be estimates, as clandestine cremations and those from house fires and other contexts tend to be not as consistent in their cremation state. It is recommended that all recovered cremains be weighed in order to have a record of the mass of such friable specimens. However, the use of these weights as a means of ascertaining the minimum number of individuals has not been validated

TABLE 5.2

Comparison of East Tennessee Mean Cremation Weights With Other Samples (drawn from Table 4, Bass and Jantz, 2004)

	Males			Females		
Group	N	Mean	S.D.	N	Mean	S.D.
E. Tenn.	151	3379.77	634.98	155	2350.17	536.43
Florida	50	2898.70	499.20	40	1829.38	406.53
California	76	2801.38	589.47	63	1874.87	528.82
Anatomical	30	3410	–	30	2297	–

scientifically. Therefore, cremations that have not been undertaken in funerary crematoria should not use cremation weights as an indicator of the minimum number of individuals.

A further technique for distinguishing funerary cremains that have been commingled has been explored by Warren et al. (2002). Proton-induced X-ray emission (PIXE) is an analytical technique that provides the elemental composition of a material. In fact, it is designed to provide an absolute determination of the concentration of each element present with a detection limit in parts per million or less. Warren et al. note that a difficulty with the identification of cremains is that their chemical composition is variable and dependent upon several factors, including trace elements present in the body (and medical history), alterations of element ratios during the process of burning the body, and even the method of collection and storage of the cremains. In cases where a family may suspect that the "ashes" provided to them are not in fact human cremains, the application of a PIXE analysis may be indicated. Warren et al. logically contend that the level of phosphorus should be a key indicator of the presence of cremains, as this element is a major component of bones and teeth. They found that the levels of P in their reference samples were at least 40 times higher than the samples in question. Further, an examination of the P: Ca concentration ratio served as an additional indicator that the sample in question did not conform to the expected values. This was even the case when it is assumed that the incineration of bone does not significantly alter this ratio. Further testing of dolomite, sand, limestone, and soil confirmed that the profile of the suspect sample was that of dolomite limestone with an admixture of sand. Although this is not a means for examining MNI specifically, it is a means of distinguishing commercially prepared cremains from a replacement filler material.

The occurrence of what has become known as the Tri-State Crematory Incident (Noble, GA, February 2001) in which over 300 bodies were not cremated and families were presented with "ashes" in place of any real cremains, spawned the use of elemental analysis using Inductively Coupled Plasma-Optical Emission Spectroscopy (ICP-OES) (Brooks et al., 2006). Their study uses ICP-OES in order to distinguish known human cremains, concrete, mixtures of the two, and questionable sets of cremains from one another. After acid digestions and analysis for 21 elements through this technique, variable cluster and principal component analysis yielded seven elements (Sb, B, Li, Mn, Sr, Tl, and V) that were used to develop discriminant functions to categorize questionable samples as being either cremains or concrete. Mixtures having 50% or less human content were classified as concrete, whereas mixtures with 90% human content were classified as human cremains. The authors caution that as this is a pilot study, Daubert standards for courtroom admissibility in the U.S. have not been met. This is an extremely important point as the Daubert standard in the U.S. or the Regina v. JLJ standard in Canada must be satisfied in order for them to be admissible. To that end, it is important to consider that, although we may have techniques for analyzing the human skeletal remains that can meet these standards, the application of these standards on cremains will not be able to satisfy that standard at this time.

5.4   CLEANING AND SORTING

As stated earlier, the field collection of materials is just the initial step in a long process of analysis. The recovery of cremains in the field is far from a clean process. Fire scenes tend to have soot, carbonized material that is black, ash, soil, metal (such as nails from building materials), rusted metal, ceramics, melted glass, plastics, and other clinkers that can adhere to or encase cremains. An analysis of the human constituents of the mass of material recovered from a fire scene needs to be separated from the nonhuman materials in order for a morphological analysis to proceed. It has been my experience that it is rare that metals actually encase human remains in such a way that they are almost inseparable. However, Stratton and Beattie (1999) found that in addition to metal, a great deal of time was spent separating human material from burned insulation found in rail cars during the Hinton train disaster in Alberta, Canada in 1986. Yet, in most house fires and clandestine fires in pits the most common material to adhere to bone is soil, and the by-products of combusting building materials. The use of water at a fire scene will result in mixing this material with the bones.

Owsley (1993) stresses the importance of making as many observations at a scene as possible. In his investigation of the cremains of two missing U.S. journalists in Guatemala, the soil from the scene was screened through one-eighth inch wire mesh and then bone, plant material, metal, and soil were all separated from one another. Radiography of the soil yielded the finding of zipper teeth and other metals. This basic methodology, as a start to the laboratory analysis, is highly adaptable and an excellent starting point.

A similar instance of a double cremation in northern Ontario demonstrates how Owsley's basic methodology can be adapted. The perpetrators of a double homicide burned the bodies of two young adults, a male and a female, and actively crushed the cremains to render them "unrecognizable." However, the commingling of these remains in a pit separate from that in which they were cremated resulted in the carbonized material, along with the bones, being combined with the burial pit soil. The resulting coating of soil and carbonized material acted to obscure the features of the bone, and in some cases, cemented disparate element fragments together into a semisolid mass. Additionally, the recovered soil also contained other evidence of burned clothing, such as grommets from jeans and backpacks, as well as jewelry. This material also had to be separated in our cleaning process from the soil and the bone. To resolve this problem, my own lab developed a water separation method that permitted the separation and retention of all materials.

5.4.1 WATER PROCESSING OF CREMAINS

The water processing referred to here is a simple system of using various geological sieves and water to wash the bone and other artifacts from the fire in such a way as to collect the items of interest, and retain the soil and debris should other analysis be required.

This process is just a further enhancement to the basic screening demonstrated by Owsley (1993). Archaeologists have used the flotation process for decades in order to separate carbonized plant remains from the soil matrix found in ancient garbage dumps (middens). The carbonized material tends to be more buoyant and hence will float to the surface of a container of water once the soil has been mixed in. The mixing of the soil results in the water loosening the soil matrix and liberating the materials previously trapped in that matrix. The idea of solubilizing the soil to liberate the encased material is exactly what is needed in the processing of cremains. To that end, a system was developed that not only resulted in the recovery of bones and artifacts down to a millimeter in size, but also allowed all separated soil to be retained should it prove to be of further value.

Soil and cremated bone from one case were collected from a secondary burial pit. Although large fragments of bone visible in the pit were collected separately in the field and packaged accordingly after screening, the soil was then collected for further processing in the laboratory in large pails. These pails were each assigned an evidence number and noted in the evidence log accordingly. Thus, the processing of the soil contained in each pit was processed according to the evidence number, hence, preserving the context.

As a great deal of sorting was done in the field at the time of recovery using a one-quarter inch hardware cloth screen, most large pieces were recovered. However, as this was done in the middle of a northern Ontario winter with temperatures at negative 20°C, inside a tent heated with propane concrete driers, and the saturated soil was being melted in order to facilitate the recovery, the bone fragments were covered with adhering materials. Hence, all washing of recovered materials and the soil from the secondary burial pit was conducted using the same process.

The start of the process was to break the evidence seal on each soil container or bag of evidence as required (noted in the catalog). The material was placed into a geological sieve with 1 millimeter openings. This sieve was held over a shallow pan that was to receive the soil and material washed from the bones and artifacts as the water was run over the bone material (see Figure 5.1). This pan would quickly overflow with the water; however, the heavier fraction of the soil would sink to the bottom of the pan (Figure 5.2). The water would then decant off the side of the pan into a sink with a silt trap. The material recovered with the sieve was then placed on a clean tray for drying and subsequent sorting (Figure 5.3). The sorting of this material was initially sorted into two sections, bone and nonbone. The nonbone

FIGURE 5.1 The water processing of cremains seen here separates the various fractions while retaining the soil and associated artifacts. (Photo by T. Oost.)

FIGURE 5.2 The course fraction is retained in a sieve with 1-millimeter openings. (Photo by T. Oost.)

FIGURE 5.3 Material from the sieve is placed on a metal tray for drying and sorting. (Photo by T. Oost.)

material was then sorted as to the type of material, metallic and nonmetallic. The nonmetallic material was largely made up of charcoal resulting from the carbonized fuel used in the cremation. Metallic items were associated with staples and nails used in furniture construction, which made sense, as furniture was a confirmed fuel source in the fire. Additionally, personal effects from the victims, including remnants of clothing, teeth from zippers, rivets from jeans, dome snapped clasps from backpacks, glasses, and even coins were recovered (Figure 5.4).

Much of the larger material was packaged at the scene in paper bags. This material was cleaned using the method described above due to the possibility of adherent material falling away from these larger pieces. In some cases, a small new toothbrush was used to dislodge some of the soil that was sticking to some of the features. However, care was taken to not press too hard so as to keep from breaking cremated bone, given its friable state.

The sorting of the bone was first done according to the type of element, if possible. Namely, flat bones with a defined inner and outer table, as well as diploic tissue, were classified as being of cranial origin. Other flat bones lacking anatomically specific features were simply classified as such until repairs with other bones facilitated further identification.

During this sorting process, a label was maintained with all bone fragments and groups of fragments that indicated its evidence (or now, catalog) number. This is essential as we did not want to lose a fragment's context, and thus lose track of the continuity of that fragment. Once a fragment was dry, an evidence number was written directly onto it in a location that was deemed to be lacking in pathology, or any feature of diagnostic importance. This is particularly important when a piece is found to mend with another fragment.

In some instances, cremains will also have adherent charred soft tissues. In some cases, the soft tissue is more pervasive than expected (Figure 5.5). These tissues, in the first instance, must be recorded in context in the field, and then in greater detail

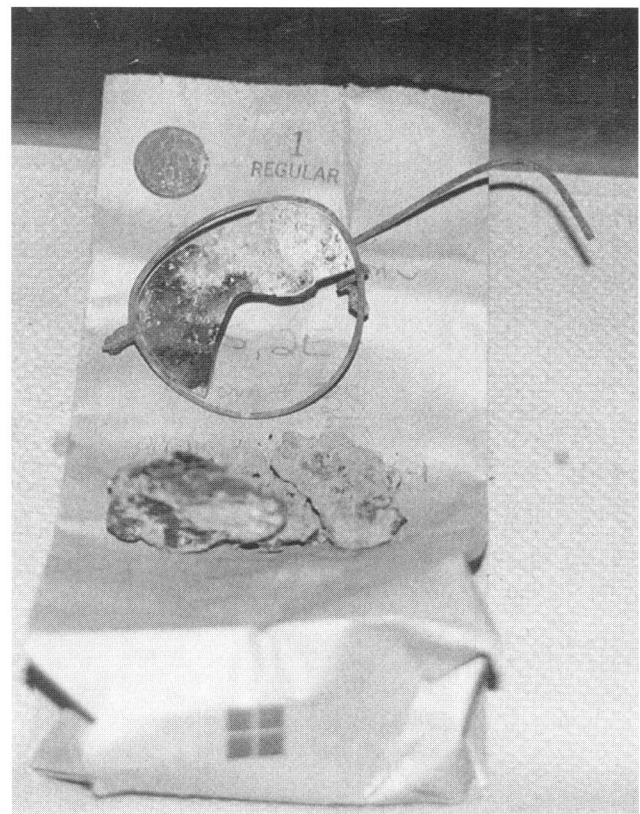

FIGURE 5.4   Artifacts such as glasses and a coin may be recovered from screen soil associated with cremated remains. (Photo by S. Fairgrieve.)

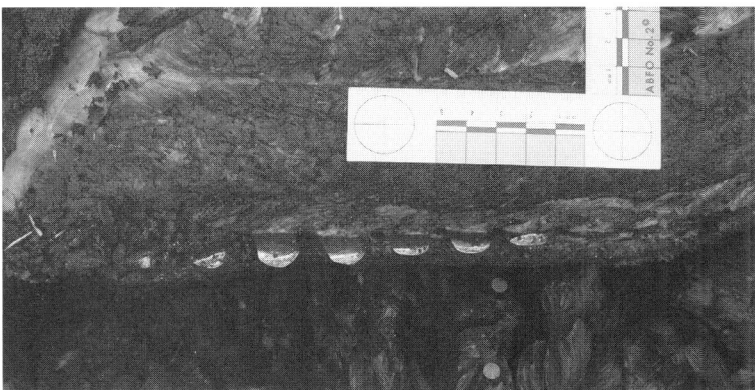

FIGURE 5.5   A portion of the thoracic cage with visible spinous processes of an experimentally cremated domestic pig. Note the large quantity of soft tissue that survived an outdoor fire of 30 minutes' duration that reached in excess of 900°C. (Photo by S. Fairgrieve.)

in the laboratory. As part of the initial examination, these fragments should also be radiographed for foreign objects and signs of trauma. The adherent tissue should not be removed unless there is sufficient reason to do so. Such reasons may include the recovery of evidence, such as bullet fragments, or to examine specific trauma. This must be judged by you and the forensic pathologist assigned to the case. Additionally, the soft tissue, likely muscle, has the potential to be a good source of DNA.

The removal of soft tissue can follow one of several methods that have been used by forensic anthropologists for years. The least caustic method of tissue removal is through the use of insects. Dermestid beetles have proven to be very effective. However, as time is usually a factor in most investigations, the time-honored traditions of soaking the specimen in water and boiling it have proven to be reliable. However, all sampling for DNA should be done prior to any method of tissue removal.

5.5   REPAIR AND RECONSTRUCTION

The repair or mending of fragments is the first step into chronicling the injuries suffered by cremation victims. As noted in a previous chapter, the idea of categorizing fractures as being heat-induced or due to a mechanical trauma has the potential to have a tremendous impact on charges that may be laid in a criminal case. In Figure 5.6 a cremated domestic pig neurocranium from a house fire is reconstructed

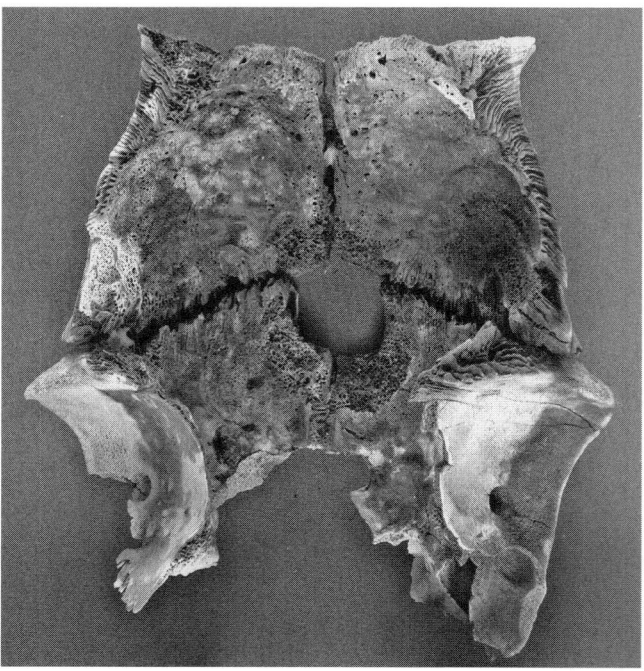

FIGURE 5.6   The reconstructed fragments of the neurocranium of a domestic pig cremated in an experimental house fire. The internal beveling clearly indicates a gunshot wound penetrating from the outer to inner table. (Photo by S. Fairgrieve.)

to demonstrate a penetrating gunshot wound. Seemingly disparate portions of the skull can be mended to yield important evidence.

There are specific procedures to follow when undertaking the mending of two bone fragments. First, the two fragments should be photographed individually (with scale) to show the nature of the fracture. The mending of the bone must consider the quality of the bone to be mended. If the margin of the bone on either specimen is too friable for mending, even after some form of consolidation, then it should not be undertaken. However, if the margins are strong enough to support an adhesive, typically white PVA glue that is water soluble, then the mend should proceed. The application of the glue should be done on clean and dry surfaces. Do not saturate the material with the glue, but apply enough to penetrate both sides of the fracture. The fragments should be supported in a medium to carry their weight so that the glue does not dry the join between the two fragments at an unnatural angle. Typically, a tub of sand is used to place the two fragments into for such support. Two parallel lines should be drawn across the location of the mend on each fragment in order to indicate that a mend between these two fragments was performed. Likewise, a note in the catalog indicating which fragments mended with other fragments must also be recorded as needed. The nature of the fracture that had separated the two fragments should also be indicated.

It is essential in all forensic cases, and particularly in cremains cases, to mend these fragments, as this will facilitate the analysis of the fracture patterns. The importance of fracture pattern analysis was briefly discussed in the previous chapter; however, I would caution that this can be a long process, especially if you are dealing with commingled cremains. Nonetheless, the mending of fragments must be taken as far as possible. The physical action of the fire, and even the perpetrator, operate to make reconstruction of the recovered elements a challenge. In many cases, the margins of the fractures may have been degraded to the point where a physical mend is not possible. However, if the fragment is determined to be from a particular element, and the position on that element is known, then a mock-up of the complete bone may be done. This is done in a similar fashion to that of fossil reconstructions. In this case, the gaps between structures are not filled, but the relative position and locations of the various fragments are photographed. Such photographs may become important for court purposes.

5.6   OSTEOBIOGRAPHICAL ANALYSIS

The osteobiographical analysis is the means by which the physical characteristics of the individual represented by the cremains are chronicled. The analysis, as with any osteological analysis of human skeletal remains, is geared to ultimately arriving at a positive identification of the cremains. Rather than outlining all of the various methods for estimating the age at death, assessing the sex of the cremains, estimating ancestry, and stature, the goal of the following sections is to provide the analyst with the various caveats that must be taken into consideration when dealing with cremains. As demonstrated in previous chapters, the alteration of bone by fire can have a profound effect on the size and shape of these elements and their fragments. Thompson (2004) found that heat-induced alterations of bone would have an

TABLE 5.3
The Influence of Heat-Induced Change on Anthropological Analytical
Techniques (drawn from Thompson, 2004, Table 2)

Heat-Induced Change	Technique Affected	Cause of Effect
Color change	Metric	Indirectly: color change implies loss of organics, which causes shrinkage
Weight loss	Metric	Indirectly: weight loss implies loss of organics, which causes shrinkage
Fracture formation	Morphological and metric	Directly: increased fragmentation reduces likelihood of technique application
Change in strength	Morphological and metric	Indirectly: weaker bone increases fragmentation, which reduces likelihood of technique application
Recrystallization	Morphological and metric	Directly: changes in microstructure may affect shape and will affect dimensions
Porosity change	Metric	Indirectly: implies loss of organics and reorganization of microstructure
Dimensional change	Morphological and metric	Directly: differential size changes may affect shape and will affect dimensions

effect on specific aspects of analytical techniques (see Table 5.3 for a summary). It is agreed that osteological analytical techniques utilized by forensic anthropologists are based on metrics and morphology. As noted by Thompson (2004), all observed heat-induced changes to bone, including color change, weight loss, fracture formation, changes in strength, recrystallization, porosity change, and dimensional change, will result in a metrical and/or morphological change that will have an effect on the application of an analytical technique or the application of established standards based on unburned bones. Therefore, the reliability of standard analytical procedures will be called into question. This fact directly affects the admissibility of such an analysis under the Daubert, R. v. JLJ and R. v. Mohan rules of admissibility.

5.6.1 AGE AT DEATH ESTIMATION

Age at death estimation is based on morphological indicators of the skeleton that have been linked to the development, growth, and maturation of osteological or odontological structures. There is a rich literature base on age at death estimation using intact and fragmentary human remains. These methods are largely metrically or morphologically based, requiring the analyst to make a determination as to the developmental status of a structure, or the appearance of various features. For example, the measurement of long bone diaphyses in juveniles has been used to provide an estimate of age at death in children. Other means of dependably estimating the age at death in children has included dental eruption, and tooth root and crown calcification. In adults, age at death estimates have been based on cranial and mandibular suture closure (synostosis), pubic symphysis metamorphosis, rib end meta-morphosis, osteon aging, cementum annulations, dental attrition, and even tooth root color, to name a few. The underlying principle behind all of these methods is that there is change that occurs to the hard tissues in a fashion that may be correlated with time. The problem is that populations differ in the rates and manifestations of these changes. If we now consider the additional factor of heat-induced alterations, there is an even more significant problem.

It is generally accepted in forensic anthropology that the younger the individual, the more accurate the age estimation. This is considered common sense, as there are many more developmentally morphological indicators on subadults than in adults. If that logic is followed, fetal development, typically characterized as being a regular process with predictable age indicators, should then afford us an opportunity to estimate age with a high degree of reliability.

Fazekas and Kósa (1978) have the most extensive database for fetal bone size and age (both gestational and lunar). The determination of fetal age is largely dependent upon measuring the length of a diaphysis. Fetal bone will react to fire in a similar manner to adult bone. The fire results in a reduction in the length and diameter of a diaphysis. In their volume on *Forensic Fetal Osteology*, Fazekas and Kósa (1978) cite an original study by Petersohn and Köhler (1965) in which fetal bones were reexamined to determine the percentage of shrinkage from fresh to carbonized and calcined states. It stands to reason that one must know the degree to which bones shrink in a fire environment if one is going to apply metrical data to make an age at death estimation. Huxley and Kósa (1999) reevaluated Petersohn and Köhler's (1965) data, as this would have implications in forensic contexts for estimating the age at death of fetal remains recovered from fire scenes.

By way of a brief summary of Petersohn and Köhler's data, Huxley and Kósa (1999) report that the percentage shrinkage of fetal bone from carbonization and calcination varies greatly by the lunar age group and the skeletal element. In fact, the percentage shrinkage of wet bone to a carbonized state varies greatly in the earliest lunar age groups. In the case of newborn remains, the average shrinkage is 2.16% ± 0.29% with a range from 1.97 to 2.72%. In the case of going from a wet state to carbonized, the trend noted in this early study was that the percentage shrinkage decreased by more than half during each lunar month (LM) between 4 to 6 LMs and then started to taper off at 7 LMs and slowly decline between 8 LMs and newborn. If the burn is taken to the point of converting a bone from the wet state to a calcine state, the shrinkage rates were found to be high over the course of fetal development. Greater shrinkage is observed in calcined bone. This trend makes sense, as carbonization and calcification result in organic components being leached out of the diaphyses and the medullary marrow (Huxley and Kósa, 1999). Table 5.4 is a compilation by Huxley and Kósa (1999) of the diaphyseal shrinkage rates for carbonized and calcined fetal bones from 4 LMs to newborns. Table 5.5 is a compilation by Huxley (1998) of Petersohn and Köhler's (1965) data showing the differences in the average percent shrinkage of specific skeletal elements by lunar age group.

This research on the dimensional reduction of fetal and newborn bones subjected to fire is a clear indication that the biological age (or rather the level of

TABLE 5.4

Comparison of Combined Diaphyseal Shrinkage Rates for Carbonized and Calcined Bones from Fetuses between 4–10 LM and Newborns (drawn from Table 13, Huxley and Kósa, 1999)

Age	Sample Size	Average ± Carbonized	SD% Calcined	Range Carbonized	SD% Calcined
4 LM	1–6	32.50 ± 12.12	40.11 ± 17.51	17.50–50.16	21.49–68.98
5 LM	16–47	14.40 ± 4.44	18.29 ± 4.42	9.65–21.40	13.91–25.24
6 LM	7–14	6.78 ± 1.06	9.84 ± 1.27	5.61–8.01	8.42–11.26
7 LM	3–8	4.18 ± 0.31	9.82 ± 0.51	3.71–4.48	0.04–10.58
8 LM	4	3.47 ± 0.42	9.42 ± 0.72	3.12–4.14	9.39–10.31
9 LM	5–6	3.05 ± 0.18	9.45 ± 0.33	2.85–3.22	9.13–10.00
10 LM	10–12	2.46 ± 0.67	8.94 ± 0.37	2.38–2.54	8.35–9.42
Newborns	1–2	2.16 ± 0.29	8.96 ± 0.49	1.97–2.72	8.37–9.52

calcification) of the decedent and the type of skeletal element will have an influence on its final dimensions. Further, the duration of the fire, producing either a carbonized or a calcined bone, dictates the amount of organic components that have been eliminated from the bone. In the case of fetal and newborn bones, the measurement of charred or calcined skeletal elements as a basis for age will be problematic, particularly in the earlier lunar age groups, as the rates of reduction can vary between 6.27%–13.85% (Huxley, 1998). In the older lunar age groups the rates range between 0.39%–2.03%.

If this trend is followed then the amount of shrinkage in the bones of mature individuals should be much less than that seen in subadults. However, the question remains, is this change in morphology enough to significantly alter the application of metrical and morphological methods of estimating age at death?

TABLE 5.5

Comparison of Shrinkage Rates (%) by Skeletal Element for Fetuses between 4–10 LM and Newborns with Sample Sizes in Brackets (drawn from Table 7, Huxley, 1998)

	4 LM	5 LM	6 LM	7 LM	8 LM	9 LM	10 LM	Newborn
Humerus	9.13 (6)	5.39 (47)	3.37 (14)	2.24 (8)	1.45 (4)	1.68 (6)	1.75 (12)	2.03 (2)
Radius	9.73 (3)	5.79 (37)	4.30 (14)	2.24 (6)	2.41 (4)	1.90 (6)	1.70 (12)	0.39 (2)
Ulna	9.23 (3)	5.65 (31)	3.46 (9)	2.25 (7)	2.21 (4)	1.82 (5)	3.09 (11)	1.06 (2)
Femur	13.85 (6)	4.59 (44)	3.56 (14)	2.46 (8)	2.28 (4)	1.67 (6)	1.72 (10)	1.48 (1)
Tibia	12.35 (3)	5.82 (44)	3.44 (14)	2.51 (8)	2.93 (4)	1.94 (6)	1.69 (12)	1.19 (2)
Fibula	6.27 (1)	7.18 (16)	2.77 (7)	2.07 (3)	1.82 (4)	1.59 (6)	1.46 (10)	1.52 (2)

In order to answer this question there are some steps that must be taken by the analyst prior to the application of an aging technique (or any analytical technique for that matter). First, when using a metrically based method, it would be prudent to examine the method for the implications of shrinkage on the measurements and the derived results from those measures. One does this by simply taking known specimens and measuring them, and applying the method. Then, to test for the effect of shrinkage, apply a conversion factor that would mimic heat-induced shrinkage, while accounting for the percentage differences for the type of bone tissue and the presumed temperature range (see Section 3.5.3.2). Next, apply these new values to the method you have chosen and examine the results. If the result is a different age at death estimate than your previous estimate, you will need to examine the maximum possible amount of shrinkage for the measurement taken. In this scenario, the baseline for your age estimate should assume that no shrinkage has occurred. This way you will have an age range based on no shrinkage and then the maximal shrinkage. Keep in mind that when you are applying this to an actual specimen, there is no way for you to assess the amount of shrinkage that has taken place. As such, you will need to assume that the maximum degree of shrinkage has occurred for that specimen considering the scene evidence for temperature as well as the color and overall condition of the bone. If the specimen in question has been warped, then no measurement should be taken or applied to an aging method.

It is important to note that providing a wide age at death estimate is not a failure of the method, but rather a conservative estimate that is used as part of the identification process. Providing a wider age estimate will give the police investigators a potentially larger list of missing individuals to consider if the cremains are in a truly isolated context with no other scene indicators.

Age at death estimation based on metrical methods is possible; however, the application of any data to such a method must be done with the aforementioned considerations. The analyst must also keep in mind that a Daubert challenge of this type of evidence is likely in the event that no positive identification is achieved and the identification is based on the osteobiographical data generated by the analysis.

The use of morphological features for estimating age at death, such as dental calcification, epiphyseal fusion, surface metamorphosis, and bone histology are all highly dependent upon the extent of heat-induced alterations. In subadults, other than long bone lengths, aging is based on ossification centers, tooth formation, dental eruption sequences, and epiphyseal union. In adults, the methods include those that evaluate changes in specific surfaces, such as the pubic symphysis, auricular surface, and sternal rib ends. In the case of suture closure, ectocranial, endocranial, and palatal sutures have been used on more mature individuals. The evaluation of histological structures in bones (cortical remodeling) and teeth (cementum annulations) depend on being able to visualize and quantify structures that may be prone to severe damage from heat. Dental evaluation is dealt with in greater detail in Chapter 7.

Rather than go into detail of the specific structures affected by heat-induced alterations, Table 5.6 has been compiled to assist forensic anthropologists by listing the surfaces likely to be affected and the implications of such alteration on various methods for estimating age at death. The methods listed are just there as examples

TABLE 5.6

Age at Death Estimation Methods and the Influence of Heat-Induced Changes

Method	Feature/Surface Affected	Heat-Induced Change
Diaphyseal lengths (Hoffman, 1979)	Length of diaphysis and metaphyseal growth plate surface	Shrinkage in length, erosion of metaphyseal growth plate, thinner cortex.
Primary ossification centers	Immature ossification centers with higher cartilage composition	Consumption by fire of cartilaginous ossification centers, such as those in the wrist and cranial bone of infants.
Tooth Formation (Moorrees et al., 1963 a,b)	Tooth crown and root in crypt and in process of erupting	Desiccation of crown and roots; may be preserved in crypt depending on condition of mandible and maxillae. Maxillae more likely to be severely fractured.
Tooth eruption (Schour and Massler, 1941; Ubelaker, 1999)	Tooth crown and root of erupted and erupting teeth; mandibular and maxillary alveolus	Desiccation of crown and roots of erupted teeth; damage to those teeth in crypts dependent upon condition of alveolus with heat-induced fractures.
Epiphyseal fusion (Buikstra and Ubelaker, 1994)	Epiphysis and epiphyseal growth plate	Heat-induced factures of epiphysis and destruction of growth plate and fracturing of fusion sites.
Pubic symphysis (Todd, 1920; Brooks, 1955; McKern and Stewart, 1957; Suchey and Katz, 1986; Brooks and Suchey, 1990; Meindl et al., 1985)	Pubic symphysis rim, face and demifaces	Heat-induced fractures, warping, obscuring ridges and furrows, and consuming of nodules.
Auricular surface (Lovejoy et al., 1985; Meindl and Lovejoy, 1989; Bedford et al., 1989)	Auricular surface, margins, and retroauricular area	Heat-induced fractures, obscuring porosity, billows, striae, transverse organization, texture, and consuming of ossific nodules.
Sternal rib ends (Iscan et al., 1984, 1985, 1987; Iscan and Loth, 1986)	Sternal surface texture, surface contour, rib edge form, and contour	Consumption by fire, heat-induced fractures, and obscuring of traits.
Cranial suture closure (Todd and Lyon, 1924, 1925a,b,c; Meindl and Lovejoy, 1985; Buikstra and Ubelaker, 1994; Galera et al., 1998)	Ectocranial and endocranial bone	Heat-induced fractures, delamination, and extreme fragmentation.
Palatal sutures (Mann et al., 1987; Gruspier and Mullen, 1991; Buikstra and Ubelaker, 1994)	Maxillary anterior alveolus, hard palate, and horizontal component of palatines	Heat-induced fracture of the anterior alveolus and hard palate, posterior portions more well-protected but also subject to heat-induced fractures and marginal abrasions.

of the most common methods utilized; hence, this is not meant to be an exhaustive list. However, the types of damage listed are indeed important considerations for the application of the methods listed. The overall trend to note is that portions of bone that are closer to the surface of the body will be more highly affected by fire than those areas embedded deep in soft tissues. The types of damage, including warping, cracking, delamination, desiccation, and contraction, have the potential to affect all exposed areas depending upon the temperature and duration of direct exposure. Regardless of the region, the application of any method for estimating age at death is a pursuit that necessitates caution.

5.6.2   SEX ASSESSMENT

Many of the caveats expressed in the previous section can be directly applied to the examination of cremains for the sex of the decedent. Assessing any skeletal remains for indicators of the decedent's sex are also based on metrical and morphological methods. However, in the case of sexing remains, the goal is to quantify, by some means, exhibited sexually dimorphic traits in order to render a conclusion. Given that by simply guessing the chance of being correct is 50%, it stands to reason that forensic anthropologists should be right more often than they are wrong, since the sexing methods should build on the aforementioned random value. Rather than use this section to discuss problems with intra- and interpopulational variance in sexually dimorphic traits and dimensions, the effects of heat-induced alterations to bones and relevant features will be discussed in light of various sexing methods used by forensic anthropologists.

Forensic anthropologists are keenly aware that sexing the skeletal remains of juvenile, or sexually immature, individuals is nowhere near as accurate as sexing the remains of a mature individual. Hence, sexing the cremains of juveniles is not recommended for two reasons: first, the bones of juveniles are not as thoroughly ossified and are subject to a greater degree of heat-induced damage; second, juveniles have not undergone the osteological changes of pubescence that result in sexually dimorphic features. This is not to say that any analysis is futile; however, it is going to be a great deal more challenging. In these cases, even DNA analysis may be precluded as a possibility. However, later in this section, recommendations have been outlined for those wishing to attempt to sex subadult cremains. Yet, sexing of cremains is more commonly applied to mature elements that are more likely to have sufficiently well-preserved dimorphic features.

The two areas of the skeleton that are the most accurate for sexing are the bones of the pelvis and those of the skull. The suite of traits that are considered sexually dimorphic are listed in most osteology books (e.g., Fairgrieve and Oost, 2001; Byers, 2005; White and Folkens, 2005). In general, sexing several skeletal elements from a population, such as those found in an archaeological ossuary, can be done on the basis of relative size and robusticity of various features. However, most forensic cremation cases deal with either a single individual or a small number of individuals, sometimes in a commingled state. Therefore, the comparative approach of relative size may not be of assistance in sexing, particularly when the fire environment is not homogeneous and the degree of preservation and heat-induced alterations demonstrate intrapersonal and interpersonal variation.

Although heat-induced fractures (HIFs) are a serious impediment to the analysis of cremains, some regions of the skeleton can still have useful features that demonstrate sexual dimorphism. If we consider the skull, there are numerous features in a variety of locations on various elements that can be used in sexing cremains. For example, Byers (2005) lists several traits that exhibit sexual dimorphism in the skull. These traits include the overall size of the skull, the mastoid process size and robusticity, brow ridge prominence, nuchal area robusticity, supraorbital margin shape, and chin relative form and dimensions. The aforementioned traits are all dependent on the experience of the forensic anthropologist and knowledge of population variation. Hence, any analysis should consider as many traits as possible. In the cremation context there is always a possibility that the relevant traits have been damaged to the point of not being utilized.

Table 5.7 lists some of the common sexually dimorphic traits of the skull and the effects of fire on those areas. It is clear that with prolonged exposure to fire, HIFs, shrinkage, fragmentation, and warping may be inevitable. However, not all traits will be rendered useless should significant heat-induced alterations occur.

The size of the overall skull may be difficult to appreciate and quantify if the skull is not reassembled. However, the reassembly will be difficult, especially if it has been subjected to differential heat exposure. As such, some mends may not permit precise alignment, due to differential shrinkage and/or warping. Yet, this feature is not one depended upon when examining an isolated specimen unless the analyst has significant experience with the range of variation for that population. The use of osteometrics would have to be considered, albeit somewhat reluctantly.

The mastoid process size and robusticity is not as susceptible to heat-induced alteration, due to its embedded nature within one end of the sternocleidomastoid muscle. However, the shrinkage of the surface with accompanying fractures has been observed. Likewise, the increase in temperature inside the mastoid air cells has resulted in further cracking and subsequent exposure of these deep structures to the calcined surface. Larger and more robust mastoid processes, as observed in males, are primarily composed of more dense compact bone and are more resilient to heat-induced stress. The size and robusticity of the mastoid process is likely

---

TABLE 5.7

The Size of Microstructural Features of Bone in Descending Order (drawn from Piekarski, 1970)

Structure	Size
Vascular canals	20–30 microns
Lacunae	4–6 microns
Canaliculi	0.5–2 microns
Fine porosity	600–800 angstroms
Spaces between mineral phase	50–100 angstroms

---

to survive house fire contexts and outdoor cremations. Cremations of remains in confined contexts, such as the inside of an automobile, may provide temperatures high enough to cause the aforementioned damage.

Taken collectively, brow ridges, frontal squama, and supraorbital margins are subjected to similar degrees of exposure as they are obviously situated around the orbits and in an area that has a relatively thin covering of soft tissue. The most highly damaged area is the region of the frontal squama. The tissue is particularly thin in this area and burns away quickly. Hence, HIFs, shrinkage, warping, fragmentation, and delamination are all common occurrences. Reconstruction may yield evidence of frontal bossing; however, the amount of bossing, if present at all, may be overexaggerated due to warping and cracking. This is the case for subadults whose frontal bones are not as well ossified. Yet, even in severe cremation contexts, brow ridges and supraorbital margins have been preserved (Figure 5.7).

The nuchal area of the occipital bone is typically one of the thickest portions of the neurocranial bones, particularly between the internal and external occipital protuberances. In spite of the extreme heat, this area usually survives so that it can be recovered and examined. Due to the relatively large mass and density of bone, delamination is common. This is due to the fact that the heat-induced changes to the outer table, including HIFs and shrinkage, proceed more expeditiously than the bone of the inner table.

The chin is a prominent structure that can be characterized as being relatively close to the surface of the skin. Yet, deep to the chin in the lingual region there is considerable soft tissue coverage. This arrangement also creates a differentially burned region. Heat-induced fractures, shrinkage, and delamination are all common for this region of the mandible. In spite of this, usable fragments may survive and be assessable. Figure 5.8 depicts the fragmented mandible from the same individual in Figure 5.7.

FIGURE 5.7   The left and right supraorbital margins and brow ridges are evident on these cremated fragments from a Caucasoid adult male. (Photo by S. Fairgrieve.)

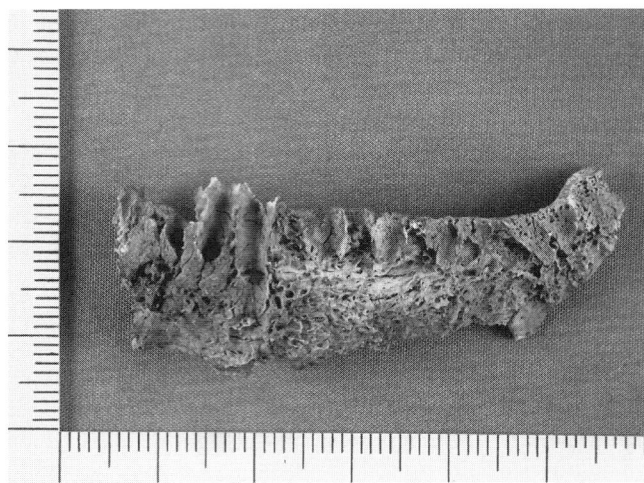

FIGURE 5.8   The anterior body fragment of a cremated mandible from the same individual shown in Figure 5.7. (Photo by S. Fairgrieve.)

The assessment of sex from cremains has typically been centered on the skull (Mayne, 1990). Accordingly, sexual dimorphism in the postcranial (actually, infracranial) skeleton can be more problematic. Without question, the bones of the pelvis are considered to be the most sexually dimorphic of the human body (e.g., Byers, 2005; White and Folkens, 2005). However, their utility in evaluating the sex of cremated remains will, once again, depend on its level of preservation. Dokládal (1969) noted that the bones of the pelvis are frequently fragmented by fire. This is due to these elements being intramembranous in origin. The outer compact bone is susceptible to cracking with rapid desiccation. Delamination and warping also occur in this region. However, the deeper areas of the pelvic structures, including the ischium, acetabulae, and sacrum are relatively well protected unlike the os pubis and the anterior iliac crests. Unfortunately, the os pubis is the one region that can provide very reliable features for sexing and an age at death estimate.

The Phenice Method (Phenice, 1969) has been reported to sex the os pubis to a high degree of accuracy (Lovell, 1989; Sutherland and Suchey, 1991; Ubelaker and Volk, 2002). It is for this reason that an attempt to recover and repair the os pubis must be made. The Phenice features that seem to survive more readily are the ventral arc, and an ischiopubic ramus ridge, both usually indicative of females. The subpubic concavity formed along the inferior margin of the inferior ischiopubic ramus, another female trait, may be difficult to assess due to warping and/or delamination damage. As this method is dependent upon assessing all three of these features and a conclusion for sex is based on at least two features favoring a particular sex, it may be possible to come to a reliable conclusion. However, if only two traits can be evaluated and they yield an equivocal result, then the conclusion will remain equivocal for this method.

The sexing of subadults, mentioned above, is considered to be precarious. Byers (2005) summarized the situation by noting "most differences in size and shape emerge at puberty." However, in spite of this, some researchers have demonstrated that it is possible to sex a subadult with at least 70% accuracy using features of the auricular surface (Weaver, 1980; Mittler and Sheridan, 1992). Using the same region, the greater sciatic notch has also been examined by researchers since the 1950s (Boucher, 1957; Weaver, 1980; Schutkowski, 1993). Regardless of the reported rates of these methods, the application of them to subadults will be plagued by the ubiquitous problem of cremated bone preservational quality. Again, subadult remains are not only more easily damaged, but may even be more highly fragmented in the fire due to their smaller size, mass, and lower level of ossification. As there is a general reluctance of forensic anthropologists to even report the sex of subadult remains, extreme caution must be exercised if one is going to evaluate subadult cremains for sex.

Although there are other methods that have been attempted to assess the sex of remains, the application of any of these methods is subject to the same caveats as outlined above. However, the use of dental remains as a source of sexually dimorphic traits will be discussed in Chapter 7 with other aspects of dental analysis.

5.6.3 ESTIMATION OF ANCESTRY

Forensic anthropologists, as part of their analysis, will provide police with some description of the "race" to which the decedent likely belonged. As the term "race" is recognized as a cultural identification rather than a biological one, forensic anthropologists will tend to use the term "ancestry." The inherent problem with this is that people tend to self-identify the group or groups to which they feel they have an affiliation. This is done in spite of the fact that they may have indeed no biologically relevant ancestry associated with that group. A further complication is that the biological variants used by police to provide descriptions of suspects or missing persons, such as skin color, hair color and style, and even eye color, are not features that are reflected well in the skeleton.

The most reliable region of the skeleton to evaluate for ancestry is the skull (e.g., Krogman and Iscan, 1986; Bass, 1995; Byers, 2005). Specifically, the anthroposcopic characteristics of the skull used by many forensic anthropologists are designed to provide a distinction between "Whites," "Blacks," and "Asians." As such, ancestry is only done in terms of very broad categories.

Many areas of the skull are commonly examined for indicators of ancestry. These areas include the nose, face, vault, and the upper and lower jaws and teeth (Byers, 2005). The overdependence on the structural features of the facial region and its periphery, although necessary for a reliable result, is unfortunate due to this region being particularly susceptible to the ravages of fire. The thin nature of the facial bones, coupled with the presence of paranasal sinuses, all promote the fracturing and fine fragmentation in cremation contexts.

One area in particular that is heavily relied upon for indicators of ancestry is the nose. The root, bridge, spine, lower border, and width of the nasal orifice are key to any evaluation of visible traits. It is possible for cremains to have elements of the nasal region preserved in spite of the cremation process. The root and bridge of the nose, located at the point of the articulation of the nasal bones with the frontal bone and the articulated nasal bones themselves, respectively, are often recoverable from cremation scenes. Likewise, the inferior margin of the nasal orifice, located on the maxilla, is worth close scrutiny for the presence of a sill, guttering, or a flat and sharp form.

Osteometrically, the face will normally provide much of the data required to apply to discriminant functions for estimating ancestry. The caveats pertaining to osteometrics from cremains still apply. This is especially true for the face and the rest of the skull as the degree of fragmentation and destruction in cremation contexts, particularly if a perpetrator is physically crushing elements, may render reconstruction impossible. These elements are highly susceptible to delamination and warping.

Therefore, in cases of more complete cremations in which the cremated remains of the skull are in a calcined state, any chance of making a successful attempt to analyze these elements for indicators of ancestry will depend on macroscopically visible traits being preserved, as opposed to osteometrically derived and interpreted data.

5.6.4 STATURE ESTIMATION

The estimation of living stature is one individual characteristic that is attempted in spite of there often being no accurate antemortem record. The use of living stature data from driver's licenses, a form of self-reported stature, can tend to actually be overreported (e.g., Willey and Falsetti, 1990; Giles and Hutchinson, 1991; Ousley, 1995). However, by utilizing anthropometric techniques, an estimate of a range of living stature, rather than a specifically assigned stature itself, may be beneficial in resolving identity issues. It should be noted that stature, in and of itself, falls into the category of class evidence in forensic science and is, therefore, not a characteristic that can be used as a sole criterion for a positive identification.

Success in achieving a stature estimate that one can have confidence in will depend on the completeness of the skeletal remains. Hence, methods have been developed that utilize the full skeleton (Fully, 1956; Stewart, 1979) to methods that utilize portions of a skeleton, such as long bone lengths or partial long bones (e.g., Jantz et al., 1995; Trotter and Gleser, 1952, 1958; Trotter, 1970; Meadows and Jantz, 1992; Byers et al., 1989; Janson and Taylor, 1995; Steele, 1970).

In addition to the raw calculation of stature, the age of the individual and any shrinkage of the bone will need to be considered. It is known that, with increasing age, people will lose stature (Byers, 2005). Although it is beyond the scope of this book to discuss various formulae for age correction factors, it is important to consider that age as well as bone shrinkage due to gradual desiccation may pale in comparison with the alterations to bones caused by fire. The rapid desiccation and subsequent shrinkage of bone tissue will act to confound most stature estimates. Hence, wider stature estimates may be necessary, if reported at all, as the goal is to have a realistic stature estimate range that has a high probability to include the record of the victim.

The application of some methods of stature estimation to fragmentary remains has been attempted by various researchers studying cremains (Lisowski, 1968;

Malinowski and Porawski, 1969; Piontek, 1975; Rösing, 1977). However, these studies recognize that the error rates for such estimates are large (Mayne, 1990).

In order to apply one of the various methods of stature estimation, such as measurement of an articular surface diameter from a limb long bone, the measurement would undoubtedly necessitate a correction factor for that measurement due to the shrinkage of the bone. Therefore, stature estimation from cremains will depend on the type and degree of alteration encountered. Correction factors may be applicable; however, these factors can only be estimated as the actual amount of shrinkage of the bone is an unknown quantity and not scientifically determined.

So, it would seem that a stature estimate should only be provided if there is a reasonably intact skeletal element that has not progressed beyond a stage at which shrinkage is a significant factor. A significant factor in this instance refers to the degree of shrinkage found with a particular burning stage that would alter the interpretation of a measurement as it is applied to a stature estimation formula. By first examining the stature estimation method one wishes to apply, it is recommended that a measurement first be made of an unburned element from a reference collection and apply it to the method of consideration. Once the value is applied to the method, and a stature estimate is concluded, one would then reduce the measurement already taken by a corresponding degree of shrinkage that would be observed in cremated bone at various stages of burn. This exercise would then permit the analyst to assess how appropriate a particular methodology is in any instance. For example, if we were to examine estimating the stature of a skeleton using an adult humerus length regression formula from Trotter (1970) for a white male as the basis of our stature estimate, the formula would be as follows:

$$Stature = 3.80 \times Hum + 70.45 \pm 4.05$$

If we measure an unburned humerus to be 32 centimeters and utilize a 95% confidence interval, the formula would be as follows:

$$Low\ end\ of\ range = 3.80(32) + 70.45 - (4.05 \times 2)$$
$$= 183.95\ centimeters = 6\ feet\ 0.5\ inches$$

$$High\ end\ of\ range = 3.80(32) + 70.45 + (4.05 \times 2)$$
$$= 200.15\ centimeters = 6\ feet\ 6.8\ inches$$

This results in a range of 6.3 inches between the two estimates. However, if we were to now do the same calculation, but alter the original measurement of 32 centimeters by a factor of 10% due to shrinkage and warping in an extreme cremation scenario, the measurement would be as follows:

$$32\ cm - (32 \times 0.10) = 32\ cm - 3.2\ cm = 28.8\ cm$$

If we now substituted in this new cremation length value for the humerus, with everything else being equal the following result is yielded:

$$\text{Low end of range} = 3.80(28.8) + 70.45 - (4.05 \times 2)$$
$$= 171.79 \text{ centimeters} = 5 \text{ feet } 7.7 \text{ inches}$$

$$\text{High end of range} = 3.80(28.8) + 70.45 + (4.05 \times 2)$$
$$= 187.99 \text{ centimeters} = 6 \text{ feet } 2 \text{ inches}$$

The resulting range once again is 6.3 inches; however, the actual estimate in stature has shifted from a minimum possible height (at 95% confidence) of 6'0.5" to a low of 5'7.7", a difference of 6.61%. In the case of the maximum possible stature, the shift was from a high of 6'6.8" to 6'2", a difference of 6.08%. In summary, using the above formula and measurements, a bone burned to the point where there is a 10% shrinkage of the overall length would produce stature estimates that are from 6 to 7% smaller than the actual estimate if made from dry, uncharred bone. The question now is whether or not this scenario is likely?

If we consider that Hummel and Schutkowski (1989) found that the length of compact bone would shrink by 5% up to a temperature of 1000°C, then the maximum of a 10% reduction in long bone length, as suggested by Buikstra and Swegle (1989), is well outside the experimental expectation. Yet, further caution must be exercised as spongy bone, such as that found at the articular ends of long bones, will be reduced by 12% (Grupe and Herrmann, 1983). Therefore, in order to validly consider the effect of shrinkage on a long bone, we would have to consider a 12% reduction of each end of the long bone with a 5% reduction in the diaphysis. This would mean that the proportion of spongy tissue that contributes to the overall length of the long bone would have to first be calculated for each population. But, is all this necessary? The goal of all this is to provide a realistic stature estimate that will help police investigators sort through missing persons cases. Hence, we need to provide police with stature estimates that will not potentially exclude our decedent from a list of possible candidates based on various characteristics, including stature.

If we were simply to adjust the maximum and minimum stature estimates up or down, respectively, by a certain percentage, what would that percentage be? It was demonstrated above, that for the measurement of an adult male white humerus, that a 10% reduction in the overall length resulted in a 6 to 7% change in the minimum and maximum stature estimates. Therefore, simply applying the percentage of shrinkage expected for a particular bone at a particular temperature is not sufficient. If one takes the minimum stature calculated based on the actual measurement of the cremated long bone, without a correction factor, this may be considered the absolute minimum for the decedent, as we do not truly know how much shrinkage has taken place. However, if one assumes that shrinkage has been 10% (an extreme situation), we would then add to our cremated long bone measurement the aforementioned value, and then calculate the maximum stature. In our example above, the stature report would cite a minimum stature of 5'7.7" and a maximum height of 6'6.8". This stature estimate has a range of 11.1 inches. It is obvious that this is not going to be terribly discriminating and would certainly not live up to the standards of a Daubert challenge. Hence, the stature estimate should only be used as a guide by police to screen missing persons files, with the knowledge that these stature estimates, if provided, are obviously not going to serve as an identifying characteristic.

5.6.5 IDENTIFYING CHARACTERISTICS

Identifying characteristics are those aspects of a skeleton that are particular to that individual and have been documented as such. This documentation is usually in the form of antemortem records. These records usually come to light as a result of a police investigation. All of the information that the forensic anthropologist has provided up to this point is designed to provide police with elements that will enable them to narrow the list of possible candidates from a list of reported missing persons. As part of that investigation procedure, it is up to the investigators to acquire any and all antemortem records that will assist with the identification process.

In the case of remains that have associated soft tissue, characteristics, such as fingerprints and DNA, are used to provide a positive identification. If the features of the face are preserved well enough, the identification may be made through a viewing of the decedent by a close relative, friend, or colleague. Other items that are associated with the remains, including a wallet, photo identification card, or personal items will usually be of great assistance.

The analysis of skeletal remains for aspects of positive identification will be entirely dependent upon antemortem records, and should the need arise, DNA analysis. Anatomically based positive identification depends on there being documented medical records that can take many forms. The most commonly sought after forms of medical records include antemortem radiographs, and records of surgical procedures or fractures that affect any of the hard tissues of the body.

As positive identification is a topic that is deserving of a thorough treatment, and is usually the pinnacle of a forensic investigation of human remains, this topic will be covered in Chapter 8 of this book.

5.7 PATHOLOGICAL INDICATORS

The examination of cremains for indicators of pathology is another aspect of the "osteobiography" of the victim. In this instance, we are interested in any pathology regardless of when it took place. To that end, a forensic examination of this sort will depend on, in the first instance, the recognition of pathological indicators on bone. The second aspect to such an analysis is distinguishing the timing of the pathology noted. When I refer to timing, I am referring to whether the insult to the body, regardless of etiology, occurred prior to death (*antemortem*), around the time of death (*perimortem*), or after death (*postmortem*).

Pathology that is evident to have occurred antemortem provides information about the individual during life. In the case of cremains, pathology that affects the hard tissues of the body, namely bones and teeth, may be preserved in spite of the physical action of the fire. The importance of these antemortem indicators of pathology will be of importance in the identification process, particularly with any antemortem radiographs or other documented sources of information. Antemortem injuries, reported or not, may also be important indicators that the decedent was a victim of a form of abuse. The key to identifying antemortem pathology is to examine the bones and teeth for evidence of healing. If evidence of healing exists, this indicates that the individual survived that particular insult to the body for a sufficiently long enough period of time that healing, to one degree or another, can take place.

Perimortem pathology, for our purposes signs of trauma, is the occurrence of some form of insult to the hard tissues of the body that cannot have its timing pinpointed to being just prior to death, at the time of death, or shortly after death. So, this term literally means, "around the time of death." Such a designation for a pathological condition means that we are unable to attest to that pathology, say a fracture, having occurred at the time of death, or shortly before or after. This is problematic as the fracture may be presented in court this way and may cause confusion to a jury. Hence, it is wise to be clear under direct examination in a court of law as to what such a categorization means. For example, a penetrating trauma to the cervical vertebrae that would result in the decapitation of the victim would certainly not be consistent with continuation of life. However, in skeletal remains, it must be indicated that if it cannot be ascertained that the decapitation happened at the time of death or shortly thereafter, such as in a mutilation, it would then be categorized as being either at the time of death or shortly thereafter. There is no suggestion that the trauma occurred prior to death.

Postmortem pathology is a label that is given to any form of skeletal alteration, such as a fracture or a cut mark, that is clearly defined as being after the death of the individual. If we use the same example of a decapitation, evidence of postmortem pathology would be further cut marks that are found inside the anterior margin of the foramen magnum. The aforementioned cut marks can only be made by first exposing the foramen magnum, and then separating the base of the skull from the cervical vertebrae. Hence, the individual would be dead in order for cut marks to be located in this position.

As mentioned in Chapter 3, the cremation process can produce a large number of fractures of hard tissues. This then presents the problem of distinguishing those HIFs from those that are traumatically produced, regardless of the timing. It is for this reason that the following section outlines the characteristics of traumatic fractures from those caused by the cremation process.

5.7.1 Differentiating Fractures and Trauma

In order for trauma analysis to be of any assistance to an investigation, one must be able to distinguish between cracks and fractures that were cause by manually induced trauma caused by an assailant, from those that have been caused by the cremation process. The key to the differentiation of heat-induced fractures from those of a traumatic origin is based in understanding the nature of the fracturing process. This process is based on the mechanisms of crack formation and propagation through hard tissues. A thorough understanding of these mechanisms and the specific role bone microstructure has to play in crack formation and propagation will act as a basis for distinguishing between the rates at which these cracks form. Further, the effect of heat-induced bone alterations and the resulting changes in microstructure will dictate the behavior of cracks formed by the cremation process itself or those of a traumatic origin.

5.7.1.1 Fracture Formation and Bone Microstructure

To reach an understanding of how fractures form and the role that bone microstructure plays in this process, the problem is best approached from the perspective of fracture mechanics through any material. It is the physical makeup of the material that will dictate how a fracture begins and how it is propagated, and ultimately, whether it terminates in the bone or proceeds through all the structures resulting in a complete fracture. Those fractures that are incomplete and terminate within the bone tissue will be referred to as cracks. Those cracks that proceed through a bone to the point where it has separated a segment from any portion of the bone in such a way that they are sequestered from one another will be termed fractures. Much of this work is based on Piekarski's (1970) work on the mechanisms of bone fracture. This work takes the approach that it is not enough to just understand the mechanisms of fracturing through any material. The material in question, specifically bone, is a composite material and, hence, will have properties that will dictate how a crack will propagate through such a composite material.

It is without question that bone is a composite material. It is not a homogenous material throughout and, as such, it consists of various phases that have differing capacities to absorb energy. Piekarski (1970) describes the phases in bone as follows:

1. Crystalline mineral phase—hydroxyapatite
2. Amorphous mineral phase
3. Crystalline organic phase—collagen
4. Amorphous organic phase—protein molecules in the form of gels and sols
5. Liquids

The nature of this structure results in various mechanisms that, in addition to its microstructure, will resist the propagation of cracks.

The structure of bone is one that is designed to make it resistant to fracture. However, this is highly dependent upon the combination of the five phases mentioned above. If one considers these proportions, the mineral phase of the bone is very much interconnected with the organic phase, which largely consists of collagen (approximately 90%). The amorphous mineral and organic phases are less than 1% of the total volume of the solid matter that makes up the bone. In addition to liquids and sols, the amorphous phase is represented by the contents of Haversian canals, Volkman's (or perforating) canals, and lacunae with their associated canaliculi (see Table 5.7 for information on the size of microstructural features in bone).

The interconnected nature of the aforementioned microstructures permits the liquid phase throughout the bone to absorb the energy from the forces encountered. This ability to dissipate energy is of key importance at the front of a propagating crack. Piekarski (1970) explained that the discontinuities in the bone microstructure, including blood vessels, lacunae, and canaliculi may act as "stress concentrators," and they may even act to divert the propagation of a crack's leading edge. The intersection of a crack with a lacuna will have its force attenuated by the lacuna and thus be slowed in its ratability to continue. The propagation of a crack along the interface between concentric lamellae testifies to the weakness of the structure between these structures. This same mechanism results in the tendency for a crack to circumvent blood vessels. Blood vessels are surrounded by concentric lamellae and, as such, the stress of a crack propagating is oriented in the direction of the long axis of the cylindrically oriented osteons. Ultimately, the rate of propagation is dependent upon the energy that overcomes the capacity of the bone to absorb that energy. Yet, cracks with high rates of propagation, and hence a greater amount of energy, will propagate through all microstructures.

Based on the above, it is reasonable for analysts to consider traumatic fractures, such as those resulting from a blow, would tend to form fractures with a high rate of propagation. Hence, they would proceed through the various microstructures and not be channeled along the interface of lamellae or alter their direction upon passing through a lacuna.

In the case of HIFs, they can proceed along the length of long bones and in a transverse direction, following the areas of the weakest interface between microstructures. It is important to consider that with the act of cremation, the microstructure is being altered and, hence, the mechanisms of crack propagation found in wet, uncremated bone, will likely differ.

5.7.1.2 Traumatic Versus Heat-Induced Fractures

The forms of trauma that can be potentially found on skeletal remains are summarized in Table 5.8. Yet, in the context of cremated remains, the signatures that characterize each of these forms of trauma may be obscured. This can impact categorization and interpreting the timing of these fractures. Specifically, the issue of differentiating perimortem fractures that have been traumatically induced from HIFs as well as situational fractures (fractures that are not directly heat-induced, but occur in the postfire recovery process [Herrmann and Bennett, 1999]) is going to have a profound effect on a forensic investigation.

TABLE 5.8

A Summary of Forms of Trauma Potentially Found on Skeletal Remains, and Their Indicators (drawn from Herrmann and Bennett, 1999)

Type of Trauma	Morphological Characteristics
Sharp-force: -cut marks -saw marks - stab wounds	Sharp margins, blade striae, kerf walls, and sheering of cortical and cancellous bones
Gunshots	Beveling, radiating fractures, concentric fractures, and confirmed by lead spatter
blunt force	Diverse fracture patterns, evidenced often by an impact point

A recent paper approached this problem by examining experimentally induced trauma on cranial bones (Pope and Smith, 2004). Through the use of 40 unembalmed cadaver heads, of which 36 were analyzed after burning, ballistic, blunt, and sharp trauma were inflicted on those specimens. Ten control crania were subjected to burning without any form of trauma. The resulting heat-induced alterations to these crania were recorded. Pope and Smith (2004) found that, not unexpectedly, the head burns in a way that is consistent with the thickness of the soft tissue in these areas. Specifically, those areas with the thinnest tissue depth, hence, covering areas that are very close to the surface, were the first to be exposed by the retraction of tissues over the scalp and forehead. Thicker areas of the lower face follow the aforementioned regions by exposing the dermis, hypodermis, and adipose and muscle tissue to direct heat.

The skull, specifically, undergoes a series of heat-induced fractures, such as delamination. This type of heat-induced fracture is cited by Pope and Smith (2004) to be the most common on the skull. As the outer table undergoes shrinkage through the dehydration of the bone, there are tensile surface cracks as well as shrinkage. This shrinkage proceeds in such a way to expose the underlying diploë. The caveat with delamination is that an external bevel may be present and thus has the potential to be misinterpreted as a ballistic or blunt trauma (Pope and Smith, 2004). The aforementioned feature may also be accompanied by linear fractures that penetrate the cranial vault, as well as fragmentation. Precremation traumatic fractures of the skull that penetrate the cranial vault will allow the passage of organic materials as they vent through this opening. Hence, calcined cranial vaults with deep black margins are evidence of that fracture being present prior to, or at the early stages of burning (Pope and Smith, 2004) (see Figure 5.9). This is also seen in cases of open sutures, and a nontraumatic heat fracture that penetrates the cranial vault.

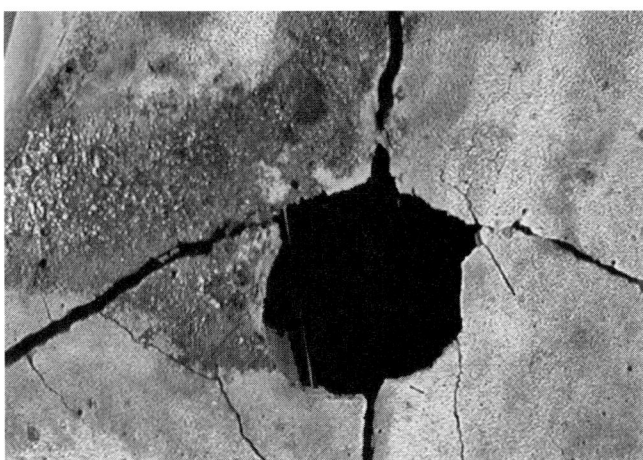

FIGURE 5.9   The outer table of a pig skull with a reconstructed gun shot wound (GSW) depicted in Figure 5.6 showing carbonized organic residue at the margins that indicate venting of organic material, likely a heat hematoma. (Photo by S. Fairgrieve.)

TABLE 5.9
Categories of Heat-Induced Fractures Based on Form
(drawn from Herrmann and Bennett, 1999)

Heat-Induced Fracture Categories
Longitudinal
Curved Transverse
Straight Transverse
Patina
Delamination

Linear fractures can result from shrinking and cracking during the burning process. Linear fractures that are present due to a previous trauma may be confused with those of a heat-induced origin. Pope and Smith (2004) logically note that heat-induced fractures will not extend into unburned bone; however, a preexisting fracture will. But what of those cases that no longer have any green (unburned) areas of bone? How does the analyst approach these cases? Recall that Herrmann and Bennett (1999) examined fractures, mechanical and heat-induced, on the basis of Piekarski's (1970) research on fracture formation rates and fracture propagation. They concluded that fractures in bone resulting from the heat of a fire should exhibit characteristics that are similar to those resulting from high-energy forces. This means that cremated bone does not have the same energy-absorbing capabilities of noncremated bone. Hence, the propagation of heat-induced fractures can be characterized as being high energy, or fast propagation. This would explain why Pope and Smith (2004) are seeing, macroscopically, patterns that may be coincidental to both traumatic and heat-induced fractures. Pope and Smith (2004) do summarize the heat-related changes to crania with different forms of trauma both during and after burning (see Table 5.10).

The margins of traumatic fractures appear to be eroded by the cremation process. This macroscopically visible characteristic is supported at the histological level (Herrmann and Bennett, 1999). This appearance is due to the masking of the margins by contaminants, such as ash and combusted particulate matter. In areas where there is little contamination or masking, the margins of the fracture demonstrate longitudinally sectioned vascular/Haversian canals that, on occasion, show vascular pullouts as described by Piekarski (1970). These are indicative of slow propagating cracks as seen in fresh bone fractures.

Heat-induced fractures are seen under transmitted light to have, what appears to be, a very smooth surface when compared to both a burned and a fresh traumatic fracture (Herrmann and Bennett, 1999). In this case, heat-induced fracture margins demonstrate cleanly sectioned vascular canals. Under Piekarski's model, these fractures are classified as being derived from fast-propagating cracks. This makes sense as heat-induced fractures occur on bone tissue that has undergone dramatic changes in moisture content and cellular degradation. The resulting dehydration of the tis-

TABLE 5.10

Summary of Differential Heat Effects for Heads With, and Without, Traumatic Injuries (drawn from Pope and Smith, 2004)

Number	Treatment	Heat-related Changes During Burning	Signatures of Trauma Type in Burned Cranial Bone
16	Ballistic	Wounds retract and shrink focally to expose bone. Exposed injuries undergo advanced thermal destruction. Open injuries accelerate color changes to bone.	Internal or external beveling from penetration. Secondary radiating or concentric fractures from impact. Organic carbonized venting of wounds or linear fractures. Juxtaposition of color in adjacent fragments. Radiating fractures into green bone. Extremely deformed, ragged, or eroded facture margins. Lead wipe or pellets embedded in bone upon X-ray.
8	Blunt	Edged weapons may create open wounds in skin. Crushing injuries may weaken skin, no open wound. Impact sites retract and shrink focally to expose bone. Exposed injuries undergo advanced thermal destruction. Open injuries accelerate color changes to bone.	Impact sites with tool marks or inwardly crushed bone. Secondary radiating or concentric fractures from impact. Organic carbonized venting of wounds or linear fractures. Juxtaposition of color in adjacent fragments. Radiating fractures into green bone. Extremely deformed, ragged, or eroded facture margins. Depression, inward crushing, patterns, tool marks.
6	Sharp	Heat causes margins of soft tissue injury to bulge; this is different than heat-related skin splitting. Incisions retract and shrink focally to expose bone. Exposed injuries undergo advanced thermal destruction. Open injuries accelerate color changes to bone.	Linear incisions, depressions, cuts, chops, tool marks, partial saw marks, complete saw marks, punctures, stabs, hacks, drill marks, etc. Features of perimortem tool marks cannot be replicated in, or mistaken for, stray postmortem marks in dry calcined bone.
10	Control	Heat creates color changes, blistering, and skin splitting. Elastic skin exposes bone earliest in thinnest areas. Skin, fat, and muscle burn according to thickness. Bone changes color according to exposure to heat.	Heat creates delamination, well-defined heat fractures, fragmentation, embrittlement, and color changes. "Exploded appearance" is created by heat fragmentation, fallen debris extinguishment, movement, recovery.

sue permits cracks to propagate at a much faster rate and, hence, they have fracture surfaces that are cleanly sectioned and lacking in pull-outs of individual osteons.

Yet, the situation for differentiating some heat-induced fractures from those of a traumatic origin may not be as clear as the above evidence would indicate. Herrmann and Bennett (1999) noted that heat fractures may develop as a result of a rapid expansion of medullary fluids while the bone is still intact. This would appear as a slow propagating fracture and thus may be confused with a traumatic fracture. In spite of this, the subsequent study by Pope and Smith (2004) indicates that fracture patterns, in concert with analysis of the fracture margins for venting evidence and a histological evaluation, will provide compelling evidence to differentiate heat-induced from traumatic fractures.

The final category associated with the aforementioned fractures is known as situational fractures. These are fractures that occur as a result of the context and recovery methodology and, as such, are not directly due to the heat. They are characterized by "sharply defined features and clean, richly colored margins" (Herrmann and Bennett, 1999). These fractures may also occur after the skeletal element has cooled. In the case of straight transverse fractures, the surface is very smooth with the vascular canals having been cleanly sectioned. Hence, situational fractures are easily differentiated from traumatic and heat-induced fractures (Herrmann and Bennett, 1999).

The examination of all fractures necessitates the reconstruction and mending of all fractures where possible; a macroscopic examination of the pattern of fractures where possible; and, finally, a microscopic examination of the margins of all uninterpreted fractures.

5.7.1.3 Sequencing of Fractures

The sequencing of fractures in forensic contexts is not new to trauma analysis in forensically relevant remains (for a review, see Maples, 1986 and Merbs, 1989). Yet, in the case of forensically relevant cremains, it is evident that distinguishing traumatically induced fractures from heat-induced fractures deserve special consideration. Once this determination is made, the analysis of traumatic fractures will commence.

Forensic anthropologists and forensic pathologists are keenly aware of the importance of interpreting traumatic fractures. They can lead to conclusions pertaining to the manner and cause of death. They can also lead to a reconstruction of the trauma suffered by the victim from the action(s) of another individual. The ability to sequence fractures allows an analyst to quantify the number of blows and the sequence of blows in order to construct a scenario with respect to the course of an assault.

The assessment for fracture sequencing begins, once again, with the reconstruction of the bone(s) in question. The most common region for such an inquiry is, of course, the skull. During the reconstruction of the skull, the analyst will typically look for patterns to distinguish gunshot wound entries and/or exits, as well as crushing injuries by means of blunt implements, and sharp-force trauma, to name a few. The act of sequencing fractures is done by noting the intersection of traumatic fractures. In fresh bone (i.e., perimortem), new fracture lines terminate at the intersection with a previous fracture line. That is to say that new fracture lines will not cross previously established fracture lines. Hence, a relative pattern of timing of fracture lines can result in a sequencing of fracturing events.

The confounding factor in this is the presence of heat-induced fractures. Heat-induced fractures may, coincidentally, present the appearance of overlapping fractures. In order to remedy this problem one must first examine all fractures to ascertain if any portions of them are due to the action of the fire or the remnant of a prefire trauma. Without making a determination as to the source of the fracture, no sequencing should be undertaken. It is conceivable that a heat-induced fracture may proceed as a continuation of a traumatic fracture. It is in these instances that an examination based on Piekarski's indicators is necessary.

5.7.1.4   Perimortem Chop Marks

The ability to discern evidence of chop or hacking wounds from bone has been studied by several researchers (e.g., Maples, 1986; Ormstad et al., 1986; Merbs, 1989; Wenham, 1989; Mayne, 1990; Mayne, Correia, 1997; Humphrey and Hutchinson, 2001; de Gruchy and Rogers, 2002). Yet, of these works, the most systematic studies in the cremation context have been relatively recent (de Gruchy and Rogers, 2002; Mayne, 1990; Mayne, Correia, 1997).

The aforementioned studies involved inflicting chop marks on bones that were subsequently subjected to cremation scenarios using either an oven or outdoor fire. Regardless of the circumstances of fire, cremated bone was found to retain the characteristics of chop marks (de Gruchy and Rogers, 2002). These marks include entry marks as seen with a smooth and flat cut surface, kerf floors, and striations perpendicularly oriented to the kerf floor, to name a few (see Wenham, 1989; and Humphrey and Hutchinson, 2001 for a review). With the burning of the bone, the area of the wound will become somewhat more susceptible to heat-induced fractures. The most common form of heat-induced fractures associated with chop marks are straight transverse fractures (de Gruchy and Rogers, 2002). This research, however, is limited to the use of a cleaver. In order to be applicable to other forensic contexts, the use of other bladed items that may be used in a chopping fashion should be examined further.

5.7.2   Does the Skull Explode When Heated?

The concept of a skull exploding during the cremation process has been cited in the cremation literature as being due to the expansion of cerebrospinal fluid (Heglar, 1984). As Rhine (1998) explains:

> In a fire of longer duration or higher intensity, temperatures will rise enough that the fluids present in the skull vaporize. The pressure inside the skull continues to build since its only outlets are plugged by various soft tissue structures. The pressure finally increases to the point when the vessel can no longer hold, and the skull explodes. This explosion flings pieces of the vault of the skull some distance from the body, leaving the bones of the skull base and the face more or less intact. Exposed only a little lon-

ger, however, the relatively thin layers of soft tissue are burned off the face, and the flames may severely damage some of the underlying bone structure. (1998: 5)

Rhine also explains that in cases where the skull is not as well fragmented that there may be a previously present traumatic fracture that is allowing the pressure to escape and thus the skull does not explode. Yet, Pope and Smith (2004) found that skulls were affected by their actual surroundings. Falling debris, heat embrittlement, the handling of cremains, the means by which the fire is extinguished, and even the action of transporting the cremains are all external forces that can act to fracture the skull. As such, they propose that it is these "external events" that create the appearance of the exploded skull (ibid.). In fact, with delamination of the outer table from the diploë and the inner table, fragments accumulate around and below the peripheral areas of the skull. Coupled with the fact that the skull fragments are fragile enough to fracture under their own weight by this point, finding fragmentation of a skull should be expected. Hence, the explosive release may not be something that has a logical basis in reality, at least not so far as the term "exploded" may be interpreted.

However, what of the concept of increased intracranial pressure and a subsequent release through a weakened area of the cranial vault? The human skull is replete with a wide array of foramina, particularly in the cranial base. Yet, during the burning of the skull, the soft tissue is consumed from the most superior aspect of the cranial vault and then proceeds inferiorly, across the face, and then laterally and posteriorly. Finally, the base of the skull is exposed only with the consumption of musculature of the neck. Therefore, the cranial vault does not have any foramina through which heat could escape during the burning and exposure of the neurocranial portion. The gaps between sutures are indeed a possible means by which increased pressure may be vented (as noted by Pope and Smith, 2004).

The venting of pressure through sutures is certainly possible, but what of older individuals who have sutures that have undergone complete synostosis (or obliteration)? There would seem to be no opportunity for there to be a release of pressure. Unfortunately, Pope and Smith (2004) do not report the ages of the ten non-traumatized heads on intact bodies observed during the cremation process.

Rhine (1998) noted that in the case of a skull looking reasonably intact, one should suspect that the skull had a perimortem, or rather a precremation, fracture of the cranial vault, thus permitting the release of pressure. As such, there would be no explosive release of pressure and the skull would survive the fire in a more intact condition. As logical as this argument may seem, there is no data to substantiate this claim. The level of intactness could be explained by the lack of external events present in a specific context. Likewise, the skull will still have to be reconstructed, as Rhine (1998) does not claim that the only traumatic fractures are due to the precremation trauma. His claim is that the size of the fragments and their distribution are such that they do not have that "exploded" appearance.

Fractures of the cranial base in cremations have been studied by Bohnert et al. (1997). They conclude that, should an investigator encounter such a situation, mechanical traumatization of some form must be considered. Further, traumatization can only be ruled as having occurred prior to the fire if sources of postmortem trauma from the recovery process or falling objects and the like can be ruled out.

Overall, the effects of fire on the skull are summarized in Table 3.3 (from Bohnert et al., 1998). This table also presents information from two previous studies (Günther and Schmidt, 1953, and Richards, 1977). Bohnert et al. (1998) observed fracture gaps in the calvaria as having widened with a "boiling liquid" and a "more solid, crumbly material exuding from the gaps." This crumbly material is likely a heat hematoma that formed as a result of the initial heating of the cranial cavity and the brain. In almost all observed cases, after 20 minutes, the skull had burst through at the coronal and/or sagittal sutures. Given that this area of the skull is highly susceptible to heat-induced changes, and that it is clear of soft tissue after 10 minutes, certainly this would render this region structurally deficient relative to the other areas of the skull. These sutural areas are inherently less dense in their structure due to the articulation of the parietals and the frontal bone. Even in older individuals used in Bohnert et al.'s (1998) study, there was "no clear correlation between the duration of the fire needed for destruction of the body on the one hand and temperature, material of the coffin, as well as sex or constitution of the deceased, on the other hand." In fact, the age of the bodies used in their study range from 68 to 100 years. So, it would appear that there is no "explosive" release of pressure even in elderly victims whose sutures would be in an advanced stage of synostosis. The heating of the bone of the cranial vault progresses to the point where the outer table is altered prior to the inner table. As a result of this heating, the outer table shrinks back and delaminates from the diploë and the inner table. With this contraction of bone, the deeper structures begin to undergo the same process and produce gaps in the cranial vault in the area of the coronal and sagittal sutures. The widening of the gaps between these bones continues with further burning and, consequently, shrinkage of the exposed bone. This then results in permitting the exuding of liquid and the remnants of a coincidentally formed heat hematoma. As the cremation process continues, the calcined bones of the vault collapse under their own weight, thereby increasing the degree of fragmentation. The region of the cranial base is the last area to be subjected to direct heat from the fire, due to its association with the cervical musculature. Heat-induced fractures may occur here once the associated musculature has been eliminated. However, the caveat here is that one must consider the context for incidental factors that may act to damage the skull further. In just such an instance, a cranial base fracture was diagnosed from the burned head of a 41-year-old woman killed by blows to the head with a bat (Iwase et al., 1998). The radiating fracture proceeded from the cranial vault along the left side of the skull to the uncharred left temporal bone and through to the cranial base along the left pyramis.

It would appear that if one is considering an exploded skull as having propelled fragments across a large area, it does not seem possible that the release of pressure from within the cranial cavity is enough to have such a result. A release through the area of the coronal and sagittal sutures is, indeed, going to occur, however, not with a force sufficient enough to propel fragments a meter or more from the skull. If fragments are found with a distribution pattern suggesting "explosion" of the skull, it would be prudent to consider that a force, such as a gunshot to the head, may be the event that had resulted in the position of cranial fragments. Other incidental forces, such as falling debris in structural fires, are also a likely source of cranial fragment translocation.

Caution also needs to be exercised in the interpretation of apparent wounds to the skull. In a recent case report, Hausmann and Betz (2002) describe an entrance wound-like defect with a diameter of approximately 1 centimeter located 2.5 centimeters above the upper edge of the right orbit on the frontal bone. The outer table surrounding this defect was detached for an area measuring approximately 5 centimeters in diameter. There were also radiating fracture lines at the rim of the lesion and some extending to the nasal or maxillary bones. Initial findings suggested that it was not atypical for a "cratering" pattern found in some bullet entrance wounds. Careful examination of the scene and the recovered bone material permitted a complete restoration of the defect; something that is not possible in a gunshot wound of this nature. Once again, this emphasizes the value of reconstruction rather than depending on the morphology of fractures and, in this case, the form of a defect that resembles a gunshot wound.

A defect similar to the one described above was diagnosed in another case as a captive-bolt injury to the frontal bone from a livestock stunner (Bohnert et al., 2002). The diagnostic finding in this case was the presence of internal beveling of the inner table and exposing this aspect of the diploë.

5.8   CHEMICAL ANALYSIS OF CREMATED BONE

Recent advances in detector sensitivity and extraction methodology have taken cremated bone from the status of an unanalyzable mass to a repository of chemical information.

One of the first instances where the concept of cremains retaining biochemical constituents of analyzable quality was with immunological detection of albumin in cremated bone from the Roman Period using ELISA and monoclonal antibodies (Cattaneo et al., 1994). Enzyme-linked immunoabsorbent assay (ELISA) utilizing monoclonal antibodies was used to study not only ancient cremated bone, but also fresh bone burnt on pyres. The purpose of this study was to assess the preservational quality of proteins from cremains. Although human albumin was shown to be preserved in some cremated material, this resulted in generating the question as to the possible presence of DNA.

The detection of albumin does have a limit based on the temperature reached in the fire and the exposure time. Antigenicity was lost between 300°C and 350°C (Cattaneo et al., 1994). As cremains in a forensic context will likely reach temperatures well in excess of 300°C, it stands to reason that there is a threshold where proteins break down and their investigative utility is lost. However, it is safe to conclude that the temperature in a bone has exceeded 300°C if albumin is not detected. Other methods examining proteins have also been explored as a means to assess temperature.

An examination of the proportion of two common constituents of Type I collagen in human cremains, namely glycine (Gly) and glutamic acid (Glu), and NH_3 were found to provide an indicator as to whether a bone had been subjected to one or more heating events (Taylor et al., 1995). The Gly/Glu proportional value below 3 was an indicator that the amino acid nitrogen content had dropped below 0.1%. This served to indicate that there was a "non-collagen-like profile" present in the sample. Hence, it was concluded that the bone was subjected to heating. Unfortunately, there is no indication of the color stage of the burned bones tested in this study. As such, the applicability to modern forensic cremains is not evident.

In scenarios where a sample of material is suspected to be cremated bone, an objective means of analysis is necessary. Recently, Warren et al. (2002) utilized proton-induced X-ray emission (PIXE) as a means of examining the elemental composition of just such suspicious material. In one case, the key element of consideration in a multielement analysis was found to be phosphorus due to its prevalence in bones and teeth. It was assumed that the concentration ratio of P:Ca would not significantly alter during the incineration process. This provided Warren et al. (2002) a basis to compare cremains to other suspected substances.

PIXE analysis has also been used by the same authors to confirm the presence of lead in a set of cremains exhibiting gunshot wounds with radiopaque material (presumably lead). Elevated levels of Pb were confirmed to indicate adherent bullet fragments in the cremains.

It appears that cremated bone can retain certain chemical properties that have utility in forensic investigations. For example, in the now infamous case of the Tri-State Crematory Incident in which "filler" material was put into urns in place of cremains, a method of analysis was needed to assess the composition of the content of urns returned to families. The use of inductively coupled plasma-optical emission spectroscopy (ICP-OES) in the elemental analysis of questionable material assisted in distinguishing legitimate (actual cremains) from contaminated cremains (Brooks et al., 2006). This study found that not all elements were equally useful for discriminating between cremains and filler. Samples were then classified based on their composition as being concrete if there was less than or equal to 50% human content; 60–75% human content had a probability of 0.14–0.51 of belonging to the cremains group; and samples with 90% human content were classified as being cremains. However, a limitation of this analysis is that it is unable to distinguish human cremains from faunal cremains. Additionally, individuals whose bodies may contain foreign material, such as bullets not excised during postmortem examination, or clandestinely burned, will alter the elemental signature and result in misclassification.

The aforementioned analyses are still relatively new to the analysis of cremains as they pertain to forensic contexts. It is anticipated that such analyses, and others, will continue to be tested and applied to forensically relevant scenarios and cases.

5.9   SUMMARY

The foregoing chapter has dealt with the laboratory analysis of cremated bone in some detail. Clearly, cremated remains have a significant probative value in forensic investigations. However, caution must be exercised by the analyst due to the altered form of the cremains. The changes in size and shape can have a dramatic effect on the interpretation for age, sex, and stature. Other biographical details, such as the estimation of ancestry, and even indicators of individuation can be either obliterated or, at the very least, obfuscated.

The key to the analysis of cremains is to undertake the analysis in a systematic fashion. The separation and curation of the cremains is done in such a way as to not compound the level of fragmentation as it exists. Once that is completed, a comprehensive inventory of all recovered materials in the form of a catalog is necessary. This will then form the basis for tracking the analytical status of all cremated material. Part of the analysis will include the identification of the skeletal elements and a recording of their physical characteristics, including weight. The fractures will then be examined in the light of any possible repairs that can be made on the basis of skeletal elements. It is at this point in time that the minimum number of individuals will be considered given that an inventory of the elements present will have been done.

The repairs of fractures will be undertaken in order to elucidate the relationship of fracture lines to the cremation context or perimortem trauma. This is typically undertaken during a protracted period in which the mends of fractures will assist in characterizing each fracture line. This is a crucial stage of the analysis as it has a direct bearing on the manner and cause of death.

The point of this chapter was to outline the methods that should be considered when undertaking the basic analysis of cremated remains. This is undertaken to ultimately provide information that can be utilized by the authorities when considering possible candidates from missing persons records. Addressing questions of pathology, as well as manner and cause of death, are relevant at this stage due to the influence they may have on the course of an investigation.

At this stage, our analysis would continue with histological indicators of the context that produced the cremains. There are specific changes at the histological level that necessitate our examination for evidence of the scenario under which the remains were burned. The examination of dental tissues may also serve in this capacity; however, they are more readily associated with their traditional role in the identification process. Positive identification on the basis of the entirety of the evidence that has been accrued to this point is one of the ultimate goals of our analysis. Subsequent chapters of this volume deal with the aforementioned issues in great detail. In many instances, case studies provide insightful glimpses into the caveats one must consider in these areas of examination.

6 Heat-Induced Alterations of Bone Microstructure

6.1 INTRODUCTION

The analysis of cremains has, so far, largely dealt with macroscopically observed alterations to bone tissue. These observations have been geared to the analysis of the cremains in order to draw conclusions concerning the nature of the fire, the duration of exposure to the fire, distinguishing precremation trauma from heat-induced fractures, and how all of the above affect an analyst's ability to construct an osteobiography of the victim. Ultimately, it is the composition and structure of bone at the histological level that will have a direct bearing on how a bone behaves in the fire environment.

This chapter deals with the effects of fire on bone microstructure. To that end, a review of the composition of bone and its histomorphology is in order. This is then followed by a discussion of the relationship between the chemical alterations of bone in the cremation environment and concomitant structural alterations. The changes associated with dental structures are covered in the next chapter.

6.2 CALCIFIED TISSUES

The special property that distinguishes calcified, or hard, tissues from all others is that they consist of an inorganic phase and one or more organic components. Of significance to human cremains is that the inorganic component of bone is hydroxyapatite, while the organic component largely consists of collagen and a few other noncollagenous proteins. In order to appreciate how these structures are altered by the heat found in a fire, a detailed understanding of these structures in unaltered tissue is necessary.

6.2.1 THE INORGANIC MATRIX

Hydroxyapatite is, in essence, a form of calcium phosphate. Yet, the structure of hydroxyapatite in bones and teeth is regarded as being an imperfect matrix. Calcium and phosphate ions have a very high affinity for one another, resulting in a stable matrix. Hence, it is not surprising that calcium hydroxyapatite has such an important role to play in the structure and physiology of bones and teeth.

Biological apatite can have a variable composition. The ideal atomic ratio of calcium to phosphorus is 10:6. This Ca:P ratio can also be shifted in favor of either side while still maintaining the physiological characteristics of biological apatite. Ions that can be considered "foreign" in this context include carbonate, citrate, sodium, magnesium, potassium, chloride, fluoride, zinc, manganese, molybdenum, iron, copper, lead, strontium, tin, aluminum, and boron. Of these, carbonate, citrate, sodium, magnesium, potassium, and chloride are the more abundant of these "foreign" ions.

Examination of the inorganic portion of bone has not only identified hydroxyapatite as the major structural component, but also includes amorphous calcium phosphate (ACP). ACP appears to exist as minute spheroids about 20 nanometers in diameter. There is evidence to suggest that the amount of mineral ACP in bone is age-dependent (Cole and Eastoe, 1988). In adult humans, approximately 40% of the mineral content is composed of ACP.

A feature of calcium hydroxyapatite that is of importance to cremation studies is the presence of firmly bound water making up what is known as the hydration shell. Within the hydration shell of hydroxyapatite there are calcium phosphate ions suspended in a dilute KCl solution. The binding of the water and other polarizable ions is a result of the high surface charge on the crystals and is the means by which this charge is neutralized. The hydration shell has been known to occupy twice the volume of the hydroxyapatite crystallite. Ions in the hydration shell are attracted to the surface of the hydroxyapatite crystal. Nevertheless, these ions are still in constant motion. Hence, the ions are always shifting from the hydration shell to the bulk solution and back again.

The structure of hydroxyapatite promotes the exchange of ions between the various layers mentioned above, but at different rates. The most rapid of these exchanges is between the hydration shell and the bulk solution. The next in line is the rate of exchange between phosphates in the hydration shell and phosphate ions in the surface of the crystal. The slowest rate of exchange is between the phosphate ions in the crystal surface and the ions in the interior of the crystal. Therefore, the four layers that make up the region of the hydroxyapatite crystallite include the crystal interior, the crystal surface, the hydration shell, and the bulk solution. Polarizable ions tend to concentrate in the hydration shell and are known as the bound ion layer. The ions in this layer include hydrated ions, such as calcium, carbonate, citrate, magnesium, and strontium. Yet, these ions are able to exchange with ions in the bulk solution.

The crystal lattice is capable of having a "foreign ion" of similar size replace an ion that is a normal hydroxyapatite constituent. This heteroionic exchange is in contrast to isoionic exchange that has an exchange of like ions. Thus, it is possible for ions other than calcium, phosphate, or hydroxyl to become part of the crystal lattice of biological apatite. This is all dependent upon the presence of such ions of a suitable size in the liquid in which the mineral forms. Subsequently, the chemical composition of biological apatite will vary according to the ions present in the liquid in which it bathes.

6.2.2 The Organic Matrix

Bone, dentine, and cementum all have a similar chemical composition and are regarded by many as calcified collagens, due to the predominance of this structural protein. Cartilage also contains high levels of collagen, yet, the higher levels of chondroitin sulphate distinguish it from the aforementioned collagenous tissues.

The structural contribution of collagen to bone, dentine, and cementum is that it is impregnated with crystallites of apatite between, within, and on the collagen fibrils.

By way of a brief review, collagen fibrils are produced by osteoblasts, odontoblasts, and cementoblasts. Calcium phosphate, in an amorphous state, and hydroxyapatite will grow into crystals that eventually increase in number, producing a heavily mineralized region.

Table 6.1 provides a list of the components of air-dried compact bone (bovine femur diaphysis) according to the percentage of each constituent by total weight. Likewise, Table 6.2 provides the composition of human dentine (drawn from Cole and Eastoe, 1988). In the case of cementum, it closely resembles bone. In living bone, water is likely in the range of 15–20% by weight.

These proportions are not static. In fact, the percentage of inorganic matter in bone is directly proportional with the length of time since each tissue has been laid down. This means that the degree of mineralization differs from one bone to another in the same animal and even within the same bone. This can be seen in microradiography of Haversian systems (osteons) in cross-sections of long bone diaphyses. The degree of radiolucency will vary according to the age of the osteons. The more highly calcified (radiodense) are older, while those newly formed osteons are less mineralized (more radiolucent). However, due to bone remodeling, an individual will demonstrate osteons of varying age.

Collagen in hard tissue is more stable than the collagen found in soft tissue. At first, this may seem surprising, as the chemical composition of these collagens is very much alike. However, hard tissue collagens are substantially more stable due to

---

TABLE 6.1
Relative Composition of Air-dried Compact Bone From a Bovine Femur Diaphysis (drawn from Cole and Eastoe, 1988)

	Percentage by Weight
Inorganic matter	70
Insoluble in hot water	68.7
Water-soluble	1.25
Organic matter	21.73
Collagen	18.64
Resistant protein material	1.02
Citrate	1.0
Preteoglycan (chondroitin SO_4)	
Sialoprotein	1.0
Mucoprotein	
Total lipid	0.07
Water (lost below 105°C)	8.18

TABLE 6.2
Relative Composition of Normal Human Dentine (drawn from Cole and Eastoe, 1988)

	Percentage by Weight
Inorganic matter	75
Ash	72
Carbon dioxide	3
Organic matter	20
Collagen	18
Resistant protein	0.2
Citrate	0.89
Lactate	0.15
Chondroitin sulphate	0.4
Lipid	0.2
Unaccounted for (water retained at 100°C, errors, etc.)	5

the higher level of cross-linkages between collagen fibrils. There are an especially high number of hydroxyallysine–hydroxylysine cross-linkeages and more cross-linkage between allysine and hydroxylysine.

6.2.3   HISTOLOGICAL MORPHOLOGY OF BONE

The histological morphology of bone is dictated by the organic and inorganic components described above. It is, without question, that there is going to be significant variation in the density and degree of distribution of these components depending on the type of bone tissue (woven or compact), the category of bone element (long, short, flat, or irregular), and the age of the individual.

As bone is a highly vascularized tissue that is physiologically active through the processes of remodeling, the health of this tissue is entirely dependent upon the nutritional status of the individual. The changeable nature of bone and its ability to adapt to the variety of functional demands in which it is found in the body will contribute to its architecture. Hence, the macroscopic appearance of various bones is very much related to its function. The density of compact bone on the surface, and the orientation of the individual trabeculae of cancellous bone found deep to the superficial compact bone will dictate how it reacts to external forces, such as heat.

The previous section covered the importance of collagen as a major organic component of bone tissue. To expand on this, the orientation of the collagen fibers actually determines the structural function in different areas of a specific bone element, be it the proximal end of a femur, or the lateral end of a clavicle. In the case of woven bone, the collagen fibers are randomly oriented in "coarse" bundles, typically found in young bone and at sites of tissue repair in fractures. Lamellar bone is, in contrast, highly ordered into parallel-fibered sheets, as seen in mature bone.

Using the example of a long bone shaped like a cylinder, the lamellar bone that is parallel to both the periosteal and endosteal surfaces is known as circumferential lamellar bone (or primary lamellae). The lamellae, found to occur concentrically around vascular canals running parallel to the length of the bone making up the layers of an osteon (Haversian System), are referred to as osteonic lamellae. Finally, the layers of bone found to occur between osteons are known as interstitial lamellae. The layered structure of lamellae, and the architecture of cancellous bone tissue, determines how a bone will respond to heat on both the microscopic and macroscopic levels.

Although the matrix of the bone has been covered, the cellular components of bone have not been considered. There are a number of types of cells found in the bone tissue (see Table 6.3 for a summary). Of these, the osteocytes have the greatest relevance with respect to the way that bone reacts to heat stress. Osteocytes are the most prominent cell type found in living bone tissue. They are scattered throughout the bone matrix and form an interconnected network resulting from dendrites that emerge from its soma (body). The body of an osteocyte is found inside a lacuna contained within the matrix. To accommodate the dendrites extending from the body of the osteocyte are up to 100 channels (canaliculi) that are approximately 0.25 μm each in diameter. This means that bone is, in fact, riddled with canaliculi and lacunae.

As with any living tissue, bone too has its own blood vessels and nerves. The circulation of blood to bone supplies nutrients to bone tissue, the marrow, perichondrium, epiphyseal cartilages (in immature bones), and partially, to the articular cartilages. The actual flow of blood follows a centrifugal model through the cortical bone in diaphyses to the surface of the bone.

TABLE 6.3
Types of Cells Found in Bone and Their Function

Cell Type	Function
Osteoprogenitor cell	Proliferation and differentiation into osteoblasts.
Osteoblasts	Occur on endosteal surfaces and deep in compact bone. Responsible for the synthesis, deposition and mineralization of bone matrix. Will transform into osteocytes.
Osteocytes	Scatters within bone matrix and interconnected to make a cellular network. Essential role in bone maintenance.
Bone lining cells	Found as continuous layers in contact with each other and neighboring osteocytes on surface not undergoing deposition or erosion.
Osteoclasts	Found where there is active erosion of bone. Responsible for the removal of bone matrix.

6.3 HISTOMORPHOLOGICAL REACTION TO HEAT

Previous chapters have covered the macroscopic changes to bone in response to extreme heat. In addition to obvious changes in color, the mechanisms of cracking and shrinkage are the most readily visible alterations to bone subjected to fire. Yet, other alterations are visible at the histological level of study.

The fact that the bone shrinks as a result of heating is not in dispute. However, it does beg the question of what is it that is shrinking? Is it the matrix, the hydroxyapatite, and/or collagen that is changing chemically to produce this contraction of the tissue? Is it the water content, as it is surely being leached out of the bones? It has been found that when bone was observed to shrink in fire, it did not seem to affect the actual osteon count, but it did seem to increase the relative size of the osteon (Bradtmiller and Buikstra, 1984). This would indicate that although the entire matrix dimensions shrank, the osteons, with their concentric lamellae, were not as highly affected as interstitial lamellae. A further examination of this found that when femoral segments were burned and then thin sectioned for examination under conventional light microscopy, the Haversian canal diameter actually increased on average by 10.5%, while the osteon diameter decreased on average by 16.7% (Nelson, 1992). The difference between this result and the Bradtmiller and Buikstra (1984) study may be due to a number of factors, including the possibility that incompletely burned bones may expand due to the heat (Nelson, 1992). The type of oven, as well as differing time and temperature exposures, are also offered as explanations. In the same study, individual lamellae were often indistinguishable in burned bone. The positive aspect of Nelson's study is that it would appear that shrinkage does not seem to affect the estimation of age using osteon counts.

The cremation process is not homogenious in its effect on the body. Given that this process differentially affects the body, it is reasonable to assume that bone will not be affected evenly. Hummel and Schutkowski (1993) found that the outer portion of cremated bone is altered in temperatures of 700°C or greater. In spite of this temperature, one is still able to distinguish different histological features. In fact, the same authors found that the "type of structural element" did not have an influence on the amount of shrinkage (Hummel and Schutkowski, 1986). In the case of incompletely burned bones, the histological features are readily visible, albeit with some residual carbon. This is not to say that aging using a method (e.g., Ahlquist and Damsten, 1969) that depends on the quantification of specific histological features is without difficulty. Hummel and Schutkowski (1993) found that qualitative methods (e.g., Drusini, 1987) produced the best results, whereas methods that require quantitation of specific structures fared worse. Hence, they concluded that a method that depends on counting osteons is preferable to one that requires the quantitation of whole and fragmentary osteons.

In addition to its utility in estimating an age at death of the fire victim, histological analysis can aid in resolving whether or not the bone is human (Cuijpers, 1995). An examination of the orientation and relative positioning of osteons will enable one to conclude, in many instances, species of origin (see Ubelaker, 1989).

It would appear that the histology of bone is still of use even in cremation contexts. Age at death estimation using osteon counts, and species identification, are both reasonable expectations from an examination of the histology of cremains. However, these expectations need to be measured against the quality of recovery from the scene.

The structures discussed to this point are observable at relatively low power using standard light microscopy. The next level of alterations is both chemical and physical. An alteration in the hydroxyapatite crystals will result in characteristic changes to the physical properties of the bone. The amount of time of exposure to fire and the temperature to which the bone reaches are critical to the extent of change of bone ultrastructure.

6.4   FIRE AND BONE MINERAL CHEMISTRY AND STRUCTURE

It has been established that there is an intimate relationship between the organic (proteinaceous) and inorganic (mineral) phases that make up bone matrix. Hence, the incineration of bone will affect both of these phases, albeit in different ways.

As bone is heated, proteins will undergo a process of denaturation. As this heating continues, the water that is found in bone is removed between 300°C and 500°C (Harsányi, 1993). This does not include the water that is part of the apatite crystals. That water is lost at temperatures in excess of 700°C. The carbon dioxide contained within the matrix is lost at around 600°C. The effect of removing water from the apatite crystals is that their conformation is temporarily lost; however, with cooling, a recrystallization takes place and their shape is reestablished. These so-called "secondary" crystals can be 50 times as large as the originals. According to previous research, apatite crystals appear to be stable at temperatures less than 1200°C (Burri et al., 1935; Harsányi, 1976, 1977).

Table 6.4 provides a summary of the effects of heat on the bone matrix. As indicated by the work of Grupe and Hummel (1991), physiological hydroxyapatite chemically alters its structure to β-tricalcium phosphate. This change results in a

TABLE 6.4
Effects of Heat on Bone Matrix

Temperature (°C)	Effect	Author
300–500	H_2O removed from nonmineralized portion.	Harsányi, 1993
600–700	Organic carbon burnt to CO_2 and eliminated from bone.	Grupe and Hummel, 1991; Harsányi, 1993
>700	H_2O removed from apatite crystals; CO_2 formation.	Harsányi, 1993; Rogers and Daniels, 2002
>800	Physiological hydroxyapatite changes to β-tricalcium phosphate; Shrinking 30% due to recrystallization and crystal fusion.	Grupe and Hummel, 1991

recrystallization and fusion of the crystals to generate a structure that is 30% smaller than the original crystal. This is part of a trend that has been observed toward what has been referred to as a more "perfect" or "crystalline" phase of hydroxyapatite at temperatures up to 1000°C (Hiller et al., 2003). These changes are considered to be "fine-scale" with respect to the ultrastructure. However, at temperatures above 700°C, CaO has been formed (Rogers and Daniels, 2002). It has been suggested that skeletal maturity is linked to the formation of CaO. Holden et al. (1995b) found that CaO occurred only in human samples over 22 years of age. This age-effect has also been found in other mammalian species once a certain level of skeletal maturity has been attained (Ravaglioli et al., 1996).

The fact that age (or, rather, biological maturity) appears to be a consideration in the burning of bone is quite logical as it is known that juvenile bones will burn more completely with less mineral residue. With advancing age comes an increase in the intermolecular cross-links between collagen chains. Hence, the greater the degree of mineralization observed, the greater the occurrence of cross-linkages between collagen fibers. As noted by Holden et al. (1995b), these cross-links do not exhibit equal energies. As such, they will not break in a simultaneous fashion under constant heating regimes. This will result in a differentiation in fiber orientation and fraying. These researchers also conclude that it is possible to determine the temperature attained by the bone to within 200°C.

It has been suggested that the same characteristics of crystal morphology may serve as a basis for estimating age at death. Specifically, the cremains may be placed in one of three categories: young (1–22 years), adult (22–60 years), or old (≥ 60 years) (Holden et al., 1995b). Yet, a practical means of applying these data is not presented by these researchers. In an attempt to resolve this, it was clear from their research that younger samples, 1–22 years, produced spherical-type crystals at ~600°C that were significantly larger than in specimens ≥ 22 years. This does not hold in cases where the temperature has reached ~800°C. The crystal size difference decreases due to increasing temperature until the crystal size approaches a constant for all ages.

In order to successfully apply the above to interpreting the age group to which cremains belong, assuming other morphological means are not available, one needs to be able to determine an estimated maximum temperature attained by the bone tissue. At 200°C the endosteum inside Haversian canals begins to disintegrate by flaking and lifting, and/or by shrinkage and splitting (Holden et al., 1995b). By 600°C the endosteum is completely destroyed. At ~800°C the lamellar structure of bone is lost due to crystal formation; however, the Haversian canals and osteocyte lacunae retain their form up to 1400°C. All of the above structural features are completely destroyed at temperatures of 1600°C and above. It was also noted that the crystal morphology has also been altered at such high temperatures that above 1200°C, crystals take on a variety of shapes including rosettes, platelets, and irregular forms.

Therefore, it is possible to analyze the ultrastructure of cremated bone in such a way to be able to consider questions of age at death and the temperature the bone reached during their process. It must be stressed that the temperatures cited here are not those of the fire, but those attained by the bone itself. Although, this will at least provide an estimated framework with which to work when considering the temperature of a fire.

6.5   SUMMATION

The microstructure of bone has the potential to provide an estimate of age at death based on the geochemical reaction of the matrix to fire. These reactions may also provide us with an estimate of the temperature the bone has achieved during the cremation process. It is clear that some earlier work by Shipman et al. (1984) provided many researchers with a basis for providing estimates of fire temperature. However, the work by Holden et al. (1995a, b) provides us with not only the color as an indicator of the temperature bone has achieved, but also the histological hallmarks of such temperature changes (Table 6.5). Therefore, it would be prudent in forensic contexts to provide broad temperature ranges based on a combination of color and histological analysis. Again, it needs to be stressed that such temperatures are those reached by the bone tissue itself and not the temperature reached by the fire upon combustion of fuel, regardless of source. The next logical step would be to pursue research using mammalian bone, with soft tissue present, in a controlled temperature environment to measure the temperature of bone in relation to an external temperature source. Further, conducting this research based on the time, temperature achieved, and the histological effects would further enhance our capacity to make meaningful comments on cremation contexts.

The histology of bone also lends itself to age at death estimation analysis, as osteons do not appear to be destroyed until the temperature exceeds 1400°C. The application of histologically based methods of age at death estimation using qualitative analysis seemed to provide the most reliable results (Hummel and Schutkowski, 1993). In even the most complete rendering of a body to calcine bone, it may be possible to have an age at death estimate based on histological structures. This is

---

TABLE 6.5
Bone Color Due to Cremation as it Relates to Crystal Morphology, and Appearance of Lamellar Pattern and Collagen Fibers in the Haversian Canal (drawn from Holden et al., 1995a, b)

Bone Color (temp. °C)	Cortical Position	Crystal Morphology	Size Range	Lamellar Pattern	Collagen Fibers in Haversian Canal
White (800–1400)	Outer	Spherical and Hexagonal	0.25 ± 0.07 μm to 0.41 ± 0.09 μm	Not observable	Indistinguishable
Gray (~600)	Mid-cortex	Spherical	~0.060 ± 0.007 μm	Not observable	Fraying
Black (200–600)	Inner	No crystals	–	Observable	No Fraying

particularly useful when a perpetrator has mechanically crushed the cremations in order to obscure the anatomy.

Continued research on histological analysis at the ultrastructural level will enable analysts to provide a greater depth of information to ultimately aid in the positive identification of cremated remains.

Bone is just one of the tissues that remain in the cremation context. Dental tissues are among the hardiest of the body's tissues. Thus, the expectation is that they would survive the cremation process, albeit in an altered and fractured form. However, as teeth traditionally provide us with the most information pertaining to the identity of an individual, they have great analytical potential.

7 Incineration of Dental Tissues

7.1 INTRODUCTION

As most references on forensic identification of human remains will tell you, the analysis of dental remains can provide information pertaining to the age of the individual, as well as identity through comparison to antemortem records. Of course, in order to do such a comparison, one must have an idea of whom the remains represent. Any information with respect to the age at death, the sex, race (or ancestry) will be of great assistance to establishing a positive identification (see Chapter 8 for complete discussion on positive identification through other methods).

As with bone tissue, teeth are also made up of an inorganic matrix of hydroxyapatite. However, a tooth is actually composed of three related hard tissues. These tissues—enamel, cementum, and dentine—will react differently from one another when exposed to heat. The nature of any one tissue's reaction is dependent upon its chemical/structural composition as well as its location on the tooth. Once again, the anatomical axiom of structure reflecting the function holds for the reaction of dental tissues to elevated heat.

Teeth are amongst the most resilient structures of the human body. As such, forensic odontologists are often called upon to undertake an examination of dental structures in order to establish an identification of remains based on a comparison of antemortem dental records. The dentition is commonly preserved, at least partially, in a variety of instances where exposure of a body to a heat source may occur. However, in forensic cremations, the heat exposure can be of such an extent that the teeth and associated alveolar bone may be highly fragmentary (Figure 7.1a and b). Such contexts necessitate careful recovery procedures, as fragmentary dental remains may yield important evidence concerning antemortem dental work that may lead to a positive identification (Fairgrieve, 1994).

This chapter provides a review of the structure of teeth and their associated tissues. The reactions of these tissues to elevated heat in a cremation context are also detailed. Specific attention is paid to the interpretation of heat-induced alterations to these dental tissues.

7.2 BASIC DENTAL ANATOMY

A tooth, in general, consists of a crown, covered by enamel, and a root covered by cementum. These two areas of the tooth meet at the neck or cementoenamel junction (CEJ). Beneath these tissues, the bulk of a tooth's structure consists of dentine. The dentine supports the enamel covering the crown and the cementum of the root.

FIGURE 7.1   A) This photograph of the mandibular region of a pig carcass subjected to a fire for 30 minutes demonstrates that the back teeth are more protected than the anterior teeth. B) This detailed photograph of an alveolar remnant from a pig carcass subjected to 50 minutes in an automobile fire exhibits severe fragmentation. (Photos by S. Fairgrieve.)

Within the dentine there is a central space known as the pulp cavity that is expanded at the coronal end and tapers down the root (a root canal) and terminates at the tip of the root as an apical foramen. In teeth with multiple roots, such as premolars and molars, each root will have an apical foramen. The roots are surrounded by a tissue, known as the periodontal ligament, that binds them to the alveolar bone that makes up the socket in which the root sits.

Humans have a heterodontic dental arcade. That is to say, we exhibit a dentition that has a variety of tooth forms rather than just one form as found in homodontic species, such as sharks. We also have teeth that are permanent, or rather, adult, and teeth that are shed during childhood; hence, they are known as deciduous teeth. The implication of this is that although teeth possess the same tissues, there is variation in the actual structure and position of the tooth in the mouth. This in turn means that teeth will not all react to heat in a uniform manner.

The human dentition consists of four morphologically functional forms: the incisors, canines, premolars, and molars. The incisors and canines make up what is known as the "anterior dentition." This anterior position makes these teeth more susceptible to heat stress, as they are directly adjacent to the opening of the mouth. In contrast, the posterior dentition, also referred to as the "cheek teeth," include the premolars and molars. This position provides enhanced protection of the teeth due to the insulative effect of the cheeks. The tongue also acts to insulate the lingual surfaces of all teeth.

The teeth are organized into upper and lower dentitions. These opposing arches are subsequently divided into halves, resulting in the four quadrants of the mouth. The arrangement of teeth in these quadrants follows the order of placement along that arch from the midline to the distal aspect. In each quadrant there are typically two incisors, one canine, two premolars and three molars. This is known as the following dental formula: 2-1-2-3. As this is the same for upper and lower dentitions, the more formal way to express this is 2-1-2-3/2-1-2-3.

The incisors are single-rooted teeth with a single incisal edge and somewhat spatulate in shape. Their function is for shearing into items to be consumed.

Distal to the lateral incisor is the larger canine with a single cusp and a long single root that acts to deeply anchor this tooth within the alveolus. The larger size of the root results in a bulge in the maxillary alveolus known as the "canine eminence." The thinned alveolus in this area is subject to fracture in fire and exposes the root of the upper canines to direct fire damage.

Distal to the canines are two premolars. These bicuspid teeth have one cusp adjacent to the cheek (buccally), and the other lingually positioned (adjacent to the tongue), separated by a mesiodistal fissure. The upper first premolars generally have two roots, whereas the second upper premolar usually has one root.

At the distal end of each quadrant of the mouth are the three molars. Of all the teeth so far described, these are the most well-protected, due to their overall mass and deep position within the mouth.

In the case of a deciduous dentition, that is, children less than age six have five teeth in each quadrant rather than eight; there are no deciduous premolars and there is one less molar. These teeth are generally smaller than adult teeth and on a smaller arch. Fire more readily affects these teeth due to their size and the smaller amount of soft tissue protecting the back teeth. In children older than five the dentition is a mix of deciduous and adult teeth. Those searching a cremation scene must be fully cognizant of the possibility of victims with a mixed dentition and permanent teeth developing within the alveolus.

It has been observed that with the heating of dental tissues they do not react in an identical fashion to one another (e.g., Fairgrieve, 1994). This is largely due to their respective microstructural anatomy. In order to understand how these tissues react to heat, a brief description of the microstructure of enamel, cementum, and dentine is outlined below.

7.2.1   ENAMEL MICROSTRUCTURE

As demonstrated in the previous chapter, we are once again dealing with composites of mineral and organic phases. This holds for enamel, cementum, and dentine. In the case of enamel, the tissue covering the crown, its hardness, and rigidity have been likened to a ceramic material. The justification of this comparison is due to 95–96% of the weight being crystalline apatite, while less than 1% is from the organic matrix, and the remainder being water (Williams et al., 1989). Once erupted, the cells responsible for the formation of enamel (ameloblasts) are lost. This means that once formed, enamel is not capable of further growth, or repair for that matter.

As a ceramic-like material, enamel is composed of tightly packed enamel prisms, or rods, that are U-shaped in cross-section, and extend from the enamel–dentine junction to within 6–12 μm of the surface. Each prism is packed with flattened hexagonal hydroxyapatite crystallites. Between these prisms is an interprismatic material that contains most of the organic material found in mature enamel.

The larger size of the crystals in enamel, relative to bone and dentine, will affect its physical properties. This larger crystal size also means that the surface of the organic phase is reduced and it is, therefore, less reactive (Cole and Eastoe, 1988). During the growth of these crystals the amelogenins (proteins that predominate in newly secreted enamel) are removed during the maturation process. It is at this stage that the enamel becomes hard.

The orientation of enamel crystals will play an important role in the manner in which it reacts to heat stress.

7.2.2   CEMENTUM MICROSTRUCTURE

Like enamel, cementum is also an outer covering, albeit of the tooth root rather than the crown. The function of cementum is to encase the root of the tooth and receive the uncalcified collagen fibers of the periodontal membrane (Sharpey's fibers) in order to anchor the tooth to the alveolus.

Cementum is approximately 50% by weight hydroxyapatite and amorphous calcium phosphates. This tissue has a yellowish appearance. As one ages, this yellow color becomes progressively deeper (Ten Cate et al., 1977).

Cementum is formed by specialized cells known as cementoblasts. The organic matrix, or precement (or cementoid) is deposited first and is subsequently mineralized. In the active growth layer of cement, cementoblasts become entrapped in developing tissue and they then become cementocytes.

Cementum deposition is a continuous process throughout the life of the individual. The thickest areas of cementum deposition are the apices of the roots and the point of bifurcation of the roots in multirooted teeth (Hillson, 1986). This is done to maintain a small degree of eruption in order to compensate for occlusal wear.

Cementum is known to occur in layers. These layers can be observed as having an incremental pattern that may be annually deposited (Hillson, 1986). This has been the basis of an age-at-death estimation technique (e.g., Charles et al., 1989). However, to my knowledge there has never been an attempt to use this technique on cremated tooth remnants. This is likely due to the highly fragmented condition that occurs when subjected to heat stress (see Section 7.3.2 below). It is of interest to note that the deposition of cementum within the apical foramen (orifice) may cause a strangulation of the vessels passing through it. Hence, this area should be examined as a possible alternative for examining cementum annulations.

7.2.3 DENTINE MICROSTRUCTURE

As with the previous two dental tissues, dentine is a mix of organic and mineral components. An examination of this composition is listed in Table 7.1. This material makes up the bulk of the tooth, as it is deep to, and in support of, both the enamel of the crown and cementum of the root.

The major structural feature of dentine is the presence of densely packed dentinal tubules. The tubules are found to be passing perpendicularly through what are described as felted mats of collagen fibrils that are piled one on top of another (Hillson, 1986). The inorganic crystallites occur within this organic matrix. Further, the tubules themselves enclose a single cytoplasmic process of an odontoblast, containing microtubules, microfilaments, and mitochondria (Williams et al., 1989). The cell body of this odontoblast is in the pseudostratified layer lining the pulpal chamber encased within the dentine.

As dentine mineralizes it takes on the form of calospherites, microscopic spherical aggregates of crystals. However, dentine is not subsequently remodeled, as is the case with bone. Dentine does form what is known as secondary dentine inside the pulpal chamber. This type of dentine is reparative in nature. It is the only mechanism by which a tooth with a microfracture, due to some form of trauma, can repair itself.

TABLE 7.1
The Composition of Normal Human Dentine (drawn from Cole and Eastoe, 1988)

	% by Weight
Inorganic matter	75
Ash	72
Carbon dioxide	3
Organic matter	20
Collagen	18
Resistant protein	0.2
Citrate	0.89
Lactate	0.15
Chondroitin sulphate	0.4
Lipid	0.2
Unaccounted for (water retained at 100°C, errors, etc.)	5

7.2.4   Dental Pulp

The material contained within the confines of the pulpal chamber consists of a loose connective tissue that is well-vascularized and known simply as the pulp. The pulp communicates with the rest of the body via the apical foramen. There are several arterioles and capillary loops along with myelinated and unmyelinated sensory nerve fibers. These nerves respond to thermal, mechanical, or osmotic stimuli of dentine by a pain response.

The pulp is of particular importance in cases involving fire, as it is a highly protected environment that may yield nuclear or mitochondrial DNA that is suitable for profiling (see Chapter 8).

7.2.5   Other Tissues

The only other tissues of concern to the dentition are the gingiva and the oral mucosa of the mouth. A healthy gingiva may be recognized by its pale pink color and lightly stippled appearance. The gingiva is continuous with the oral mucosa via the muco-gingival junction. The mucosa consists of stratified squamous epithelium that has a smooth texture and red appearance due to vascularization.

The mucosa, along with the tissues that make up the cheeks, act to insulate the teeth from heat stress during the initial stages of the cremation process. The only gap in that protection is through the opening of the mouth.

7.3   INCINERATION OF DENTAL TISSUES

It has been recognized in the professional literature that teeth are indeed the most reliant structure of the human body. In fact, enamel is often described as the hardest substance of the body. This statement is supported through the paleontological recovery of teeth exceeding that of bone. As part of their inherent resiliency, teeth are resistant to fire, desiccation, decomposition, and prolonged immersion in water (Robinson et al., 1998). The experience of individuals involved with the recovery of bodies from fires and blast events is that dental remains are often going to play a key role in the identification process, and may help in answering other questions relating to the scene.

This section outlines the effects that various temperatures have on dental tissues. Each tissue is dealt with in turn.

7.3.1   Incinerated Enamel

One of the most important papers in surveying the effects of heat on dental tissues is by Harsányi (1975). In this study Harsányi exposed intact incisors and premolars from fresh corpses from 35 to 45 years of age, representing both sexes, to a heat source. An electric incinerator was used for these teeth to reach specific temperatures. It took 5 minutes for the oven to reach each target temperature; once reached, that temperature was maintained for 55 minutes. The teeth were then weighed and examined. Table 7.2 is a compilation of Harsányi's results for enamel.

TABLE 7.2

The Effects of One Hour of Exposure at Specific Target Temperatures on Enamel at Macroscopic and Microscopic Levels (drawn from Harsányi, 1976)

Temperature	Macroscopic Observations	Microscopic Observations
200°C	Color changes	None
300°C	Dark grayish brown; small crevices; enamel starts to peel off via small crevices; carries are not narrowed	Small crevices; enamel intact from crevice to crevice
500°C	Gray enamel; longitudinal furrows	Divided by crevice network; multiangular plates
700°C	Light grayish-white; broken into fragments	Consists of fine grained granules; original surface unrecognizable
900°C	Almost white (equal in color to cementum and dentine); enamel in smaller pieces	Enamel grains start to fuse-structure unrecognizable
1000°C	Enamel porcelain-white (equal in color to cementum and dentine)	"Structureless" smooth plates
1100°C	Small fragments, porcelain-white color	Same as at 1000°C
1300°C	Minute smooth porcelain-white fragments; glass-like surface	Inorganic salts are fused into round formations

Enamel appeared to go through a series of color changes ranging from a dark grayish-brown at 300°C to porcelain-white at 1000°C. Structurally, the enamel begins to crack and eventually break into fragments, separating from the underlying dentine. Microscopically small crevices appear at 300°C and increase in size and number as the temperature increases. The formation of granules on the surface of the enamel occurs at 700°C, while a fusion of these granules appears at 900°C. At 1000°C the enamel microstructure is unrecognizable.

If a comparison is made to the results of a similar study by Shipman et al. (1984), summarized in Table 7.3, many of the same types of physical alterations are noted, albeit under heating regimes that were slightly different. Shipman et al. refer to temperature ranges as opposed to a specific peak temperature as seen in Harsányi's study. However, the individual temperatures are within the range outlined in Shipman et al.'s study, save those in Harsányi's study, that are in excess of 900°C. Both studies note that there is a structural change at temperatures below 200°C. However, as 300°C is approached, there are changes to the surface of the enamel ranging from "dimple" development to the initiation of crevices. As temperatures approach 500°C, the presence of rounded particles is noted by Shipman et al. At this same level, Harsányi reports a gray color and the establishment of a microcrevice network. Shipman et al. also note the presence of fissures (crevices) and enamel beginning to break into small fragments. Both studies agree that previously formed particles (granules) will coalesce into larger, smooth globules and eventually fuse below 1000°C. Once above that temperature, the enamel is "porce-

TABLE 7.3

Heating Stages of Enamel: Microscopic Morphology (drawn from Shipman et al., 1984)

Stage	Temperature	Description
I	20–< 185°C	Normal and unaltered
II	185–< 285°C	Enamel develops dimples, but overall surface texture is smoother than in Stage I
III	285–< 440°C	Rounded particles appear, covering the surface
IV	440–< 800°C	Appearance of vitrified or glassy particles separated by many pores and fissures; enamel closer to CEJ, breaks into smaller fragments
V	800–940°C	Particles coalesce into larger, smooth-surfaced globules and these fuse into an irregularly shaped mass pierced by rounded holes

lain-white" and has fragmented. The effects of the heat on the hydroxyapatite are the same as observed in bone. Ultimately, with temperature in excess of 1100°C and up to 1300°C, the fusion of these salts results in the enamel developing a glass-like consistency.

Although these studies examine the effects of varying temperatures on the enamel, they do not indicate what will be observed in the field. The differing chemical composition of each of the three dental tissues will dictate how they will each react at a given temperature. Of these three tissues, enamel has the smallest amount of water. This is part of the reason that enamel, in relation to cementum and dentine, does not retract to the same degree. It is therefore quite common to encounter enamel crowns separated from underlying dentine (Figure 7.2). In cases where the enamel has some form of dental work, such as a filling composed of some sort of amalgam, the separation of the enamel from the dentine will still occur, with the

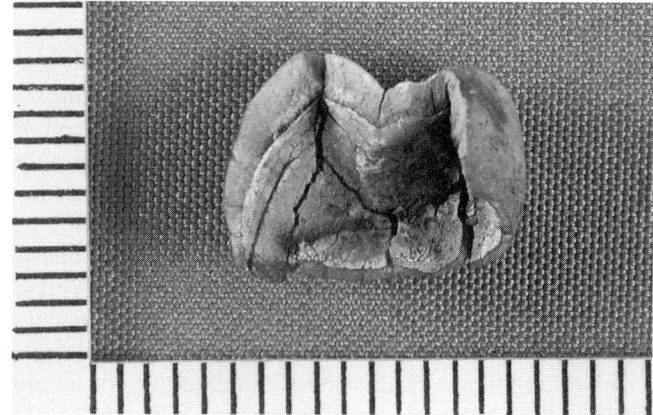

FIGURE 7.2   This enamel crown has separated completely from its underlying dentine. This is a common occurrence in forensic cremations. (Photo by S. Fairgrieve.)

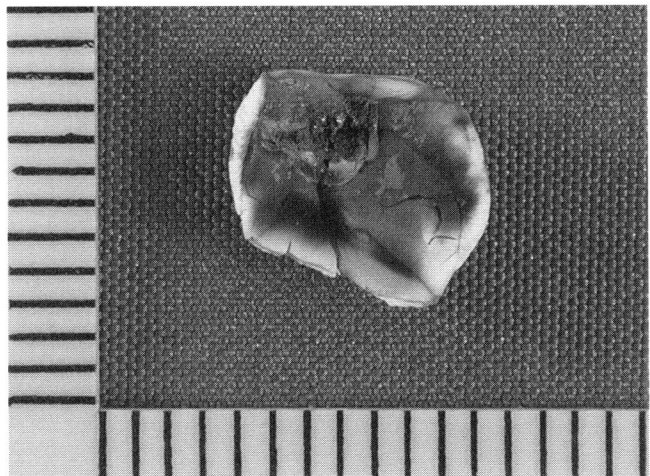

FIGURE 7.3   This section of a crown exhibits the remnants of an occlusal filling that has been eliminated during the cremation process. (Photo by S. Fairgrieve.)

additional separation of the filling from the enamel itself (Fairgrieve, 1994; Bush et al., 2006) (Figure 7.3).

The alterations of enamel during incineration may appear to be dramatic on a histological level; however, the enamel is nonetheless recoverable from cremation scenes. Analysis of such enamel may provide indications of peak temperatures as well as dental morphology that can be utilized as part of the identification process.

7.3.2   INCINERATED CEMENTUM

Cementum is protected by the gingiva, periodontal ligament, and the alveolus of the mandible, or maxilla. As the soft tissue features of the face and parietal aspects of the oral cavity are consumed by fire, the cementum is not directly affected until the gingiva is consumed.

As mentioned above, the enamel of the crown is the first of the dental tissues to be assaulted by the fire, starting with the anterior dentition. The cementum, the second tissue to be direly affected by fire, would first be exposed at the CEJ and then as the periodontal ligament and surrounding alveolus are eliminated; the remaining portions of the cementum are subjected to the heat down to the apex of each root. This explains the differentially shaded appearance of cremated tooth roots that have not been completely incinerated to the porcelain-white stage.

Table 7.4 summarizes the effects of an hour of exposure of cementum to fire. Early on in the process, at 300°C, the evaporation of water from the cementum results in a lifting of this tissue layer from the underlying dentine. At this stage the cementum has a "dark grayish-brown" color (Harsányi, 1975). At 500°C the root canal and apical foramen are preserved. The root appears to have large plates with deep furrows in between (Figure 7.4). With a tooth having been liberated from the alveolus, the root is now going to be directly accessible to the flame. With this increased heat to 700°C the cementum becomes a grayish-white color with a fine

TABLE 7.4

The Effects of One Hour of Exposure at Specific Target Temperatures on Cementum at Macroscopic and Microscopic Levels (drawn from Harsányi, 1976)

Temperature	Macroscopic Observations	Microscopic Observations
200°C	Color changes	None
300°C	Dark grayish brown	Evaporating water lifts cementum from dentine, "vesicles" with disrupted walls are formed; denuded surface exhibits tubular orifices
500°C	Light brownish-gray; root canal is preserved	Aggregated into large plates, divided by deep furrows; single plates are multiangular and are 30 to 60 μm in diameter
700°C	Light grayish-white; root canal narrowed but recognizable	Fnely granular surface; original structure no longer visible
900°C	Light, almost white color; root broken into large pieces	Granular surface penetrated by deep and wide crevices; original structure is decomposed
1000°C	Porcelain-white color	Covers dentine as a homogeneous, melted unconnected layer; some open orifices of dentine tubules are visible
1100°C	Porcelain-white color	No change
1300°C	Minute smooth porcelain-white fragments	Structure is decomposed; round formations of various sizes

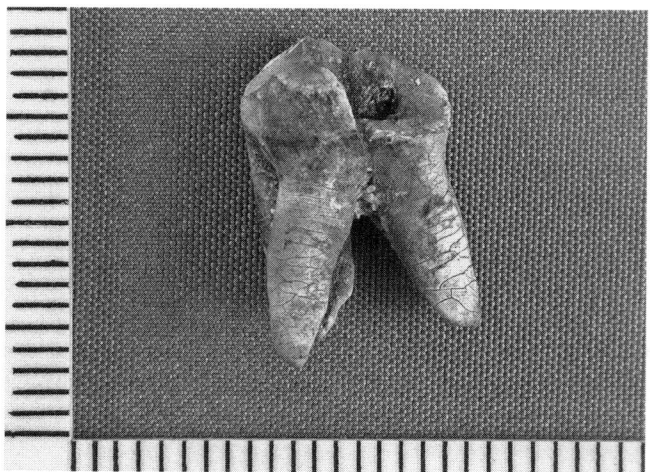

FIGURE 7.4   The roots of this upper first molar exhibit the platelike fragmentation of the cementum. The graded shades from white to gray from the CEJ to root apex indicates the differential exposure to heat due to its location in the alveolus. (Photo by S. Fairgrieve.)

granular surface at the microscopic level. In excess of this temperature, approximately 900°C, the color of the cementum is white and the root has disintegrated into large fragments. As the temperature increases the cementum becomes "porcelain-white" and appears to have undergone some form of fusion of surface particles producing a melted layer over the dentine.

It is important to stress that the studies undertaken by Harsányi (1975) and Shipman et al. (1984) used teeth that were already isolated from the alveolus. Any conclusions drawn from those studies should be considered estimates in actual casework where teeth are likely to be situated in the alveolus during cremation.

7.3.3 Incinerated Dentine

As cementum is likely to persist over dentine, albeit in a fragile state, dentine will typically be fully exposed at the crown once the enamel has separated. This is not to say that the dentine is not subjected to any heat while the enamel is still present. Heat will still reach the dentine via conduction through the enamel. As each of the dental tissues has been treated separately, in order to facilitate an explanation of this dynamic process, the tooth is a matrix of tissues, the majority of which consists of dentine.

At temperatures up to 200°C the dentine is unaffected by the heat (Table 7.5). Surface alterations of color are possible, but they are dependent upon the condition of the superficial surfaces of enamel and cementum for the crown and root, respectively. Such a tooth would be an excellent candidate from which to extract DNA from the pulp.

As 300°C is approached the dentine may become more of a light grayish-brown color, due to the heating of material within dentine tubules. This coincides with an opening of the tubules. However, the overall morphology is unaffected. The microscopic examination of the peritubular matrix demonstrates a contraction in size and separation from the intertubular matrix. The somewhat roughened appearance to the dentinal surfaces are due to the openings (or asperities) of the tubules.

The pulp cavity remains intact up to 500°C. The dentine has shifted to a dark grayish-black color, indicative of the carbonization of organic components. The asperities have melted and created a smooth surface. By this temperature Shipman et al. found that tubule openings had elongated and the intertubercular matrix had formed bars of fused material between these openings.

A further rise in temperature to approximately 700°C seems to have eliminated the majority of the organics present inside the dentine as demonstrated by the gray color. The root canal and pulp chamber persist, and yet they are narrowed. The tubules are narrowed inside, but with elongated and enlarged openings. The surface has what is described by Shipman et al. as a "frothy" appearance due to the alteration of the tubule openings. Some openings are irregularly shaped with a glassy texture (Table 7.6).

Upon reaching approximately 900°C the dentine, as with the other dental tissues, is white. Dentine tubules are narrowed and the frothy areas mentioned above have coalesced into globules that fuse into nodular spikes. The spaces between

TABLE 7.5

The Effects of One Hour of Exposure at Specific Target Temperatures on Dentine at Macroscopic and Microscopic Levels (drawn from Harsányi, 1976)

Temperature	Macroscopic Observations	Microscopic Observations
200°C	Color changes	None
300°C	Light grayish-brown	Structure preserved; tubules opened horizontally or longitudinally; morphology unaffected
500°C	Dark grayish-black; pulp chamber and root canal are preserved and not narrow	Preserved-open dental canalicules, without narrowing
700°C	Pale gray color; parts of pulp chamber and root canal recognizable but narrow	Tubules are narrowed but visible; peritubular zone is heat-resistant relative to intertubular dentine, which contains more organics and water
900°C	Almost white; large pieces with root	Narrowed dentine tubules 1.5 to 1.7 μm in diameter; anastomoses between tubules cannot be seen
1000°C	Porcelain-white; narrow pulp chamber; root canal slightly distinguishable	Tubular structure preserved; minute "pearls" of material connected (0.1–0.2 μm) in a string formation
1100°C	Root is porcelain-white; narrow pulp chamber and root canal can be observed	Tubular structure preserved; narrow portions and anastomoses are not observable; round plates and granules of varying sizes are formed
1300°C	Minute smooth porcelain-white fragments; remains of narrowed pulp chamber and root canal may be observed	Structures have decomposed and fused into granules of varying size

these spikes are the remnants of the tubules and the spikes are the remnants of intertubular bars.

Temperatures in excess of 1000°C produce dentine that is porcelain-white with a narrowed pulp chamber. The organic components have been eliminated at these temperatures.

The temperatures noted above are those achieved by the tissue and should not be used as an indicator of the amount of heat produced by a specific fuel, such as a volatile ignitable liquid (VIL).

7.3.4 INCINERATION OF DENTAL RESTORATIONS

The level of damage to dental tissues from fire is a combination of the heat being generated, the length of exposure, the type of tooth, the position of the tooth in the

TABLE 7.6

Heating Stages of Dentine: Microscopic Morphology (drawn from Shipman et al., 1984)

Stage	Temperature	Description
I	20–< 185°C	Pulp cavity dentine surface is unaltered; calcospherites are visible and pierced by smooth-edged dentine tubules
II	185–< 285°C	Peritubular matrix is shrunken and separated from the intertubular matrix; small asperities produce a roughened appearance
III	285–< 440°C	Asperities have melted and smoothed out; tubule openings are elongated; intertubular matrix forms a network of bars between openings
IV	440–< 800°C	Surface has a frothy appearance due to particles and increasing elongation and enlargement of tubule openings; some portions exhibit a glassy texture and irregularly shaped openings
V	800–940°C	Frothy areas have coalesced into globules that fuse nodular spikes; spaces between spikes are remnants of tubules and the spikes are remnants of intertubular bars

mouth, the physical condition of the tooth, and the presence of restorative materials such as dental amalgam for fillings.

The presence of fillings, be they from an amalgam of metals or a composite of resins and other materials, will yield fragments of teeth that differ in morphology from those of unrestored teeth (e.g., Fairgrieve, 1994; Robinson et al , 1998; Bush et al., 2006; Savio et al., 2006). The ability to recognize dental fragments and their associated restorative materials will enhance the interpretation of the fire and, ultimately, assist in establishing a positive identification (see Chapter 8).

Teeth incinerated to the point of fragmentation and elimination or restorative materials may be assessed for the type and position of a lost filling through the use of scanning electron microscopy (Fairgrieve, 1994). Although a filling may detach from the enamel to which it has been previously bonded, the striations left behind by the dental drill used to prepare the carious lesion for filling may still be observed. The usefulness of this technique is to enable analysts to identify teeth that have had dental restorations, as well as the type and position of that restoration from incinerated enamel fragments (Figure 7.5).

Initial examinations of dental restorative materials, such as amalgam and porcelain, seemed to indicate that the former could resist temperatures of up to 870°C, and the latter would maintain stability up to 1100°C (Robinson et al., 1998). Dental resins have become more popular and have largely replaced dental amalgam. These resins are as varied in their composition as they are in listed types and brand names. Many of these brands produce X-ray spectra that assist in the identification of such resins from incinerated remains (Bush et al., 2006). Structural and elemental compositions of these resins are capable of being identified. When high temperatures are applied to these resins, the elemental composition is still capable of being identified through energy dispersive X-ray spectroscopy (EDS).

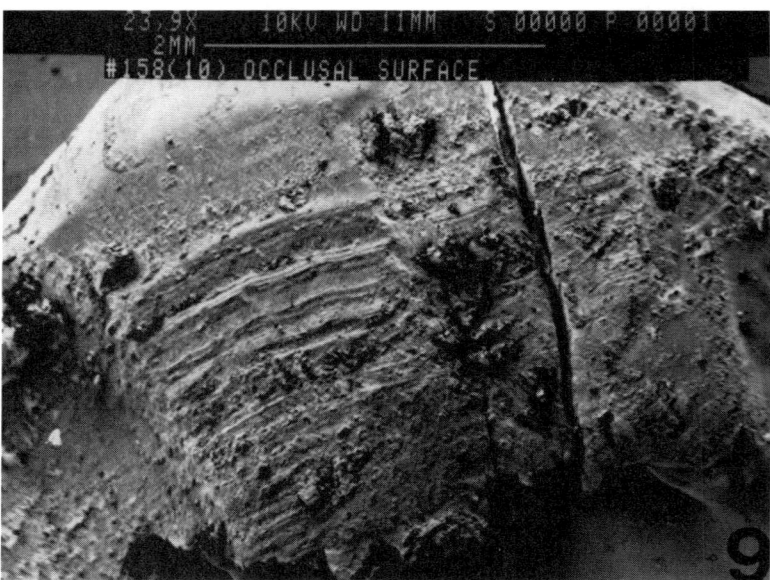

FIGURE 7.5   Scanning electron micrograph of a human and upper right second premolar with visible drill striations. This evidence of an occlusal filling on this tooth was consistent with the dental records of a victim of a cremation homicide. (Photo by S. Fairgrieve.)

Resins have been found to undergo color changes during heating that are brand-specific (Bush et al., 2006). These colors include white, gray, and dark gray. If still adhering to the tooth, distinguishing resin material from tooth matrix will be easily done. However, if the resin is dislodged from the tooth, it will be more challenging to locate this material amongst other debris. This is particularly true when a perpetrator is actively crushing dental structures.

The elemental composition seems to be the best hope of identifying the type of resin used. The production of a list of resins and their respective spectra would seem to be of value. Just such a listing was initiated by Bush et al. (2006) in their study of ten commercially available resins (see Table 1 of their article). Yet, not all resins lent themselves to EDS analysis. Those resins containing barium glass were not able to be identified individually, due to changes in their elemental composition during heating. Clearly, caution in undertaking an EDS analysis is called for when barium glass may be indicated.

The basis for any comparison of dental samples with restorations must begin with an understanding of heating regimes and their effects on unrestored teeth. In a recent study that examined the radiographic appearance of teeth subjected to high temperatures, a baseline study of unrestored teeth was done (see Table 7.7). As with the studies cited in the previous section, no changes were observed at 200°C. fissures between the crown and the underlying dentine formed at 400°C. It was not until 600°C that fissures within the root dentine were observed. Fissures within dentine of the crown were also observed at the same temperature. Fractures through root dentine did not appear until 800°C, while the crown still exhibited the same

TABLE 7.7

Differences Observed in the Radiographic Appearance of Postmortem vs. Antemortem Unrestored Teeth after the Thermal Stress (drawn from Savio et al., 2006)

Temperature	Crown	Root
200°C	No changes	No changes
400°C	Fissures between enamel and dentine	No changes
600°C	Fissures between enamel/dentine and within dentine	Fissures within dentine
800°C	Fissures between enamel/dentine and within dentine	Fractures through dentine
1000°C	Reduced to fragments	Large fractures through the dentine
1100°C	Reduced to fragments	Large fractures through the dentine

effects as at 600°C. The crown was not reduced to fragments until 1000°C. Larger fractures through root dentine were formed at 1000°C and continued to 1100°C.

Using an identical temperature regime, Savio et al. (2006) examined the effects of heat on postmortem and antemortem restored teeth having amalgam fillings, composite resin fillings, and endodontic treatments (treatments of the pulp chamber) (Table 7.8). They found that composite fillings were in place and maintained their shape up to 600°C while amalgam fillings maintained their shape and position up to 1000°C. Endodontic treatments, due to their protected context within the tooth, were recognizable up to 1100°C (the upper temperature limit of their study). At this highest temperature the amalgam fillings demonstrated a partially altered shape while the composite fillings remained in place despite being altered from a solid to a fluidic state. The endodontic treatments were slightly altered in all samples from 400°C by having less regular radiopacity, radiotransparent areas, and their shape and dimensions minimally altered. However, a "honeycomb" appearance to the endodontic treatment became apparent at 600°C. This is due to the change of the material to a fluid and/or it boiling as the temperature increased.

It is clear from the foregoing that restorative materials, be they amalgams, composite resins, or even endodontic restorations, will persist and serve as an aid to both positive identification and an estimate of the temperature attained by the dental structures in question. In the latter of these studies, Savio et al. (2006) heated their test teeth in an oven at a rate of 30°C per minute until the target temperature was reached and then immediately removed them from the oven. Further experimentation with heating regimes to mimic different types of fire contents would be useful given this baseline in the literature. Variation in size of restoration, and position, will also be needed to fully elucidate the fate of restorative materials in fire contexts.

For now, estimates of temperature are possible. However, the fact that restorative materials are hardier than some may imagine, detailed recovery of dental fragments and their associated restorations is essential.

TABLE 7.8

Differences Observed in the Radiographic Appearance of the Postmortem vs. Antemortem Restored Teeth after the Thermal Stress (drawn from Savio et al., 2006)

Temperatures	Amalgam	Composite	Endodontic treatments
200°C	No changes in shape and dimension	No change in shape and dimension	No changes
400°C	No changes in shape and dimension	No change in shape and dimension	Radiopacity less regular, presence of radiotransparent areas, shape, and dimension slightly altered
600°C	No changes in shape and dimension (even in samples with detachment of crown and fillings)	No change in shape and dimension	Radiopacity less regular, presence of many radiotransparent areas, "honeycomb" appearance, shape and dimension slightly altered
800°C	Large fissures between dental tissue and fillings—no changes in shape and dimension (even in samples with detachment of crown and fillings)	In place in an altered shape (state changing)	Radiopacity less regular, presence of many radiotransparent areas, "honeycomb" appearance, shape and dimension slightly altered
1000°C	Large fractures between dental tissue and fillings—no changes in shape and dimension (even in samples with detachment of crown and fillings)	In place in an altered shape (state changing)	Radiopacity less regular, presence of many radiotransparent areas, "honeycomb" appearance, shape and dimension slightly altered
1100°C	Crowns reduced in fragments—shape partially maintained	In place in a remarkably altered shape (state changing)	Radiopacity less regular, presence of many radiotransparent areas, "honeycomb" appearance, shape and dimension slightly altered

7.4   RECOVERY OF DENTAL CREMAINS

As mentioned above, the recovery of dental fragments is an issue that needs to be addressed. Most forensic identification officers do not have training in the recognition of bone, cremated or otherwise, let alone expertise in the recognition and recovery of ashed teeth. Mincer et al. (1990) found that 66% of responders to a survey on incinerated teeth considered the fragility of such specimens to be a significant forensic issue. Other respondents thought that difficulties may be overcome by careful handling, *in situ* photography, and/or removal of the tongue through the floor of the mouth, in order to facilitate radiography of the mandibular and maxillary dentitions. Some of the responders may not have encountered any problem due to the protection of the premolars and molars afforded by their position in the dental arcade. With the persistence of roots in the alveolus, comparative radiography would be possible.

The aforementioned comments do seem to indicate that cremains are more typically found with soft tissue, such as the tongue, demonstrating brief fire incidents. However, in forensic cremations where the remains have reached Stage 5 of the Crow–Glassman Scale, dental cremains will be in a highly fragmentary state and may require some form of consolidation.

Consolidation was found by Mincer et al. (1990) to be beneficial in the recovery of cremated teeth. Using a series of suggested materials (Table 7.9) they found that all were able to increase the physical stability of the teeth in order to preserve their macroscopic characteristics and features. Overall, the most convenient stabilizer to use was clear acrylic spray paint. The second of these was cyanoacrylate cement (Mincer et al., 1990). If the setting time is not an issue, polyvinyl acetate (PVA, or white school glue) is a good choice as it is also water soluble.

Perpetrators are not above manually destroying dental tissues using implements before, during, and after the cremation of a body. In fact, commingling of elements and actively crushing structures are not atypical in these types of scenes.

TABLE 7.9
Materials Tested for Stabilizing Incinerated Teeth
(drawn from Mincer et al., 1990)

Material	Application
Cyanoacrylate (Superglue®, liquid)	tube/drop
Acrylic spray (Krylon®, clear No. 1303)	spray*
Hair spray (Style Superhold®, unscented)	spray*
Spray varnish (Illinois Bronze®, clear, satin)	spray*
Fingernail polish (Hard as Nails®, clear)	brush
Epoxy cement (Devcon 5-Minute®)	brush
Epoxy cement (Devcon 5-Minute®) 1:1 in acetone	brush
Household cement (Duco®)	brush
Household cement (Duco®) 1:1 in acetone	brush
PVA polymer (Union Carbide®) ~5% in acetone	brush
PVA polymer (Union Carbide®) ~1% in acetone	brush
Acrylic resin (Coe®, orthodontic, self-cure, clear)	brush

*Applied in 3 coats with 3-min. drying between coats.

The implication of this is that the recovery of dental cremains need not be confined to a single area of the scene itself. This poses many challenges in the recovery of cremated teeth.

Cremated dental remains can be scattered through many layers of a scene, particularly if obfuscated by the perpetrator. Once the likely boundaries of the human cremains have been determined, areas peripheral to this region should be cleared. The region containing the cremains can then be approached systematically proceeding from the highest to the lowest levels. If the cremains are buried, forensic archaeological procedures must be followed (see Chapter 4).

The use of finer brushes to remove ash will be necessary to expose cremated dental tissues. Alveolar tissue can be extremely fragile and may flake away on contact. Consolidation should be considered at this time.

Individual padded containers for teeth will help to protect them from fragmenting during transportation to the laboratory. If one is not confident on how to proceed, it is best to consult a forensic odontologist or forensic anthropologist.

Once in the laboratory, the sorting and reconstruction of dental cremains can begin.

7.5   RECONSTRUCTION OF DENTAL CREMAINS

Highly fragmented dental cremains may first be sorted according to the roots that have been recovered. The conformation of roots may often be fitted with a portion of alveolus that contains intact or partial sockets (Figure 7.6). As roots are going to

FIGURE 7.6   A pair of cremated tooth roots from the same individual. Roots often possess dentine that supports the enamel of the crown that has previously separated. (Photo by S. Fairgrieve.)

be the most complete dental structures to recover, they will likely serve as the best means of achieving a positive identification (Smith, 1992). Root form and position, along with preserved endodontic treatments, are readily visible in antemortem radiographs, particularly when centered on the periapical area of a root (see Chapter 8 for aspects of positive identification from cremains).

Once the roots have been sorted as to possible tooth type, the crowns are then sorted in a similar fashion. As the roots will often have the dentine that was deep to a now separated enamel crown, it may be possible to simply match these to one another. However, as stated above, the enamel and dentine contract at different rates and extents when subjected to fire. It is for this reason that the enamel crown will not be a perfect size match to the dentine. A consistency in fit may be achieved. If dental restorations are present, or only a fragment of enamel with evidence of a previously adherent restoration, they may be matched for consistency with antemortem dental records once the position on the dental arch has been considered.

Reconstruction of enamel is possible with collected fragments. This is particularly important to do for the anterior dentition as the form of these teeth may be compared to antemortem photographs exhibiting the incisors and canines of the victims. This reconstruction may be undertaken using any sort of adhesive. The use of PVA glue will make it possible to separate fragments should the need arise.

7.6 SUMMARY

The incineration of dental tissues initially presents a daunting challenge for recovery and analysis in those cases in which a body has been subjected to high heat for a prolonged period. Nonetheless, dental cremains are recoverable and may be utilized in estimating temperature, and in the process of establishing a positive identification. Ultimately, dental cremains will play an important role in the identification process, as DNA analysis may not be possible in these cases.

With careful attention at the scene and thoughtful reconstruction, dental cremains may also provide evidence of a thorough recovery strategy. This will lend further credibility of the analysis in the minds of a judge and jury.

8 Positive Identification of Cremains

8.1 INTRODUCTION

The establishment of identity is one of the most significant aspects of a forensic investigation. The identity of remains, cremated or otherwise, permits authorities to begin tracing a series of events that led to the demise of the identified victim. If the remains are forensically relevant, the identity allows the authorities to contact family, friends, co-workers, and even casual acquaintances and contacts about the actions of a decedent, and who may have been associated with those actions. Hence, identity is a pivotal aspect in the analysis of human remains.

The means of establishing a positive identification (i.e., an identification that has been proven beyond any reasonable doubt and to the exclusion of all other possibilities) has changed significantly with advances in science and technology. In the latter nineteenth century, Bertillon had introduced a system of measurements (or anthropometry) of the body with full-length and profile photographs accompanied by a detailed description, in order to confirm an individual's identity if they were subsequently arrested or their remains were recovered in some context (Saferstein, 2007). The premise of using anthropometry rested on the assumption that measurements of the skeletal structure of an individual would remain the same from postadolescence to death. Although this statement may have a degree of validity to it, Bertillon's system was somewhat inconvenient due to the act of measuring and storing the various types of data collected. This system was only in use for 20 years or so when it was replaced by a new system of identification based on the friction ridge patterns found on digits (a.k.a. fingerprints).

Fingerprints revolutionized the field of human identification like no other system. Fingerprints are relatively easy to record and store. They also provide a degree of uniqueness that has been accepted by the courts for nearly a century.

More recently, the second revolution in human identification has been in the science of genetics. The direct analysis of DNA and its bases, the fundamental source of variation in all living things, is now the gold standard of forensic identification.

The use of fingerprints, DNA, and even Bertillon's system are all dependent upon finding and utilizing antemortem data from individuals who are candidates for identification. The advantage of DNA is that known blood relatives may also act as a source of known DNA to compare to the DNA from an unidentified individual. The other obvious drawback is that the source of data for comparison is derived from soft tissue. When it comes to positive identification from hard tissues alone, it can become somewhat more challenging.

It is true that forensic scientists do not have the luxury of choosing the quality of the specimens that they will use in their analysis. Information and specimens from the scene usually have limitations in completeness or preservational quality. fire is a notoriously efficient mechanism of destroying biological specimens that are depended upon for traditional means of establishing a positive identification. The one advantage of hard tissues is that they do persist in fire, although to varying degrees. In victims who have undergone some form of decomposition to the extent that facial features are not sufficient to allow a visual identification, the use of surviving dental work or DNA is considered.

Of course, modern methods of positive identification are not restricted solely to those methods mentioned above. Additional methods under research or used to assist in the identification process include stable isotope ratios, ear prints, soft and hard tissue pathology, surgical procedures and implants, radiographic comparisons, facial imagery analysis, iris patterns (in living individuals), footwear patterns, body modifications, and biometrics, including retinal comparisons (for a review, see Thompson and Black, 2007). However, it is fair to say that those methods that are based on soft tissue structures will not be applicable to cremated remains, especially those that have reached Stage V of the Crow–Glassman Scale.

This chapter presents the issues of establishing a positive identification from charred and cremated remains. The ability to apply these various methods is entirely dependent upon the condition of the remains and the availability/suitability of antemortem records.

The most common of these methods is based on dental comparisons. However, as discussed in the previous chapter, dental cremains present their own set of difficulties. Other comparisons use osteological structures, as seen in antemortem radiographs as a basis for identification. One of the most commonly applied of these is the use of frontal sinuses. Other structures such as palatal rugae morphology recorded through orthodontic casts may be of use as well.

The reconstruction of cremains from fragments (see Chapter 5) has been the basis of establishing morphological characteristics of remains in support of *de facto* identifications. Some of these characteristics may include evidence of antemortem trauma.

Finally, the application of genetic analysis to DNA recovered from cremains has become increasingly important in the identification of charred bodies. There have also been attempts to obtain analyzable DNA from dental remains.

Ultimately, attempts to identify human cremains can take an analyst down many analytical pathways. It is the discretion of the analyst and their own experience with cremains that will dictate how this process is undertaken.

8.2   RADIOGRAPHIC COMPARISONS

8.2.1   INTRODUCTION

The utilization of antemortem radiographs necessitates that the cremains be carefully collected from the scene, cleaned ultrasonically, and then reconstructed to a level permitted by the recovered fragments (Grévin et al., 1998). This may prove to be more difficult than it sounds due to the level of fragmentation that can occur (see Chapter 5). However, reconstruction is the first step in the identification process of cremains.

The comparison of antemortem and postmortem radiographs is done to examine, in detail, points of structural congruity between the images being compared. A reconstruction of as much of the skeleton as possible is essential for this process to have any validity. Assuming that an analysis of age, sex, and ancestry have permitted the generation of a list of candidates for identification, reconstruction of cremains may prove to be of sufficient quality to lend itself to a comparison of radiographs.

The most common radiographic comparison used for identification would be dental records. However, as dental identifications have many considerations that need to be examined in greater detail, those details may be found in Section 8.3. The next most common type of radiographic comparison is through structurally conservative features. Such features must have a lasting quality with slow to negligible alterations through time. In other words, these features need to last and not undergo structural changes that will render them useless for comparison purposes.

The simple fact of the matter is that the skeletal structures of the body are physiologically active. As such, bone has a rate of turnover, albeit an uneven one, throughout the entire skeleton. The question is whether or not this turnover of bone is going to significantly alter any of the structures that will be of interest to us for making a comparison. This means that the age of the individual will have an effect on our ability to identify cremains by this method. The most obvious individuals who would not be good candidates for radiographic comparison would be preadolescent children. Children's skeletal structures are not only less well ossified than those of adults, but are also still very much in the process of developing the very structures that we would evaluate in adults. For example, frontal sinuses (see below) are not present in infants and young children. However, with growth, paranasal sinuses are being formed into the adolescent stage and beyond (Williams et al., 1989). Another area of consideration is the comparison of the trabecular structure orientation found within vertebral centra. Again, postadolescent individuals who have had radiographs of the spinal column may have these used as a basis of comparison if the corresponding area of the skeleton is recovered.

Regardless of the area, the comparison of skeletal structures may be used in the identification process. However, the strength of such an evaluation must be considered in light of other studies of variation in the structures being examined, and the extent to which those structures have been preserved.

8.2.2 FRONTAL SINUS COMPARISON

One of the earliest notations of the potential of frontal sinus radiographs as a means of establishing an identification was by Schuller (1943). Recognizing the potential of such a system, Ubelaker (1984) applied the comparison of frontal sinuses from found human remains to antemortem radiographs of a suspected identification. A match was noted in this case. Part of Ubelaker's study was to examine the frontal sinus patterns of skulls from the Terry Collection at the Smithsonian. This study failed to find any other frontal sinus patterns that matched that of the identified remains. Other studies have examined the use of frontal sinuses as a means of identifying remains (e.g., Kirk et al., 2002; Harris et al., 1987a; Marlin et al., 1991; Harris et al., 1987b; Yoshino et al., 1987). More recently, the use of frontal sinuses as a means of identification and, subsequently, testifying to the validity of this methodology in court has come under scrutiny (Christensen, 2004). Under the current U.S. *Federal Rules of Evidence*, there is concern that the methodology used by forensic anthropologists, pathologists, and radiologists, in applying frontal sinus comparison, has not sufficiently established the uniqueness of the patterns to establish identity. The reason for this concern is that there is a lack of standardized methods. Without a standardized methodology it is difficult for us to apply the results in a reproducible manner such as found in other sciences as chemistry and toxicology. However, this will only become an issue in the courts if identifications are challenged and the forensic anthropologist must demonstrate how the identity was determined with this methodology. In the meantime, the examination of frontal sinuses will continue to provide evidence of identity in cases where it is unchallenged.

The frontal sinuses are often exposed in Stage V cremains (Figure 8.1). In fact, the recovery of the entire frontal bone may not be possible. Hence, only a portion of the frontal sinuses may be present for comparison. The same may be said of the antemortem radiographs that are available for comparison. A complete P–A view (posterior–anterior view) of the skull in which the skull was placed with the forehead placed directly onto the radiographic cassette will typically provide a suitable image for comparison (Figure 8.2). However, in some cases, the antemortem radiographs are in the form of CT-scan images (Figure 8.3). If the scanned images are available in electronic format, they may be compiled in order to enhance the area of the frontal sinuses for comparison. Likewise, a CT scan of the reconstructed frontal bone (or fragment) may yield images of the frontal sinuses from the unidentified cremains. CT-scan images have nonetheless been used to confirm human identification (Haglund and Fligner, 1993; Tatlisumak et al., 2007).

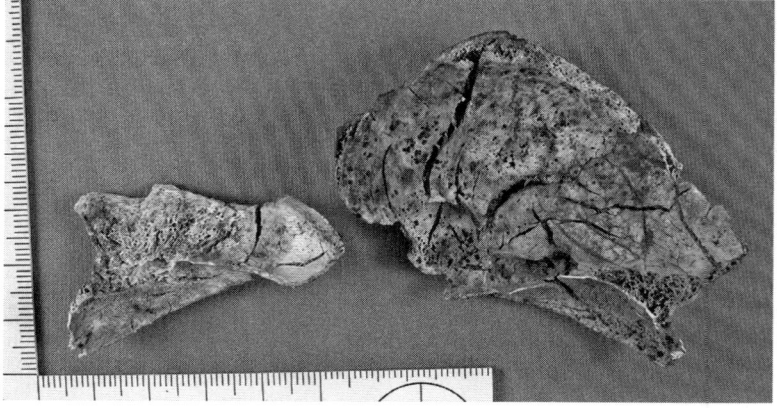

FIGURE 8.1 Partial frontal sinuses are evident in this fragmentary frontal bone from a cremation homicide victim. (Photo by S. Fairgrieve.)

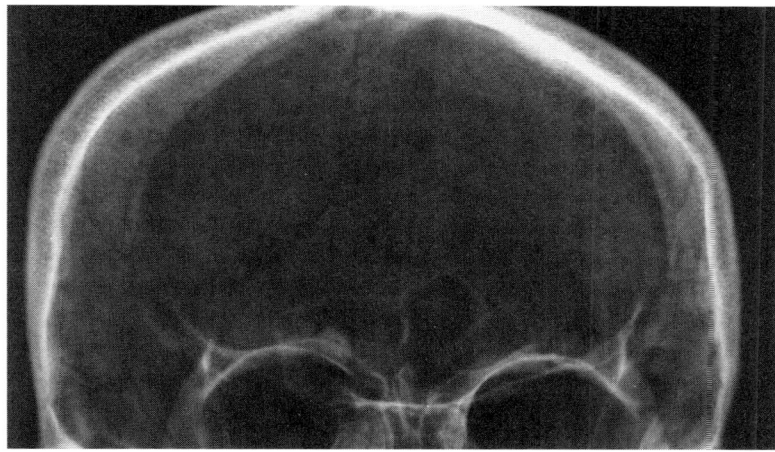

FIGURE 8.2 A P.A. radiograph of a human skull demonstrating a clear outline of the frontal sinuses. (Photo by S. Fairgrieve.)

Other complicating factors to the evaluation of frontal sinuses in complete skulls would include the positioning of postmortem radiography of the skull to mimic the antemortem position (Kirk et al., 2002). Likewise, the position of the head of the living patient may not be at an optimal angle for the purposes of comparison, but be of sufficient exposure for diagnostic purposes. One would then have to try to mimic the same position and orientation if measured comparisons are to be made. Therefore, measurements made on the antemortem and postmortem radiographs for purposes of comparison may produce a degree of error. This makes inherent sense, as a radiograph is a two-dimensional representation of a three-dimensional object. Those areas deep to the glabellar portion of the frontal bone will tend to have the clearest margins, as they are in a plane that is approximately parallel to the X-ray cassette. The lateral margins of the frontal sinuses will tend to lack clarity if they extend to the curvature of the frontal bone away from the cassette.

A caveat to keep in mind with cremated remains is that the frontal sinuses are in a position that is extremely close to the surface of the skull and lacks the protection of a thick layer of tissue to protect that area from the heat of cremation. The skull is one of the most vulnerable areas of the body and is often the first to undergo heat-induced fractures (see Chapter 4). It is for this reason that caution must be exercised, as there are no studies of the postcremation form of the frontal sinuses and their utility in identification.

The presence of unusual morphological features that may contribute to the uniqueness of the individual should also be considered in an assessment. Owsley found this to be the case in examining cremains with a fragmentary frontal bone (Owsley, 1993). In this case, an asymmetrical frontal sinus and a well-defined sulcus were evident on the antemortem radiographs and the fragmented frontal bone. However, if challenged, one must be prepared to provide other evidence that would support the identification.

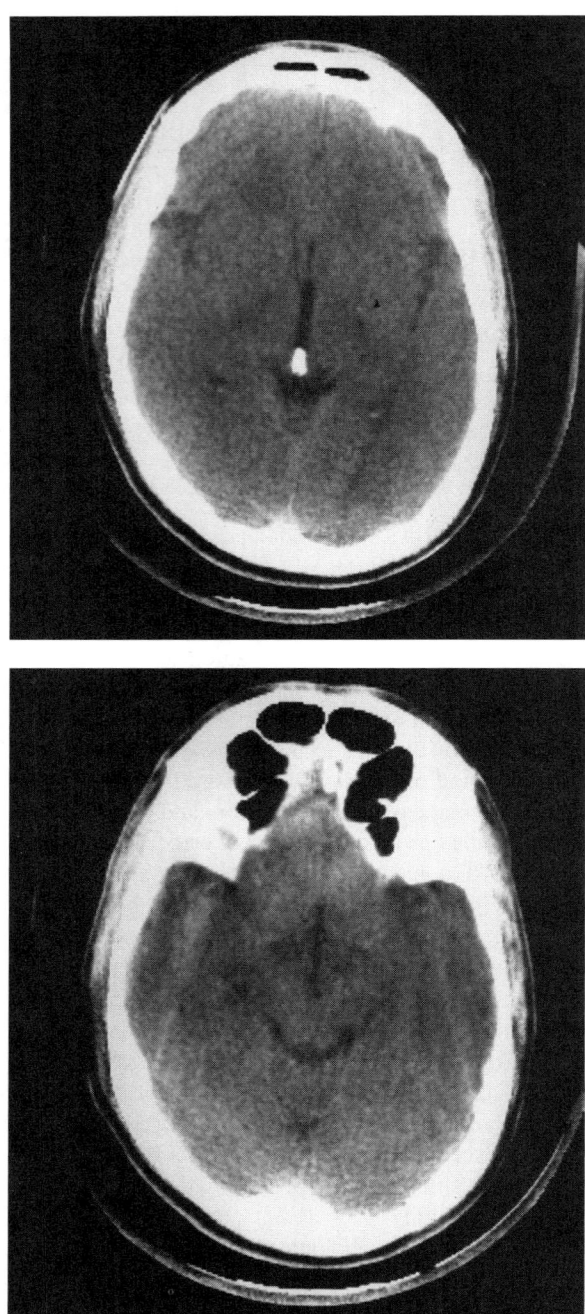

FIGURE 8.3   These CT-scan images are the only antemortem record of the frontal sinuses in Figure 8.1. Unfortunately, these images were not saved electronically with other views. (Photos by S. Fairgrieve.)

If there is sufficient material to reconstruct the frontal bone, and hence the frontal sinuses, it is recommended that a comparison is made of ante- and postmortem radiographs of this area. However, due to the lack of sufficient scientific examination of this technique on cremains, it is recommended that this type of examination be used to assist in confirming, or at least failing to exclude, the individual in question as the identity of the cremains.

8.2.3 Other Radiographic Comparisons

Certainly, other areas of the body that have been radiographed have been used as a basis for identification. The overall form and radiographic features have served as points of comparison to at least note structural similarities. Ubelaker (1990) utilized the axillary (or lateral) border of a recovered human scapula and its distinctive morphology as the basis for identification with the antemortem radiograph showing the same characteristics. The argument justifying the use of these features was that they were compared to 100 right scapulae from the Smithsonian's Huntington Collection and 100 right scapulae from skeletal collections of American Indians in the Smithsonian. Because of the uniqueness of the axillary border of the recovered skeleton, when compared to the 200 scapulae cited above, Ubelaker considered the "well-developed extended notch" to be sufficient for identification in this case.

The above case was done on a set of human remains that were subjected to carnivore scavenging, but not cremation. The effects of cremation on skeletal features have been documented in Chapter 4 and Chapter 5. There is no way of knowing if the act of cremation has sufficiently altered the morphology of bone such that a comparison to antemortem radiographs is without justification.

Anatomical features particular to a specific bone are most certainly preserved in the cremated remains. In Figure 8.4, the distal end of a humerus from a homicide cremation victim was found to have a preserved septal aperture. This feature, in life, permits the person to hyperextend their elbow joint. If the decedent is known to have been able to perform such an action, then this would be further congruence of the presumed identity, but not sufficient for identity.

Further investigation of anatomical features and their recognition after cremation is certainly recommended. A recent study by Muthusubramanian et al. (2005) of the palatal rugae of burn victims was compared to cadavers. However, this study did not extend to taking the cadavers to Stage V cremains. Superficial burning that does not affect the bone directly is of interest to cases of identification in which the charred remains are at Stage III and lower.

Identification from any area of the body for which there are any antemortem radiographs should certainly be attempted. However, the question of a particular feature's or set of features' validity for use as a means of individuating remains must be approached through further study of documented collections. Again, without the scientific studies, the analyst may, at best, fail to reject an identification rather than state that a positive identification has been established.

Trabecular pattern recognition from antemortem radiographs has been recognized as a means of identification. For example, the trabecular pattern of the distal femur and the proximal tibia (the knee joint) has been found to be distinctive (Mann,

FIGURE 8.4   The cremated remains of a distal right humerus *in situ*. A septal aperture joining the olecranon fossa with the coronoid fossa would have permitted hyperextension of the elbow joint in life. (By permission, Regional Supervising Coroner, Northern Ontario.)

1998). In fact, a minimum of four distinct "osseous features" were found by Mann (1998) to be reliable indicators for identity from that area of the skeleton.

In a recent study to validate the use of antemortem and postmortem radiographs of the hand as a basis for identification, the authors found that it is indeed a valid method for identification (Koot et al., 2005). Further, the use of the hand has the potential of employing features present in 27 bones. A significant feature of this study is that it compared "fleshed" cadaver hands that were radiographed, and subsequently removed and defleshed to simulate decomposition. This fact coupled with a test of the reliability for identification by other forensic anthropologists satisfies the Daubert guidelines. This is a further enhancement to the use of trabeculae in identification. Certainly, this method holds much promise. However, given the level of damage (shrinkage, warping, and cracking) that goes on in a cremation, care would have to be exercised in applying such a methodology to cremains.

Trabecular densitometry has been undertaken using image analysis software as a basis of comparison for antemortem and postmortem radiographs (Kahana and Hiss, 1994) and radiographs of the wrist in living subjects taken years apart (Kahana et al., 1998). As these methods and direct comparisons of trabecular patterns have been successfully developed and used on noncremated remains, the question is how differing levels of cremation will affect these methodologies.

Other anatomical features such as mastoid sinus and meningeal artery patterns (Rhine and Sperry, 1991), vertebral body and spinous process form (Mundorff et al., 2006), and even pathological conditions affecting the morphology of osteological structures (Sudimack et al., 2002; Hulewicz and Wilcher, 2003) have been used to confirm identification.

Features such as those listed above have been applied in cases that have yielded human remains that have been extensively fragmented and been bent and warped through taphonomic processes (Owsley et al., 1993). A case in which human remains were purposefully rendered down to such a condition by Jeffrey Dahmer, demonstrated that a positive identification can be made even from remains that are in a condition similar to that of cremains (Owsley et al., 1993).

In one extreme example, cremated and commingled human remains eventually resulted in positive identifications based on a comparison of antemortem and post-mortem radiographs in addition to medical, dental, and other background records (Owsley et al., 1995). In this incident, members of the Branch Davidian sect had secluded themselves in Mount Carmel, Texas, and were eventually cremated in a fire on that property. It was demonstrated that there were many points of concor-dance in the comparison of premortem and postmortem radiographs for individual MC27. Hence, the process of cremating remains did preserve enough detail of osteo-logical features for identification. However, it is worth noting that apparently not all the regions of the remains from the Branch Davidian compound were reduced to calcinated bone. Some soft tissue, albeit charred, did survive; however, crania and other areas of the body susceptible to cremation did indeed reach Crow–Glassman Stage V.

Finally, the use of cranial suture pattern matching from radiographs has been examined from the perspective of Daubert criteria (U.S.A.) and the Mohan ruling (Canada) (Rogers and Allard, 2004). It has yet to be explored in cases of cremated cranial fragments. However, cranial fragments with sutures are typically salvaged from cremations. As lambdoidal sutures are associated with the occipital bone it is more likely to be preserved due to the thickness of that region of the vault.

8.3 DENTAL IDENTIFICATION

The use of dental tissues as a means of establishing a positive identification is a common enough practice that there are full-time forensic odontologists. Although forensic odontologists are involved with examining dental structures in deceased individuals, they are also involved with assessing injuries to teeth, jaws, and oral tissues in living victims (Hardy, 2007). In the case of cremation analysis, forensic odontologists will work closely with forensic anthropologists, as the latter will have been involved with the recovery and curation of dental cremains.

A forensic odontological examination of dental features used as a basis of com-parison comprises a substantial list of features, many of which are based on the assessment of soft tissues (for a review, see Table 10.1 in Hardy, 2007). Yet, in the context of forensic cremations, many of these features are either lost or significantly altered. Those features that are more likely to be encountered in Stage V cremains are summarized in Table 8.1. Although this table would seem to indicate that there is a plethora of details that may provide a basis for identification, in practice, many of these features are obscured or eradicated in the cremation. It is nonetheless pos-sible for cremated dental tissues to exhibit some of these features.

The actual analysis of dental cremains will follow a specific set of procedures that will facilitate identification. The following section details those procedures and the dental tissues to which they apply.

TABLE 8.1
Tooth and Periodontal Features Typically Encountered in Human Cremains (drawn from Table 10.1 in Hardy, 2007)

Teeth

Teeth present
- a. Erupted
- b. Unerupted
- c. Impacted

Missing teeth (based on sockets)
- a. Congenitally
- b. Lost antemortem
- c. Lost postmortem

Tooth type
- a. Permanent
- b. Deciduous
- c. Mixed
- d. Retained primary
- e. Supernumerary

Tooth position
- a. Malposition

Crown morphology
- a. Size and shape
- b. Enamel thickness
- c. Contact points
- d. Racial variation

Crown pathology
- a. Caries
- b. Attrition, abrasion, erosion
- c. Atypical variations, enamel pearls, peg lateral, etc.

Root morphology
- a. Size
- b. Shape
- c. Number
- d. Divergence of roots

Root pathology
- a. Dilaceration
- b. Root fracture
- c. Hypercementosis
- d. Root resorption
- e. Root hemisections

(Continued)

TABLE 8.1
(Continued)

Pulp chamber/root canal morphology

    a. Size, shape, and number

    b. Secondary dentine

Pulp chamber/root canal pathology

    a. Pulp stones, dystrophic calcification

    b. Root canal therapy

    c. Retrofills

    d. Apicectomy

Periapical pathology

    a. Abscess, granuloma, or cysts

    b. Cementomas

    c. Condensing osteitis

Dental restorations

1. Metallic

    a. Nonfull coverage

    b. Full coverage

2. Nonmetallic

    a. Nonfull coverage

    b. Laminates

    c. Full Coverage

3. Dental implants

4. Bridges

5. Partial and full removable prosthesis

Periodontal Tissues

Alveolar process and lamina dura

    a. Trabecular bone pattern and bone islands

    b. Residual root fragments

Maxillary sinus

    a. Size and shape

    b. Relationship to teeth

Anterior nasal spine

    a. Incisive canal (shape) (likely damaged)

    b. Median palatal suture

Mandibular canal

    a. Mental foramen

    b. Diameter, anomalous

    c. Relationship to adjacent structures

(Continued)

TABLE 8.1

(Continued)

Coronoid and condylar process

    a. Size and shape

    b. Pathology

Temporomandibular joint

    a. Size, shape

    b. Hypertrophy/atrophy

    c. Ankylosis, fracture

    d. Arthritic changes

Other pathologies

    a. Evidence of surgery

    b. Trauma – perimortem or antemortem (wires, pins, and other implanted materials)

8.3.1 Tooth Root Analysis

Dental crowns, as established in the previous chapter, are quite commonly fractured. Although these crowns may be reconstructed, if recovered, they may not be complete due to the absence of dental restorative materials.

Tooth roots are more commonly preserved intact due to the protected nature of being situated in an alveolus. Roots may also be in poor condition due to the actions of the fire context or the actions of a perpetrator. Root repairs may also be undertaken if the roots have only been partially recovered. Single rooted teeth tend to have well-preserved roots, as they will drop out of the alveolus more readily. Although this would seem to make them more vulnerable, it has been my experience with cremation homicides in which the perpetrator fragments the cremains, that single tooth roots are reasonably intact. However, where a tooth has multiple roots, each one of these roots tends to be broken off from the rest of the tooth. All roots must be collected and an attempt be made to match these with broken root fragments.

Tooth roots may also be retained in the alveolus of the mandible or maxilla. In this case, it will be desirable to radiograph such a fragment for direct comparison to antemortem radiographs. Should the socket be intact and the root of the tooth be missing, an alternative would be to use a method such as that suggested by Smith (1992). This method requires the analyst to place inside the tooth socket a radiopaque substance, such as barium sulfate, in order for a radiograph to be taken, simulating the presence of the tooth root.

Tooth roots may also preserve evidence of antemortem dental work. Figure 8.5 demonstrates some tooth roots from a cremation homicide in which a post has been preserved. These may then be compared to dental records for concordance. Other evidence of dental restoration that may be helpful would include discontinuities in the surface adjacent to, or part of, the cemento-enamel junction (CEJ). Such areas may be the remnants of fillings that are no longer present. Figure 8.6a demonstrates a tooth from a cremation homicide with a crescent-shaped concavity that conforms to a resin-based composite filling at the CEJ. The location of that filling on an ante-

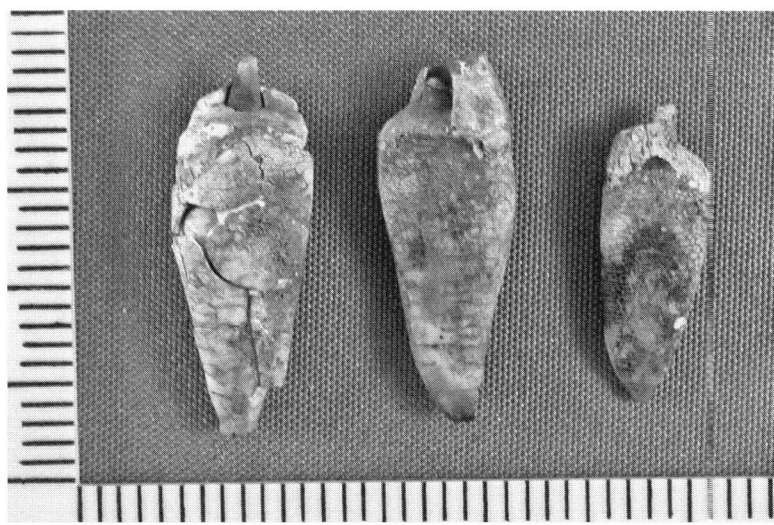

FIGURE 8.5   Dental posts are often preserved in cremated tooth roots such as these from a cremation homicide. (Photo by S. Fairgrieve.)

mortem radiograph is demonstrated in Figure 8.6b. Confirmation of evidence of dental work using a scanning electron micrograph (SEM) is recommended in these situations (Fairgrieve, 1994).

8.3.2   CROWN ANALYSIS

Although the challenges of crown repair have been outlined above, the crown fragments may be key indicators of antemortem dental restorations.

The most common form of dental restoration to the crown is a filling As outlined in the previous chapter, dental fillings may range from a metal amalgam of varying composition to composite resins. Regardless of the type of filling material, the carious lesions to be treated must be prepared in order to receive the restorative agent.

The preparation of a carious lesion is undertaken by drilling directly inside the lesion and creating a chamber that will accommodate the restorative material. The action of drilling directly inside the lesion and creating a chamber that will be filled by the restorative material will leave behind a physical signature of this action directly on the enamel. This signature is in the form of bore marks and striations. The head of the drill, as it proceeds down into the enamel, will leave a well-defined cylindrical mark. As several passes of the drill may be needed to clean out the lesion, the bore marks will overlap. Examination of the inside of one of these bore marks will yield evidence of horizontal, parallel striations from the rotational action of the drill-head. These can be easily distinguished using an SEM or even a light microscope at 40X magnification. The examination of a cremated tooth fragment will show evidence of these indicators even under low magnification (see Figure 8.7).

In particularly hot fires, the dental crown will fragment into small pieces. It is unusual to find a crown, not only in one piece, but sill attached to a tooth root.

A

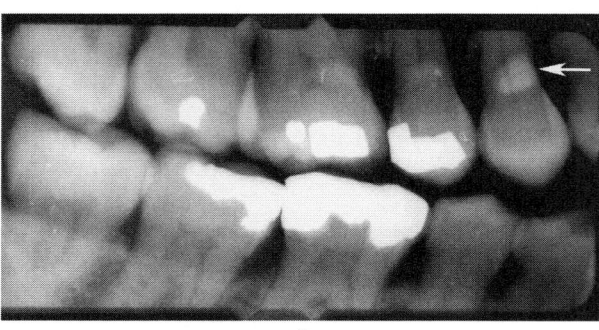

B

FIGURE 8.6   A) The crescent shape concavity at the CEJ of this tooth is indicative of a filling in this position. B) The corresponding location is demonstrated by the arrow as the confirmed location of such a filling. (Photos by S. Fairgrieve)

Figure 8.8 is a lingual view of an upper incisor from a cremation homicide victim. Note that the area of the crown adjacent to the CEJ has a metallic look to it and also exhibits a gap between the crown and the root. This is an artificial crown that has survived the cremation process and remained affixed to the underlying root post. Although the surface of the crown has some persistent adherent material, the form of the crown has been perfectly maintained.

The fragmentation of the crown, as described above, also means that resins will be present amongst the detritus of the cremation. Bush and colleagues (2006), recognizing this fact, subjected various restorative resins to incineration and compared the pre- and postincineration energy dispersive x-ray spectroscopy (EDS) elemental analysis. They found that the elemental analysis is not only unique to the manufacturer of the resin, but, it was also "almost unchanged" after incineration. This is yet another factor that may be used to assist in the identification process. It is their feeling that the wear, alignment, and combination of missing, restored, and unrestored

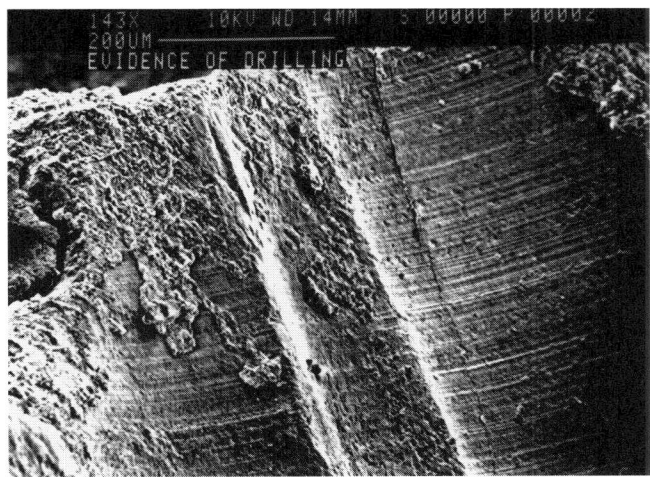

FIGURE 8.7 An SEM of a first molar demonstrating vertical bore marks and striation in a uncremated tooth. (Photo by S. Fairgrieve.)

FIGURE 8.8 An upper first incisor with an artificial crown mounted on a post in the root.

TABLE 8.2

Description of the Steps Included in the Four Stages of Examination and Documentation of the Charred Dentition (drawn from Delattre, 2000)

Stage I:	Noninvasive extra-oral visual examination
	Preliminary charting of visible teeth
	Extra-oral photography
Stage II:	Soft tissue removal for direct visualization of dentition
	Continue documenting and photographing the dentition
	Attempt to pry open the jaws for intra-oral access; if successful go to Stage III
Stage III:	Mandibular/maxillary resection
	Radiographs and more photographs as needed
	Loose, individual teeth should be identified and radiographed
Stage IV:	Place all loose dentition and resected items in a labeled container

teeth are as unique as a fingerprint. The chemical signature of restorative materials is surely another factor to add to the above suite of traits.

In the case of remains that have been charred, but not necessarily to Crow–Glassman Stage V, the procedures followed are outlined in Table 8.2 (from Delattre, 2000). However, in the case of forensic cremains, removal of soft tissue and resection are not necessarily steps that will need to be taken.

8.4 DNA AND IDENTIFICATION

The goal of DNA analysis is to differentiate between individuals who have 99.5% of their DNA in common. The fact that a differentiation can be made is testimony to the amount of DNA a person has in a single cell. Hence, only a small portion of DNA is going to exhibit any variability that forensic geneticists will exploit in differentiating between individuals.

The variability of DNA is in the form of short tandem repeats (STRs). The STR is typically characterized by having a short sequence of base pairs (four in most cases) that repeat a variable number of times. A specific locus may have a variety of possible alleles (segments that differ in the number of repeats). These segments of DNA with repeating short sequences are bounded by nonrepeating sequences known as flanking DNA.

As the method of analysis depends on analyzing the occurrence of various alleles at specific loci that are relatively short, such a sample is not only easy to characterize and interpret, but it is also ideal for profiling samples of poor quality, as is often the case with forensic contexts. Amongst these contexts is the cremation scenario.

The source of DNA in unburned human remains usually comes from muscle tissue, skin, hair, biological fluids, and even bones and teeth. In forensic cremations, this will leave us with bones and teeth as a source of DNA. The extraction of DNA from hard tissues has been studied in forensic and archaeological contexts (e.g., Alonso et al., 2001; Pääbo, 1989; Pääbo et al., 1989; Hagelberg et al., 1991; Jeffreys et al., 1992; Hummel et al., 1999).

8.4.1 DNA from Cremains

It has only been recently that the technology for isolating, detecting and quantifying DNA from burned human remains has been pursued (for a review, see von Wurmb-Schwark et al., 2004).

The extent of the cremation is a major determining factor in the success of isolating and amplifying DNA. In house fires, an examination of a scene can yield cremated bone to the calcine stage as well as some charred soft tissue, as related in some reports (e.g., Wickenheiser et al., 1999). If there is surviving fibrous muscle tissue and cartilaginous material, then there is a strong possibility of obtaining DNA. The use of surviving soft tissue from charred bodies is more commonly used for DNA identification (Barbaro et al., 2003).

The elimination of all soft tissue during the cremation process or soft tissue charred to the point of being of no value for DNA extraction will require us to consider the remaining bones and teeth as a potential source of DNA. Because bone houses the marrow, it may act as an insulator, for a time, from the severe heat of a fire. Hence, attempts at extracting DNA from the innermost regions of a bone may hold some promise (Staiti et al., 2004). As would be expected, larger bones found deep inside soft tissues will be better candidates for such extractions. Therefore, based on the model of cremation presented in Chapter 3, the bones of the lower axial skeleton, such as the lumbar vertebrae, are ideal candidates to test. Additionally, parts of the ilium, ischium, and os pubic may also be worth considering. In general, bones closer to the surface and those in the appendicular skeleton are less likely to yield usable DNA.

In extreme cases of forensic cremations, the perpetrator has managed to eliminate the body of all adherent soft tissue. The most extreme cremation of a body takes place in commercial cremations. Once the body has been reduced to calcined bone the fragments are then ground in a mill. In one test of such remains, the DNA extracted prior to cremation was compared with that extracted from commercially prepared cremains (von Wurmb-Schwark et al., 2004). It should not be too surprising that the postcremation DNA did not conform to that of the precremation DNA that was profiled using STRs. The postcremation samples were likely contaminated through processing and handling. To this point in time, DNA extraction from cremains from commercial crematoria is unreliable at best.

This only leaves us with DNA from teeth as a possible means of identification. It makes sense that the tooth pulp chamber of a tooth would be a highly protected environment and, hence, a possible source of DNA (Duffy, 1989; Sweet and Sweet, 1995). Sweet and Sweet (1995) used the dental pulp from incinerated human remains in order to generate a DNA profile. Although the soft tissue was degraded to the point of being considered useless for DNA extraction, the dentition was preserved and in the alveolus. Further, the teeth were not shattered and the roots appeared to be intact. In particular, a third molar that was as yet unerupted was extracted for DNA analysis. Teeth still situated within the alveolus and unerupted would be the most ideal candidates. In general, teeth that are in the anterior dentition are more likely to be affected by heat stress than those located distally on the dental arch. Molars are certainly preferable, due to their overall size and thickness of dental tissues.

The use of DNA from incinerated deciduous dentition as a means of sexing cremains was pioneered by Williams et al. (2004). They found that they were able to isolate and analyze DNA, specifically the amelogenin locus, to determine sex. Deciduous teeth were subjected to temperatures from 100–500°C for 15 minutes. Although not always successful, some teeth that were heated to 400°C were able to have their DNA profiled.

The insulative properties of teeth were demonstrated by Duffy et al. (1991) in their study of fleshed pigs' heads subjected to an open fire. A fire temperature of 500–700°C produced a temperature of only 75°C in the pulp chamber of the pigs' teeth. It was also found that intact nuclei were found in unextracted teeth in fleshed jaws of pigs subjected to 300°C for over an hour. As encouraging as this study may be, forensic cremations with dental remains that are calcined, and exhibit heat-induced fractures, are not candidates for DNA analysis of any type.

8.5 MASS DISASTERS AND IDENTIFICATION OF CREMAINS

A mass disaster is usually recognized as any event in which there is a sudden occurrence of large numbers of deceased individuals. One usually thinks of plane and train crashes; however, more recently, the events of 9/11 have added terrorist attacks to our collective consciousness.

Large numbers of dead may also occur in industrial accidents and, of course, conflicts. Natural disasters such as earthquakes, tornados, floods, forest and brush fires, and even avalanches can produce a large number of dead in a short period of time (Wagner and Froede, 1980).

One of the most challenging aspects of mass disaster scene processing is the coordination of resources in an efficient manner. Although the process of mass disaster scene processing is beyond the scope of this book, it is nonetheless important for readers to familiarize themselves with these procedures (for a review, see Wagner and Froede, 1980; and Mackinnon and Mundorff, 2007).

The identification of human remains from mass fatalities is largely accomplished using dental remains. This task is made somewhat easier if there is some record of the occupants of a building, or even a crashed aircraft. The implication of having some form of manifest is that there is a list of potential candidates, and hopefully, associated medical/dental records. Logistically, the task is now to sort the remains and determine identity. Fragmentary human remains undergo an inventory and cataloguing process in order to reconstitute individuals with the recovered anatomical structures.

The charring of human remains in these events tends to be uneven. In cases of aircraft crashes and fires, jet fuel will act as a very fast-burning and extremely hot accelerant. Cremation of remains to the point of calcination may occur, but it is more likely that the body will burn differentially. Of course, there are instances in which a body will be engulfed by a fire and be subjected to explosive forces. However, the differential cremation of a body at a mass disaster scene is a real possibility (Figure 8.9).

Aircraft crash victims are usually identified through the use of recovered dental structures (e.g., Barsley et al., 1985). More recently, the use of DNA on a wide scale has been used to assist in establishing the identification of highly fragmented remains (e.g., Mackinnon and Mundorff, 2007). DNA analysis in combination with dental, anthropological, and pathological analysis will continue to be used in mass fatality incidents.

As noted above, the challenge of any mass fatality incident is the documentation and collection of remains. When those remains have been cremated, such as in the Hinton, Alberta train crash in 1986, and commingled with wreckage, the challenge is now separating and sorting the cremains from melted plastics and metal (Stratton and Beattie, 1999). Although separation of cremains from other materials may be time consuming, the process of identifying remains is a challenging task due to their cremated state.

Nonmetric features have been suggested by Stratton and Beattie (1999) to be the only means possible for the identification of cremains. Sex and age may be assigned to cremains should the morphological features be present to do so. In addition to these clinical x-ray comparisons, even associated personal effects can be of importance in the identification process.

It is clear from the foregoing that the condition of cremains in mass disaster scenarios is of paramount importance to the identification process. One must be open

FIGURE 8.9   A cranial vault fragment from a small plane crash. Note the charred and uncharred areas present on the vault. (Photo by S. Fairgrieve.)

to the use of many analytical avenues in order to pursue a positive identification. It is equally clear that a team approach to the identification of disaster victims, particularly when cremated, will enhance the chances of arriving at an identification. For cremains that have reached Crow–Glassman Stage V, the use of DNA will be a foregone conclusion. However, morphological comparisons to antemortem records may still be possible.

8.6   IMPLANTS AS A MEANS OF IDENTIFICATION

As with dental restorations, surgical procedures may also require the implantation of materials in the body that may be of assistance in the identification of cremains. The usefulness of orthopedic devices, due to manufacturer logo and a means of tracking these devices to specific patients through unique serial and lot numbers, has been documented as a likely source of information for positively identifying associated human remains (Ubelaker and Jacobs, 1995). Pacemakers have been a commonly traced implant in the identification of remains (Sathyavagiswaran et al., 1992).

Although there are many forms of implants, one would have to consider the likelihood of survival of such implants in cremation contexts. Fixative devices, screws, and surgical plates are ideal candidates for examination in cremains. However, even more complicated devices, such as an osteostimulator, an implanted device that is used to induce the regeneration of bone tissue by means of a stimulating electrical current, have been of assistance in the identification of cremains (e.g., Bennett and Benedix, 1999).

All materials that are directly associated with human cremains that can possibly be a component of an implanted device must be explained in the analysis of recovered materials. The challenge is to recognize these cremated components from amongst other fire-altered materials associated with, or around, the human cremated material.

8.7   IDENTIFYING CREMAINS OF HISTORIC FIGURES

On occasion human cremains are recovered in a context that is consistent with an expected or purported individual. The challenge is no less difficult in attempting to identify these remains as with many others. To serve as examples of the challenges of such identifications, I have chosen to summarize the cases of attempting to identify the charred remains once purported to be those of King Philip II of Macedonia, father of Alexander the Great (Andronicos, 1994; Bartsiokas, 2000), and the attempts to identify the cremains of Adolf Hitler (Laurier et al., 1994; Kaleka, 1993).

The cremated remains of what was subsequently identified as belonging to an adult male were discovered in "Royal Tomb II" at Vergina, Greece, in 1977 by Andronicus (1994). The richness of the grave goods and the context (ca. 336 B.C.) served to identify the tomb as that of King Philip II of Macedonia. As noted by Bartsiokas (2000), this conclusion has been challenged due to another estimated date of 317 B.C. and, hence, belonging to King Philip III Arrhidaeus, a half-brother of Alexander the Great. As Philip II is said to have suffered an arrow wound to his right eye, the detection of evidence of such an injury on the cremains would be thought to have served as a strong indicator of the identity of these cremains. In a forensic context, if a pathology is noted in a medical record with accompanying radiographs, one would be more confident of utilizing a pathology as a basis for identification. The strongest possible conclusion that could be made in this case, should the cremains provide unequivocal evidence of an antemortem eye injury that is consistent with that reported in history, would be that we failed to exclude Philip II as the identity of the cremains. Examination of the margins of the supraorbital margin of the right eye did not yield any evidence of a healed fracture or callus formation (Bartsiokas, 2000). However, is it possible for an arrow to enter the right orbit and result in the loss of an eye without leaving any evidence on the bone? The obvious answer is yes. Although it may not seem likely, documentation of the incident is not sufficient to say one way or the other. Another point of consideration is the interval of time that has passed from the incident to the time of death. A lack of evidence of a callus formation on the bone may indicate that sufficient time has passed for resorption of the bony callus. Although Bartsiokas (2000) concludes that there is no evidence to support traumatic injuries to the face, and any asymmetries can be attributed to the warping and shrinkage associated with the cremation process. It is true that cranio-facial skeletal elements are highly susceptible to the aforementioned heat-induced changes. However, given the above, it cannot be categorically stated one way or another that the cremains are, or are not, those of Philip II of Macedonia. A rigorous forensic approach would prevent us from rendering a conclusion one way or another. Hence, the cremains should be considered as unidentified.

In the twentieth century, the most infamous person whose charred remains were under severe scrutiny for identification were those of Adolf Hitler. In spite of such interest, the purported cranial and dental fragments held by Russian authorities still have questions related to identification issues (for a review, see Marchetti et al., 2005). The issues surrounding Hilter's remains lie in the fact that the remains recovered were subjected to fire, using gasoline as an accelerant. According to Bezymenski (1968), the charred remains recovered represented an adult male of approximately 50–60 years of age with a stature of approximately 165 centimeters. Enough soft tissue was present in order for there to be an examination of internal organs, even to note the absence of the left testicle. The skull consisted of an occipital, left temporal, "lower cheek bones," nasal bones, and the mandible and maxilla. The dental remains are of significance due to the presence of bridgework, artificial teeth, crowns, and fillings. Given the above condition of the remains, this would put them into either level 2 or 3 of the Crow–Glassman Scale.

A reexamination of documents concerning the discovery of the grave containing the corpses of a man and a woman outside of Hitler's Berlin bunker yielded a reference to two fragments from a skull found at a depth of 50 to 60 centimeters (Petrova and Watson, 1996). One fragment is noted as having a bullet hole. This hole, interpreted as being an exit wound, is from a close contact gunshot through the mouth or the chin. The original autopsy report, cited by Bezymenski (1968) makes no mention of such fragments. However, mention was made of splinters from a glass ampule in the mouth of the male body (presumably containing cyanide). Further, cranial vault fragments representing the "back of the parietal and part of the occipital" were discovered and examined in 1995 (Petrova and Watson, 1996).

The nature of the conflicting reports as to whether or not Hitler shot himself or took cyanide (or both), is very much dependent upon an identification of the mandibular and maxillary fragments as well as those of the skull. An identification based on mtDNA from Hitler's maternal cousins, as suggested by Marchetti et al. (2005) would be an important step in resolving this problem. However, this case is a classic example of poor controls at a scene and subsequent chain of custody. By dissociating the remains, questions such as the above become issues of intense interest. Modern forensic science would hopefully not let things get this far.

The two cases outlined above are merely examples of some of the problems that are inherent to such work. Even remains that are charred and comparatively low on the Crow–Glassman Scale (i.e., Hitler's remains) may be more problematic due to the methods of recovery and curation of materials.

8.8 SUMMATION

The identification of cremains is a very credible pursuit. Although it is a challenge that faces any forensic analyst, it is indeed the case that success will depend upon the suitability of the recovered specimens, and the availability and quality of medical and dental records. Care must be taken when examining morphological features in light of the degree of shrinkage and warping that may occur during the cremation process.

References

Ahlquist, J., and O. Damsten. 1969. A modification of Kerley's method for the microscopic determination of age in human bone. *Journal of Forensic Sciences* 14:205–212.

Alonso, A., S. Andelinovic, P. Martin, D. Sutlovic, L. Erceg, E. Huffine, L. F. deSimon, C. Albarran, M. Definis-Gojanovic, A. Fernandez-Rodriquez, P. Garcia, L. Drmic, B. Rezie, S. Kuret, M. Sancho, and D. Primorac, 2001. DNA typing from skeletal remains : evaluation of multiplex and megaplex STR systems on DNA isolated from bones and teeth samples. *Croatian Medical Journal* 42:260–266.

Andronicos, M. 1994. *Vergina: The Royal Tombs*. Athens: Ekdotike Athinon.

Avila, F. W., and M. L. Goff. 1998. Arthropod succession patterns onto burnt carrion in two contrasting habitats in the Hawaiian Islands. *Journal of Forensic Sciences* 43(3):581–586.

Babrauskas, V. 1996. Fire modeling tools for FSE: are they good enough? *Journal of Fire Protection Engineering* 8(2):87–96.

Baby, R. S. 1954. Hopewell Cremation Practices, Columbus, OH: Ohio Historical Society, Papers in Archaeology, No. 1.

Baby, R. S. 1956. A Unique Hopewellian mask headdress. *American Antiquity* 21(3):303–304.

Barbaro, A., P. Cormaci, and A. Barbaro. 2003. Identification of a carbonized body found inside a car. *International Congress Series* 1239:869–871.

Barillo, D. J., and R. Goode. 1996. Fire fatality study: demographics of fire victims. *Burns* 22(2):85–88.

Bartsiokas, A. 2000. The eye injury of King Philip II and the skeletal evidence from the Royal Tomb II at Vergina. *Science* 288(5465):511–514.

Barsley, R. E., R. F. Carr, J. A. Cottone, and J. A. Cuminale. 1985. Identification via dental remains: Pan American flight 759. *Journal of Forensic Sciences* 30(1):128–136.

Bass, W. M. 1984. Is it possible to consume a body completely in a fire? In: Rathbun, T. and J. E. Buikstra, editors. *Human Identification: Case Studies in Forensic Anthropology*. Springfield, IL: Charles C. Thomas, p. 159–167.

Bass, W. M. 1987. *Human Osteology: A Laboratory and Field Manual*. 3rd edition. Columbia, MO: Missouri Archaeological Society.

Bass, W. M. 1995. *Human Osteology: A Laboratory and Field Manual*. 4th ed. Columbia, MO: Missouri Archaeological Society.

Bass, W. M., and P. A. Driscoll. 1983. Summary of skeletal identification in Tennessee 1971–1981. *Journal of Forensic Sciences* 28(1):159–168.

Bass, W. M., and R. L. Jantz. 2004. Cremation weights in East Tennessee. *Journal of Forensic Sciences* 49(5):901–904.

Becker, R. F. 1995. *The Underwater Crime Scene: Underwater Crime Investigation Techniques*. Springfield, IL: Charles C. Thomas.

Bedford, M. E., K. Russell, and C. O. Lovejoy. 1989. The utility of the auricular surface aging technique. Poster presented at the 58th Annual Meeting of the American Association of Physical Anthropologists, San Diego.

Bennet, J. L. 1999. Thermal alteration of buried bone. *Journal of Archaeological Science* 26:1–8.

Bennet, J. L., and D. C. Benedix. 1999. Positive identification of cremains recovered from an automobile based on presence of an internal fixation. *Journal of Forensic Sciences* 44(6):1296–1298.

Berryman, H. E., J. O. Potter, and S. Oliver. 1988. The ill-fated passenger steamer *Sultana*: an inland maritime disaster of unparalleled magnitude. *Journal of Forensic Sciences* 33(3):842–850.

Bezymenski, L. 1968. *The Death of Adolf Hitler. Unknown Documents from Soviet Archives*. London: Michael Joseph.

Binford, L. R. 1963. *An analysis of cremations from three Michigan sites*. Wisconsin Archaeology 44(2):98–110.

Blackmore, D. J. 1973. The determination of carboxyhemoglobin and its importance in aviation accidents. In: Mason, J. K., and W. J. Reals, editors. *Aerospace Pathology*. Chicago: College of American Pathologists Foundation, p. 190–202.

Bohnert, M., T. Rost, M. Faller-Marquardt, D. Ropohl, and S. Pollak. 1997. Fractures of the base of the skull in charred bodies—post-mortem heat injuries or signs of mechanical traumatization? *Forensic Science International* 87:55–62.

Bohnert, M., T. Rost, and S. Pollak. 1998. Degree of destruction of human bodies in relation to the duration of the fire. *Forensic Science International* 95(1):11–21.

Bohnert, M., U. Schmidt, M. G. Perdekamp, and S. Pollak. 2002. Diagnosis of a captive-bolt injury in a skull extremely destroyed by fire. *Forensic Science International* 127:192–197.

Bonar, L. C., and M. J. Glimcher. 1970. Thermal denaturation of mineralized and demineralized bone collagens. *Journal of Ultrastructure Research* 32:454–461.

Bonucci, E., and G. Graziani. 1975. *Comparative thermogravimetric, X-ray diffraction and electron microscope investigations of burnt bone form recent, ancient and prehistoric age*. Atti Memorie Accademia Nazionale die Lincei Scienze, Fisiche, Matematiche Naturali, Ser. 8, Sec. 2A (Roma) 59:517-534.

Boucher, B.J. 1957. Sex differences in the fetal pelvis. *American Journal of Physical Anthropology* 15:581-600.

Bowler, J. M., R. Jones, H. Allen, and A. G. Thorne. 1970. Pleistocene human remains from Australia: a living site and human cremation from Lake Mungo, western New South Wales. *World Archaeology* 2: 39–60.

Bradtmiller, B., and J. E. Buikstra. 1984. Effects of burning on human bone microstructure: a preliminary study. *Journal of Forensic Sciences* 29:535–540.

Brandt, J. 1960. Das urnengräberfeld von Preetz in Holstein, 2. bis. 4 Jahrhundert nach Christi Gerburt. Neumunster: Offa-Bücher 16.

Brooks, S. T. 1955. Age at death: reliability of cranial and pubic age indicators. *American Journal of Physical Anthropology* 13:567–597.

Brooks, S. T., and J. M. Suchey. 1990. Skeletal age determination based on the os pubis: A comparison of the Ascádi—Nemskéri and Suchey—Brooks methods. *Human Evolution* 5:227–238.

Brooks, T. R., T. E. Bodkin, G. E. Potts, and S. A. Smullen. 2006. Elemental analysis of human cremains using ICP-OES to classify legitimate and contaminated cremains. *Journal of Forensic Sciences* 51(5):1–7.

Buikstra, J. F., and M. Swegle. 1989. Bone modification due to burning: Experimental evidence. In: Bonnichsen, R., editor. Bone Modification. Maine: *Peopling of the Americas* Publication: Center for the Study of First Americans. Institute of Quaternary Studies, University of Maine, p. 247–258.

Buikstra, J. F., and D. H. Ubelaker. 1994. Standards for data collection from human skeletal remains. Fayetteville, AR: *Arkansas Archaeological Survey Research* Series 44.

Burri, C., J. Jakob, R. L. Parker, and H. Strunz. 1935. Über hydroxylapatit von der kemmeleten bei hospenthal. *Schweiz Mineral Petrogr Mitt* 15:327–339.

Bush, M. A., P. J. Bush, and R. G. Miller. 2006. Detection and classification of composite resins in incinerated teeth for forensic purposes. *Journal of Forensic Sciences* 51(3):636–642.

Byers, S. N. 2005. *Introduction to Forensic Anthropology*, Second Edition. Toronto: Pearson, p. 476.

Byers, S. N., K. Akoshima, and B. K. Curran. 1989. The determination of adult stature from metatarsal length. *American Journal of Physical Anthropology* 79(3):275–279.

Carr, R. F., R. E. Barsley, and W. D. Davenport, Jr. 1986. Postmortem examination of incinerated teeth with the scanning electron microscope. *Journal of Forensic Sciences* 31(1):307–311.

Cattaneo, C., S. Di Martino, S. Scali, O. E. Craig, M. Grandi, and R. J. Sokol 1999. Determining the human origin of fragments of burnt bone: a comparative study of histological, immunological and DNA techniques. *Forensic Science International* 102(2–3):181–191.

Cattaneo, C., K. Gelsthorpe, P. Phillips, P. Sokol, and R. J. Sokol. 1994. Immunological detection of albumin in ancient cremations using ELISA and monoclonal antibodies. *Journal of Archaeological Science* 21:565–571.

Charles, D. K., K. Condon, J. M. Cheverud, and J. E. Buikstra, J.E. 1989. Estimating age at death from growth layer groups in cementum. In: Iscan, M.Y., editor, Age Markers in the Human Skeleton. Springfield, IL: Charles C Thomas p 277–301.

Chiba, T., N. Nishida, K. Gonmori, and N. Yoshioka. 2003. Intracerebral hemorrhage as the cause of death in a severely burned body. *Legal Medicine* 5:108–109.

Christensen, A. M. 2004. The impact of Daubert: Implications for testimony and research in forensic anthropology (and the use of frontal sinuses in personal identification). *Journal of Forensic Sciences* 49(3):427–430.

Clark, M. A., D. A. Hawley, J. L. McClain, J. E. Pless, D. C. Marlin, and S. M. Standish. 1994. Investigation of the 1987 Indianapolis Airport Ramada Inn incident. *Journal of Forensic Sciences* 39(3):644–649.

Clayton, T. M., J. P. Whitaker, and C. N. Maguire. 1995. Identification of bodies from the scene of a mass disaster using DNA amplification of short tandem repeat (STR) loci. *Forensic Science International* 76:7–15.

Cole, A. S., and J. E. Eastoe. 1988. *Biochemistry and Oral Biology*. London: Butterworth and Company (Publishers) Limited, p. 555.

Council of Canadian Fire Marshals and Fire Commissioners. 2001. 2001 *Annual Report*. Ottawa: Fire Protection Services, Human Resources and Skills Development Canada.

Correie, P. M. M. 1997. Fire modifications of bone: a review of literature. In: Haglund, W. B., and M. H. Sorg, editors. *Forensic Taphonomy*. Boca Raton, FL: CRC Press, p. 275–294.

Craig, E. A., and N. Vezaro. 1998. Use of an alternate light source to locate bone and tooth fragments. *Journal of Forensic Identification* 48(4):451–458

Cujipers, H., A. E. Cujipers, and H. Schutkowsky. 1993. Histological age determination in cremated remains. *Helinium* XXXIII:99–107.

Cuijpers, S. A. G. F. M. 1995. Possibilities of histological research on diaphyseal fragments in cremated remains. In: Smits, E., E. Iregren, and A. G. Drusini, editors. *Proceedings of the Symposium Cremation Studies in Archaeology*, Padova, IT.: Logos Edizioni. pp. 73–85.

Davis, J. H. 1962. Suicide by fire. In: Symposium—fire and incendiarism. *Journal of Forensic Science* 7(4):379–430.

de Gruchy, S., and T. L. Rogers. 2002. Identifying chop marks on cremated bone: a preliminary study. *Journal of Forensic Sciences* 47(5):933–936

DeHaan, J. D. 2002. *Kirk's Fire Investigation*, fifth edition. Upper Saddle River, NJ: Prentice Hall, p. 638.

DeHaan, J. D., S. J. Campbell, and S. Nurbakhsh. 1999. Combustion of animal fat and its implications for the consumption of human bodies in fires. *Science and Justice* 39(1):27–38.

Delattre, V. F. 2000. Burned beyond recognition: systematic approach to the dental identification of charred remains. *Journal of Forensic Sciences* 45(3):589–596.

Dix, J., and R. Calaluce. 1999. *Guide to Forensic Pathology*. Boca Raton: CRC Press, p. 257.

Dokládal, M. 1969. Über die heutigen möglichkeiten der personenidentifikation auf grund von verbrannten knochen. In: *Aktuelle kriminologie*. Hamburg: Kriminolog Verlag, p. 223–246.

Dokládal, M. 1970. Ergebnisse experimenteller verbrennungen zur feststellung von form- und grössenveränderungen von menschenknochen unter fem einfluss von hohen temperaturen. *Anthropologie* 8(2):3–17.

Dokládal, M. 1971. A further contribution to the morphology of burned bones. Anthropologic Congress, Prague and Humpolec, 1969, Prague, Academia, 1971. In: Novotny, V., editor. *Proceedings of the Anthropological Congress Dedicated to Ales Hrdlicka*, 1970, p. 561–568.

Dominguez, A. M. 1962. Problems of carbon monoxide in fires. *Journal of Forensic Sciences* 7(4):379–392.

Drusini, A. 1987. Refinement of two methods for the histomorphometric determination of age in human bone. *Zeitschrift für Morphologie und Anthropologie* 77:167–176.

Duffy, J. 1989. Potential for postmortem gender identification from human tooth pulp. *Canadian Society of Forensic Science Journal* 22(2):109–117.

Duffy, J., J. D. Waterfield, and M. F. Skinner. 1989. Sex determination of tooth pulp: forensic usages. Presented at the 1989 Annual General Meeting of the Canadian Society of Forensic Science, Edmonton, Alberta. *Canadian Society of Forensic Science Journal* 22(3):278.

Duffy, J. B., J. D. Waterfield, and M. F. Skinner. 1991. Isolation of tooth pulp cells for sex chromatin studies in experimental dehydrated and cremated remains. *Forensic Science International* 101:733–737.

Dunlop, J. 1978. Traffic light discoloration in cremated bone. *Medicine, Science and the Law* 18:163–173.

Dunne, M. J., and R. R. McMeekin. 1977. Medical investigation of fatalities from aircraft-accident burns. *Aviation, Space, Environmental Medicine* 48(10):964–968.

Dupras, T. L., J. J. Schultz, S. M. Wheeler, and L. J. Williams. 2005. *Forensic Recovery of Human Remains: Archaeological Approaches*. Boca Raton: CRC Press, p. 256.

Eckert, W. G., S. James, and S. Kathis. 1988. Investigation of cremations and severely burned bodies. *American Journal of Forensic Medicine and Pathology* 9:188–200.

Emson, H. E. 1978. Problems in the identification of burn victims. *Canadian Society of Forensic Science Journal* 11(3):229–236.

Fairgrieve, S. I. 1994. SEM analysis of incinerated teeth as an aid to positive identification. *Journal of Forensic Sciences* 39(2):557–565.

Fairgrieve, S. I., editor. 1999. *Forensic Osteological Analysis: A Book of Case Studies*. Springfield, IL: Charles C. Thomas, p. 340.

Fairgrieve, S. I. 2000. Forensic Anthropology Report, Re. O.P.P. Case #236645-4: Human Skeletal Remains, Havilland Bay, Ontario, Plane Crash, June 3, 1969. Acting for Dr. Barry McLellan, Regional Coroner, Northeastern Ontario.

Fairgrieve, S. I., and E. Molto. 1994. Burning Point: Canadian Case Studies of Intentionally Cremated Human Remains. In: Herring, A., and L. Chan, editors. *Strength and Diversity: A Reader in Physical Anthropology*. Toronto: Canadian Scholars Press Inc., p. 385–402.

Fairgrieve, S. I., and T. S. Oost. 2001. *Human Skeletal Anatomy: Laboratory Manual and Workbook.* Springfield IL: Charles C. Thomas, p. 166.

Fazekas, I. G., and F. Kósa. 1978. *Forensic Fetal Osteology.* Budapest: Akadémiai Kiadó p. 414.

Fechner, G. G. P., and D. J. Gee. 1989. Study on the effects of heat on blood and on the postmortem estimation of caroxyhemoglobin and metahaemoglobin. *Forensic Science International* 40: 63–67.

Fereira, J., A. Ortega, A. Avila, A. Espina, R. Leendertz, and F. Barrios. 1997. Oral autopsy in unidentified burned human remains: A new procedure. *The American Journal of Forensic Medicine and Pathology* 17(1):306–311.

Fisher, R. S., W. U. Spitz, R. Breitenecker, and J. E. Austin. 1965. Techniques of identification applied to 81 extremely fragmented aircraft fatalities. *Journal of Forensic Sciences* 10(2):121–135.

Fitzpatrick, J. J., D. R. Shook, B. L. Kaufman, S.-J. Wu, R. J. Kirschner, H. MacMahon, L. J. Levine, W. Maples, and D. Charletta. 1996. Optical and digital techniques for enhancing radiographic anatomy for identification of human remains. *Journal of Forensic Sciences* 41(6):947–959.

Fully, G. 1956. Un nouvelle methode de determination de la taille. *Ann Méd Lég.* 35:266–273.

Galera, V., D. G. Ubelaker, and L. A. C. Hayek. 1998. Comparison of macroscopic cranial methods of age estimation applied to skeletons from the Terry Collection. *Journal of Forensic Sciences* 43:933–939.

Gejvall, N.-G. 1969. Cremations. In: Brothwell, D., and E. Higgs, editors. *Science in Archaeology.* London: Thames and Hudson, p. 468–479.

Gilchrist, M., and H. Mytum. 1986. Experimental archaeology and burnt animal bone from archaeological sites. *Circaea* 4:29–38.

Giles, E., and D. L. Hutchinson. 1991. Stature- and age-related bias in self-reported stature. *Journal of Forensic Sciences* 36(3):765–780.

Glassman, D. M., and R. M. Crow. 1996. Standardization model for describing the extent of burn injury to human remains. *Journal of Forensic Sciences* 41(1):152–154.

Gormsen, H., N. Jeppesen, and A. Lund. 1984. The causes of death in fire victims. *Forensic Science International* 24:107–111.

Graham, D., and S. M. Corless. 1970. The use of radioactive iodine 125 for dental identification in mass disasters. *Journal of Forensic Sciences* 15(4):553–564.

Grévin, G., P. Bailet, G. Quatrehomme, and A. Ollier. 1998. Anatomical reconstruction of fragments of burned human bones: a necessary means for forensic dentification. *Forensic Science International* 96(2–3):129–134.

Grupe, G., and B. Herrmann. 1983. Über das schrumpfungsverhalten experimentell verbrannter spongiöser knochen am beispiel des caput femoris. *Zeitschrift für Morphologie und Anthropologie* 74(2):121–127.

Grupe, G., and S. Hummel. 1991. Trace element studies on experimentally cremated bone. I. Alterations of the chemical composition at high temperatures. *Journal of Archaeological Science* 18:177–186.

Gruspier, K. L., and G. J. Mullen. 1991. Maxillary suture obliteration: a test of the Mann method. *Journal of Forensic Sciences* 36:512–519.

Günther, H., and O. Schmidt. 1953. Die zerstörung des menschlichen gebisses im verlauf der einwirkung hoher temperaturen. *Deutsche Zeitschrift für gerichtliche Medizin* 42:180–188.

Gupta, R. K., and A. K. Srivastava. 1988. Study of burns in Kanpur (India). *Forensic Science International* 37:81–89.

Hagelberg, E., I. C. Gray, and A. J. Jeffreys. 1991. Identification of the skeletal remains of a murder victim by DNA analysis. *Nature* 352:427–429.

Haglund, W. D., and C. L. Fligner. 1993. Confirmation of human identification using computerized tomography. *Journal of Forensic Sciences* 38(3):708–712.

Haglund, W. D., and M. H. Sorg. 1997. *Forensic Taphonomy: The Postmortem Fate of Human Remains*. Boca Raton: CRC Press, p. 636.

Haines, D. H. 1967. Dental identification in the Stockport air disaster. *British Dental Journal* 123:336–338.

Hardy, J. H. 2007. Odontology. In: Thompson, T., and S. Black, editors. *Forensic Human Identification: An Introduction*. Boca Raton: CRC Press, p. 177–198.

Harris, A. M. P., R. E. Wood, C. J., Nortje, and C. J. Thomas. 1987a. The frontal sinus forensic fingerprintÉ—a pilot study. *Journal of Odontostomatology* 5:9–15.

Harris, A. M. P., R. E. Wood, C. J. Nortje, and C. J. Thomas, 1987b. Gender and ethnic differences of radiographic image of the frontal region. *Journal of Forensic Odontostomatology* 5:51–57.

Harsányi, L. 1976. Scanning electron microscopic investigation of thermal damage of the teeth. *Acta Morphologica Academiae Scientiarium Hungaricae* 23(4):271–281.

Harsányi, L. 1977. Scanning electron microscopic investigation of thermal damage of the bone tissue. *Morphologica Ig Orv Szle* 17:26–32.

Harsányi, L. 1993. Differential diagnosis of human and animal bone. In: Grupe, G. and A. N. Garland, editors. *Histology of Ancient Human Bone: Methods and Diagnosis*. New York: Springer-Verlag, p. 79–94.

Hausmann, R., and P. Betz. 2002. Thermally induced entrance wound-like defect of the skull. *Forensic Science International* 128:159–161.

Hayden, S. 1892. Cremation as an incentive to crime. A paper presented to the Society of Arts, England, November 1892. As cited by *The Lancet*. 1893. 141(3627):478.

Heglar, R. 1984. Burned remains. In: Rathbun, T. and J. E. Buikstra, editors. *Human Identification: Case Studies in Forensic Anthropology*. Springfield, IL: Charles C. Thomas, p. 148–158.

Henderson, J., R. Janaway, and J. Richards. 1987. A curious clinker. *Journal of Archaeological Science* 14:353–365.

Herrmann, B. 1970. Anthroplogische bearbeitung der Leichenbräden von Berlin-Rudow. *Ausgrabungen in Berlin* 1:61–71.

Herrmann, B. 1976. Experimentelle und theoretische beiträge zur leichenbrand unter schung. *Homo* 27:114-118.

Herrmann, B. 1977. On histological investigations of cremated human remains. *Journal of Human Evolution*. 6:101–103.

Herrmann, N. P., and J. L. Bennett. 1999. The differentiation of traumatic and heat-related fractures in burned bone. *Journal of Forensic Sciences* 44(3):461–469.

Hiatt, B. 1969. Cremation in aboriginal Australia. *Mankind* 7:104–119.

Hiller, J., T. J. U. Thompson, M. P. Evison, A. T. Chamberlain, and T. J. Wess. 2003. Bone mineral change during experimental heating: an X-ray scattering investigation. *Biomaterials* 24(28):5091–5097.

Hillson, S. 1986. *Teeth*. Cambridge: Cambridge University Press.

Hoffman, J. M. 1979. Age estimations from diaphyseal lengths: two months to twelve years. *Journal of Forensic Sciences* 24:461–469.

Holden, J. L., P. P. Phaky, and J. G. Clement. 1995a. Scanning electron microscope observations of incinerated human femoral bone: a case study. *Forensic Science International* 74:17–28.

Holden, J. L., P. P. Phaky, and J. G. Clement. 1995b. Scanning electron microscope observations on heat-treated human bone. *Forensic Science International* 74:29–45.

Holland, T. D. 1989. Use of the cranial base in the identification of fire victims. *Journal of Forensic Sciences* 34(2):458–460.

Hooft, P. J., E. K. Noji, and H. P. van de Voorde. 1989. Fatality management in mass casualty incidents. *Forensic Science International* 40:3–14.

Hulewica, B., and G. W. Wilcher. 2003. The use of thoracolumbar and hip joint dysmorphism in identification. *Journal of Forensic Sciences* 48(4):842–847.

Hummel, S., and H. Schutkowski. 1993 Approaches to the histological age determination of cremated human remains. In: Grupe, G., and A. N. Garland, editors. *Histology of Ancient Human Bone: Methods and Diagnosis*, Berlin: Springer-Verlag, p. 111–123.

Hummel, S., T. Schultes, B. Bramanti, and B. Herrmann. 1999. Ancient profiling by megaplex amplifications. *Electrophoresis* 20:1717–1721.

Hummel, S., and H. Schutkowski. 1986. Das verhalten von knochengewebe unter demeinfluss höherer temperaturen, bedeutungen füdie leichenbranddiagnose. *Zeitschrift für Morphologie und Anthropologie* 77(1):1–9.

Humphrey, J. H., and D. L. Hutchinson. 2001. Macroscopic characteristics of hacking trauma. *Journal of Forensic Sciences* 46: 228–233.

Huxley, A. K. 1994. Analysis of ceramic substrate found in cremains. *Journal of Forensic Sciences* 39(1):287–288.

Huxley, A. K. 1998. Analysis of shrinkage in human fetal diaphyseal lengths from fresh to dry bone using Petersohn and Köhler's data. *Journal of Forensic Sciences* 43(2):423–426.

Huxley, A. K., and F. Kósa. 1999. Calculation of percentage shrinkage in human fetal diaphyseal lengths from fresh bone to carbonized and calcined bone using Petersohn and Kohler's data. *Journal of Forensic Sciences* 44(3):577–583.

Icove, D. J., and J. D. DeHaan. 2004. *Forensic Scene Reconstruction.* Upper Saddle River NJ: Pearson, Prentice Hall, p. 369.

Iscan, M. Y., and S. R. Loth. 1986. Determination of age from the sternal rib in white females: a test of the phase method. *Journal of Forensic Sciences* 31:990–999.

Iscan, M. Y., S. R. Loth, and R. K. Wright. 1984. Age estimation from the rib by phase analysis: white males. *Journal of Forensic Sciences* 29:1094–1104.

Iscan, M. Y., S. R. Loth, and R. K. Wright. 1985. Age estimation from the rib by phase analysis: white females. *Journal of Forensic Sciences* 30:853–863.

Iscan, M. Y., S. R. Loth, and R. K. Wright. 1987. Racial variation in the sternal extremity of the rib and its effect on age determination. *Journal of Forensic Sciences* 32:452–466.

Iwase, H., Y. Yamada, S. Ootani, Y. Sasakai, M. Nagao, K. Iwadate, and T. Takatori. 1998. Evidence for an antemortem injury of a burned head dissected from a burned body. *Forensic Science International* 94(1–2):9–14.

Jaalskelainen, A. J. 1968. A method for the estimation of age in the identification of mass casualties. *Journal of Forensic Sciences* 13(4):528–530.

Jablonski, N. G., and B. S. F. Shum. 1989. Identification of unknown human remains by comparison of antemortem and postmortem radiographs. *Forensic Science International* 42:221–230.

Jantz, R. L., D. R. Hunt, and L. Meadows. 1995. The measure and mismeasure of the tibia: implications for stature estimation. *Journal of Forensic Sciences* 40:758–761.

Jason, D. R., and K. Taylor. 1995. Estimation of stature from the length of the cervical, thoracic, and lumbar segments of the spine in American whites and blacks. *Journal of Forensic Sciences* 40:59–62.

Jeffreys, A. J., M. Allen, E. Hagelberg, A. and Sonnberg. 1992. Identification of skeletal remains of Josef Mengele by DNA analysis. *Forensic Science International* 56:65–76.

Jerkic, S. M. 1999. Identity crisis: two cases studies; success and failure in personal identification determination. In: Fairgrieve, S., editor. *Forensic Osteological Analysis: A Book of Case Studies.* Springfield, IL: Charles C. Thomas, p. 251–266.

Johanson, G., and T. Saldeen. 1969. Identification of burnt victims with the aid of tooth and bone fragments. *Journal of Forensic Medicine* 16:16–25.

Johanson, G., and T. Saldeen. 1969. A new method for the radiological detection and identification of fragments of teeth and bone recovered from burnt victims. *Journal of Forensic Medicine* 16:26–28.

Jones, N. L. 1996. *Atlas of Forensic Pathology*. New York: Igaku-Shoin.

Kaczmarek, M., and J. Piontik. 1982. Human cremated remains and the diversity of man. *Homo* 33:230–236.

Kahana, T., and J. Hiss. 1994. Positive identification by means of trabecular bone comparison. *Journal of Forensic Sciences* 39(5):1325–1330.

Kahana, T., J. Hiss, and P. Smith. 1998. Quantitative assessment of trabecular bone pattern identification. *Journal of Forensic Sciences* 43(6):1144–1147.

Kaleka, R. 1993. Autopsie d'Hitler : les médicins légistes russes savaient compter les dent. *Semaine des Hopitaux de Paris* 69(37) :1359–1361.

Karhunen, P. J., I. Lukkari, and E. Vuori. 1991. High cyanide level in a homicide victim burned after death: evidence of post-mortem diffusion. *Forensic Science International* 49:179–183.

Kennedy, K. A. R. 1996. The Wrong Urn: Commingling of cremains in mortuary practices. *Journal of Forensic Sciences* 41(4):689–692.

Kennedy, K. A. R. 1999. The Wrong Urn: Commingling of cremains in mortuary practices. In: Fairgrieve, S., editor. *Forensic Osteological Analysis: A Book of Case Studies*. Springfield, IL: Charles C. Thomas, p. 141–150.

Killam, E. W. 1990. *The Detection of Human Remains*. Springfield, IL: Charles C Thomas Publisher.

Kirk, N. J., R. E. Wood, and M. Goldstein. 2002. Skeletal identification using the frontal sinus region: A retrospective study of 39 cases. *Journal of Forensic Sciences* 47(2):318–323.

Knight, B. 1997. *Simpson's Forensic Medicine* 11th edition, New York: Oxford University Press.

Komori, H. 1960. On the changes of hard tissue of extracted human teeth under high temperatures. *Japanese Journal of Legal Medicine* 14:5.

Kondo, T., and T. Oshtrima. 1994. Epidural herniation of the cerebral tissue in a burned body: a case report. *Forensic Science International* 66:197–202.

Koot, M. G., N. J. Sauer, and T. W. Fenten. 2005. Radiographic human identification using bones of the hand: a validation study. *Journal of Forensic Sciences* 50(2):263–268.

Korszun, A.-K., B. E. Causton, and P. J. Lincoln. 1978. Thermostability of ABO(H) blood-group antigens in human teeth. *Forensic Science* 11:231–239.

Krogman, W. M. 1943. Role of the physical anthropologist in the identification of human skeletal remains, Part II. *FBI Law Enforcement Bulletin* 12(4):12–28.

Krogman, W. M., and M. Y. Iscan. 1986. *The Human Skeleton in Forensic Medicine*, Second Edition. Springfield, IL: Charles C. Thomas.

Lancet, The. 1893. Burial, cremation and the detection of crime. *The Lancet* 141(3627):478.

Lange, M., H. Schutkowski, S. Hummel, and B. Herrmann. 1987. *A Bibliography on Cremation*. Journal of the European Study Group on Physical, Chemical, Biological and Mathematical Techniques Applied to Archaeology. Strasbourg, p. 168.

Laurier, E., V. Hedouin, D. Gosset, and P. H. Muller. 1994. Etude critique médico-légale du rapport d'autopsie d'Hitler. *Journal de Médicine Légale Droit Médical* 37(1) :65–67.

Levin, B. C., P. R. Rechani, J. L. Gurman, F. Landron, H. M. Clark, M. F. Yoklavich, J. R. Rodriguez, L. Droz, F. de Cabrera, and S. Kaye. 1990. Analysis of carboxyhemoglobin and cyanide in blood from victims of the Dupon Plaza Hotel Fire in Puerto Rico. *Journal of Forensic Sciences* 35:151.

Lim, K. L., P. Jaya, B. Kassim, L. H. Seah, Y. H. Lee, and O. K. Chee. 2000. Identification of severely burned bodies from a vehicle collision using the RFLP technique. Forensic Science Communications [serial from the internet], [cited 2007 Apr 23] 2(3):6p. Available from: http://www.fbi.gov/hq/lab/fsc/backissu/july2000/lim.htm.

Lisowski, F. P. 1968. The investigation of human cremations. Anthropologie und Humangenetik 4:76–83.

Lovejoy, O. C., R. S. Meindl, R. Mensforth, and T. J. Barton. 1985. Chronological metamorphosis of the auricular surface of the ilium: a new method for the determination of adult skeletal age at death. American Journal of Physical Anthropology 68:15–28.

Lovell, N. C. 1989. Test of Phenice's technique for determining sex from the os pubis. American Journal of Physical Anthropology 79:117–120.

Lundquist, P., R. Lennart, and B. Sorbo. 1989. The role of hydrogen cyanide and carbon monoxide in fire casualties: a prospective study. Forensic Science International 43:9–14.

Mackinnon, G., and A. Z. Mundorff. 2007. The World Trade Centre—September 11, 2001. In: Thompson, T., and Black, S., editors. Forensic Human Identification: An Introduction. Boca Raton: CRC Press Taylor & Francis Group. p 485–499.

Maeda, H., K. Fukita, S. Oritani, K. Nagai, and B.-L. Zhu. 1996. Evaluation of post-mortem oxymetry in fire victims. Forensic Science International 81:201–209.

Malik, M. O. A. 1970. Histochemical changes as evidence of the antemortem origin of skin burns. Journal of Forensic Sciences 15(4):489–499.

Malinowski, A., and R. Porawski. 1969. Identifikationsmöglichkeiten menschlicher brandknochen mit besonderer berücksichtigung ihres gewichts. Roma: Archivio di Medicina legale, sociale criminological, Zacchia 5 Ser. 3(3):1–19.

Mann, R. W. 1998. Use bone trabeculae to establish positive identification. Forensic Science International 98(1-2):91–99.

Mann, R. W., S. A. Symes, and W. M. Bass. 1987. Maxillary suture obliteration: aging the human skeleton based on intact or fragmentary maxilla. Journal of Forensic Sciences 32:148–157.

Maples, W. R. 1986. Trauma analysis by the forensic anthropologist. In: Reichs, K. J., editor. Forensic Osteology: Advances in the Identification of Human Remains. Springfield, IL: Charles C. Thomas, p. 218–228.

Marchetti, D., I. Boschi, M. Polacco, and J. Raino. 2005. The death of Adolf Hitler—Forensic Aspects. Journal of Forensic Sciences 50(5):1147–1153.

Marlin, D. C., M. A. Clark, and S. M. Standish. 1991. Identification of human remains by comparison of frontal sinus radiographs: a series of four cases. Journal of Forensic Sciences 36(6):1765–1772.

Marsh, S. M., and S. Klem. 2002. The effects of temperature and duration of heat exposure on bone collagen yield. Unpublished manuscript. Sudbury, ON: Department of Biology, Laurentian University.

Martin-de las Heras, S., A. Valenzuela, E. Villanueva, T. Marques, N. Exposito, and J. M. Bohoyo. 1999. Methods for identification of 28 burn victims following a 1996 bus accident in Spain. Journal of Forensic Sciences 44(2):428–431.

Maruta, T., Y. Ohno, and I. Yamamoto. 1996. A case of identification of cremated bones. Research and Practice in Forensic Medicine 39:67–70.

Mavin, T. 2001. Fluorescence of bone and teeth with ultraviolet and alternate light sources including cremated human bone. Identification Canada October/November/December:12–13.

Mayne, P. 1989. The identification of traumatic fractures in cremated remains—preliminary results. Presented at the Annual General Meeting of the Canadian Society of Forensic Science, 1989, Edmonton, Alberta. Canadian Society of Forensic Science 22(3):279.

Mayne, P. 1990. The Identification of Precremation Trauma in Cremated Bone. MA Thesis, Department of Anthropology, University of Alberta, Edmonton, Canada, p. 142.

Mayne, P. M. 1990. *The identification of precremation trauma in cremated bone.* Unpublished M.A. Thesis, Department of Anthropology, University of Alberta.

Mayne, Correia P. 1997. Fire modification of bone: a review of the literature. In: Haglund, W. D., and M. H. Sorg, editors. *Forensic Taphonomy: The Postmortem Fate of Human Remains.* Boca Raton: CRC Press, p. 275–293.

McCarty, V. O., A. P. Sohn, R. S. Ritzlin, and J. H. Gauthier. 1987. Scene investigation, identification, and victim examination following the accident of Galaxy 203: disaster preplanning does work. *Journal of Forensic Sciences* 32(4):983–987.

McKern, T., and T. D. Stewart. 1957. Skeletal age changes in young American males, analyzed from the standpoint of identification, *Technical report EP-45.* Natick, MS: Headquarters, Quartermaster Research and Development Command.

McKinley, J. I. 1994. The Anglo-Saxon cemetery at Spong Hill, North Elmham Part VIII: The Cremations. *East Anglian Archaeology Report* No. 69, GB.

Meadows, L., and R. L. Jantz. 1992. Estimation of stature from metacarpal lengths. *Journal of Forensic Sciences* 37:147–154.

Meindl, R. S., and O. C. Lovejoy. 1985. Ectocranial suture closure: a revised method for the determination of skeletal age at death based on the lateral-anterior sutures. *American Journal of Physical Anthropology* 68:57–66.

Meindl, R. S., and O. C. Lovejoy. 1989. Age changes in the pelvis: Implications for paleodemography. In: Iscan, M. Y., editor. *Age Markers in the Human Skeleton.* Springfield, IL: Charles C. Thomas, p. 137–168.

Meindl, R. S., O. C. Lovejoy, R. P. Mensforth, and R. A. Walker. 1985. A revised method of age determination using the os pubis with a review and tests of accuracy of other current methods of pubic symphyseal aging. *American Journal of Physical Anthropology* 68:57–66.

Melbye, J., and S. B. Jimenez. 1997. Chain of custody from the field to the courtroom. In: Haglund, W. D. and M. H. Sorg, editors. *Forensic Taphonomy: The Postmortem Fate of Human Remains.* Boca Raton: CRC Press, p. 65–75.

Merbs, C. F. 1967. Cremated human remains from Point of Pines, Arizona: A new approach. *American Antiquity* 32(4):498–506.

Merbs, C. F. 1989. Trauma. In: Iscan, M. Y. and K. A. R. Kennedy, editors. *Reconstruction of Life from the Skeleton.* New York: Alan R Liss, Inc., p. 161–189.

Mercer, J. O., J. D. Reid, and K. F. M. Uttley. 1954. The identification of exhumed bodies: a brief report of the exhumation of the unidentified dead after the Tangiwai railway accident. *New Zealand Medical Journal* 53:329–334.

Mincer, H. H., H. E. Berryman, G. A. Murray, and R. L. Dickens. 1990. Methods for physical stabilization of ashed teeth in incinerated remains. *Journal of Forensic Sciences* 35(4):971–974.

Mittler, D. M., and S. G. Sheridan. 1992. Sex determination in subadults using auricular surface morphology: A forensic science perspective. *Journal of Forensic Sciences* 37:1068–1075.

Moorrees, C., E. A. Fanning, and E. E. Hunt, Jr. 1963a. Formation and resorption of three deciduous teeth in children. *American Journal of Physical Anthropology* 21:205–213.

Moorrees, C., E. A. Fanning, and E. E. Hunt, Jr. 1963b. Age variation of formation stages for ten permanent teeth. *Journal of Dental Research* 42(6):1490–1502.

Morovic-Budak, A. 1965. Experience in the process of putrefaction in corpses buried in earth. *Medicine, Science and the Law* 34(2):399–406.

Morse, D., J. Duncan, and J. Stoutamire. 1983. *Handbook of Forensic Archaeology and Anthropology.* Tallahassee, FL: Rose Printing.

Muhlemann, H. R., E. Steiner, and M. Brandestini. 1978. Identification of mass disaster victims: the Swiss identification system. *Journal of Forensic Sciences* 24(1):173–181.

Mundorff, A. Z., G. Vidoli, and J. Melinek. 2006. Anthropological and radiographic comparison of vertebrae for identification of decomposed human remains. *Journal of Forensic Sciences* 51(5):1002–1004.

Murad, T. A. 1998. The growing popularity of cremation versus inhumation: some forensic implications. In: Reichs, K. J., editor. *Forensic Osteology: Advances in the Identification of Human Remains*, second edition. Springfield, IL: Charles C. Thomas, p. 86–105.

Murphy, W. A., F. G. Spruill, and G. E. Gantner. 1980. Radiological identification of unknown human remains. *Journal of Forensic Sciences* 25(4):727–735.

Murray, K. A., and J. C. Rose. 1993. The analysis of cremains: a case study involving the inappropriate disposal of mortuary remains. *Journal of Forensic Sciences* 38(1):98–103.

Muthusubramanian, M., K. S. Limson, and R. Julian. 2005. Analysis of rugae in burn victims and cadavers to simulate rugae identification in case of incineration and decomposition. *Journal of Forensic Odontostomatology* 23(1):26–29.

Myers, S. L., J. M. Williams, and J. S. Hodges. 1999. Effects of extreme heat on teeth with implications for histological processing. *Journal of Forensic Sciences* 44(4):805–809.

Nagano, T., T. Tsuji, and K. Ieda. 1975. Blood group determination of badly charred bodies. I. Activity changes of A-, B-, AF-, and O(H)-active glycolipids and A- and B-active glycoproteins by heat. Abstracts, 7th International Meeting of Forensic Sciences, Zurich, Sept. 8–12, 1975. *Forensic Science* 5:103–180.

Nelson, R. J. 1992. A microscopic comparison of fresh and burned bone. *Journal of Forensic Sciences* 37(4):1055–1060.

Nortomme, H. L., and F. Strom. 1946. Exhumation and identification of 183 persons executed by the Germans at Trandum (Norway). *International Criminal Police Review* (English Edition) 1(3):7–14.

Office of the Fire Marshal of Ontario. 2006. *Ontario Fatal Fire Summary.* http://www.ofm. gov.on.ca/english/Publications/Statistics/fatalfires/default.asp.5/8/(2006).

Ormstad, K., L. Karlsson, L. Enkler, J. Rajs. 1986. Patterns of sharp force fatalities—a comprehensive forensic medical study. *Journal of Forensic Sciences* 31:529–542.

Ousley, S. 1995. Should we estimate biological or forensic stature. *Journal of Forensic Sciences* 40:768–773.

Owsley, D. W. 1993. Identification of the fragmentary, burned remains of two U.S. journalists seven years after their disappearance in Guatemala. *Journal of Forensic Sciences* 38(6):1372–1382.

Owsley, D. W., R. W. Mann, R. E. Chapman, E. Moore, and W. A. Cox. 1993. Positive identification in a case of intentional extreme fragmentation. *Journal of Forensic Sciences* 38(4):985–996.

Owsley, D. W., D. H. Ubelaker, M. M. Houck, K. L. Sandness, W. E. Grant, E.A. Craig, T. J. Woltanski, and N. Peerwani. 1995. The role of forensic anthropology in the recovery and analysis of Branch Davidian compound victims: techniques of analysis. *Journal of Forensic Sciences* 40(3):341–348.

Pääbo, S. 1989. Ancient DNA. Extraction, characterization, molecular cloning and enzymatic amplification. *Proceedings of the National Academy of Science* (USA) 86:1939–1953.

Pääbo, S., R. G. Higuchi, and A. C. Wilson. 1989. Ancient DNA and the polymerase chain reaction. The emerging field of molecular archaeology. *Journal of Biological Chemistry* 264:9709–9712.

Parks, J. G., T. T. Noguchi, and E. C. Klatt. 1989. The epidemiology of fatal burn injuries. *Journal of Forensic Sciences* 34(2):399–406.

Petersohn, F., and J. Köhler. 1965. Die bedeutung der veräderungen an fetalen röhrenknochen nach trocknung und hitzeeinwirkung für die forensische begutachtung der fruchgrösse. *Archive für Kriminologie* 134:143.

Petrova, A., and P. Watson. 1996. *The Death of Hitler. The Full Story with New Evidence from Secret Russian Archives.* New York, London: W. W. Norton and Company.

Phenice, T. W. 1969. A newly developed visual method of sexing the os pubis. *American Journal of Physical Anthropology* 30:297–302.

Piekarski, K. 1970. Fracture of bone. *Journal of Applied Physics.* 41(1):215–223.

Pinorini, M. T., C. J. Lennard, P. Margot, I. Dustin, and P. J. Furrer. 1994. Soot as an indicator in fire investigations: physical and chemical analyses. *Journal of Forensic Sciences* 39(4):933–973.

Piontek, J. 1975. Polish method and results of investigations of cremated bones from prehistoric cemeteries. *Glasnik Anthropoloskog Drustva Jugoslavise Sveska* 12:23–34.

Pless, J. E. 1982. Hazards of X-ray comparison of partially incinerated human remains. *Abstract, G42,* American Academy of Forensic Sciences Program, p. 94.

Polson, C. G., and D. J. Gee. 1973. *The Essentials of Forensic Medicine.* Toronto: Pergamon Press, p. 729.

Pope, E. J., and O. C. Smith. 2004. Identification of traumatic injury in burned cranial bone: an experimental approach. *Journal of Forensic Sciences* 49(3):431–440.

Purves, J. D. 1975. Dental identification of fire victims. *Forensic Science* 6:217–219.

Quatrehomme, G., M. Bolla, M. Muller, J. P. Rocca, G. Grevin, P. Bailet, and A. Ollier. 1998. Experimental single controlled study of burned bones: contribution of scanning electron microscopy. *Journal of Forensic Sciences* 43(2):417–422.

Ravaglioli, A., A. Krajewski, G. C. Celotti, A. Piancastelli, B. Bacchini, L. Montanari, G. Zama, and L. Piombi. 1996. Mineral evolution of bone. *Biomaterials* 17(6):617–622.

Reinhard, K. J., and T. M. Fink. 1994. Cremation in southwestern North America: aspects of taphonomy that affect pathological analysis. *Journal of Archaeological Science* 21(5):597–605.

Revised Statutes of Ontario, 1990. 2002. *Coroners Act,* Chapter C.37, Queen's Printer for Ontario, January 18, 2002.

Rhine, S. 1998. *Bone Voyage: A Journey in Forensic Anthropology.* Albuquerque: University of New Mexico Press, p. 268.

Rhine, S., and K. Sperry. 1991. Radiographic identification by mastoid sinus and arterial pattern. *Journal of Forensic Sciences* 36(1):272–279.

Richards, N. F. 1977. Fire investigation—destruction of corpses. *Medicine, Science and the Law* 17: 79–82.

Riddick, L., B. G. Brogdon, J. Laswell-Hoff, and B. Delmas. 1983. Radiographic identification of charred human remains through use of the dorsal defect of the patella. *Journal of Forensic Sciences* 28(1):263–267.

Robinson, F. G., F. A. Rueggeberg, and P. E. Lockwood. 1998. Thermal stability of direct dental esthetic restorative materials at elevated temperatures. *Journal of Forensic Sciences* 43(6): 1163–1167.

Rodge, S., and J. H. Olving. 1996. Characteristics of fire victims in different sorts of fires. *Forensic Science International* 77(1–2):93–99.

Rogers, K. D., and P. Daniels. 2002. An X-ray diffraction study of the effects of heat treatment on bone mineral microstructure. *Biomaterials* 23(12):2577–2585.

Rogers, T., and T. T. Allard. 2004. Expert testimony and positive identification of human remains through cranial suture patterns. *Journal of Forensic Sciences* 49(2):203–207.

Roh, L. 1983. Letter, Detection of accelerants on a burn victim. *Journal of Forensic Sciences* 28(3):292.

Rösing, F. W. 1977. Methoden und aussagemöglichkeiten der anthropologischen leichengrandbearbeitung. *Archaeologie und Naturwissenschaften* 1:53–80.

Rossi, D., S. De Gruchy, and N. C. Lovell. 2004. A comparative experiment in the consolidation of cremated bone. *International Journal of Osteoarchaeology* 14:104–111.

Saferstein, R. 2007. *Criminalistics: An Introduction to Forensic Science*. 9th edition. Upper Saddle River, NJ: Pearson Prentice Hall.

Sajantila, A., M. Strom, B. Budowle, P. J. Karhunen, and L. Peltonen. 1991. The polymerase chain reaction and post-mortem forensic identity testing: application of amplified D1S80 and HLA-DQ alpha loci to the identification of fire victims. *Forensic Science International* 51:23–34.

Salomone, III, J., A. P. Sohn, R. Ritzlin, J. H. Gauthier, and V. McCarty. 1987. Correlations of injury, toxicology, and cause of death to Galaxy flight 203 crash site. *Journal of Forensic Sciences* 32(5):1403–1415.

Salley, J. J., F. J. Filipowicz, and H. N. Karnitshnig. 1963. Dental identification of mass disaster victims. *Journal of the American Dental Association* 66:827–832.

Sathyavagiswaran, L., B. Florentine, J. Taylor, and N. Romero. 1992. Identifying "Does" with help of dentures. *Journal of Forensic Sciences* 38(5):1018.

Saul, F. P., and J. M. Saul. 1989. Osteobiography: a Maya example. In: Iscan, M. Y., and K. A. R. Kennedy, editors. *Reconstruction of Life from the Skeleton*. New York: Alan R. Liss, p. 287–302.

Saul, J. M., and F. P. Saul. 1999. Biker's bones: an avocational syndrome. In: Fairgrieve, S., editor. *Forensic Osteological Analysis: A Book of Case Studies*. Springfield, IL: Charles C. Thomas, p. 237–250.

Savio, C., G. Merlati, P. Danesino, G. Fassina, and P. Menghini. 2006. Radiographic evaluation of teeth subjected to high temperatures: experimental study to aid identification processes. *Forensic Science International* 158: 108–116.

Schaffer, M. B., X. J. Li, W. S. S. Jee, S. W. W. Ho, and P. J. Stern. 1988. Skeletal tissue responses to thermal injury: an experimental study. *Bone* 9(6):397–406.

Schour, I., and M. Massler. 1941. The development of the human dentition. *Journal of the American Dental Association* 28:1153–1160.

Schuller, A. 1943. A note on the identification of skulls by x-ray pictures of the frontal sinuses. *Medical Journal of Australia* 1:554–556.

Schutkowski, H. 1993. Sex determination of infant and juvenile skeletons: I, morphognostic features. *American Journal of Physical Anthropology* 90:199–205.

Shahack-Gross, R., O. Bar-Yosef, and S. Weiner. 1997. Black-colored bones in Hayorium Cave, Israel: differentiating between burning and oxide staining. *Journal of Archaeological Science* 24(5):439–446.

Shipman, P., G. Foster, and M. Shoeninger. 1984. Burnt bones and teeth: an experimental study of color, morphology, crystal structure and shrinkage. *Journal of Archaeological Science* 11:307–325.

Shkrum, M. J., and K. A. Johnston. 1992. Fire and suicide: a three-year study of self-immolation deaths. *Journal of Forensic Sciences* 37:208–221.

Siedlick, E., and C. A. Anderson. 1983. What happened? Investigating fire disaster. *Fire Engineering* 136:33–38.

Skinner, M. 1995. Expert witnessing in cremains cases (abstract). Paper presented at the 42nd Annual Meeting of the Canadian Society of Forensic Science, Toronto, Ontario, 1995. *The Canadian Society of Forensic Science Journal* 28(4):239–240.

Skinner, M, and R. A. Lazenby. 1983. *Found! Human Remains*. Burnaby: Archaeology Press, Simon Fraser University.

Smith, B. C. 1992. Reconstruction of root morphology in skeletonized remains with post-mortem dental loss. *Journal of Forensic Sciences* 37(1):176–184.

Solheim, T., S. Ronning, B. Hars, and P. K. Sundnes. 1982. A new system for computer aided dental identification in mass disasters. *Forensic Science International* 20:127–131.

Sonek, A. 1992. *The weight(s) of cremated remains*. Paper presented at the 44th annual meeting of the American Academy of Forensic Sciences. Feb. 21, New Orleans, LA.

Sopher, I. M. 1973. Dental identification of aircraft-accident fatalities. *Journal of Forensic Sciences* 18(4):356–363.

Spennemann, D. H. R., and S. M. Colley. 1989. Fire in a pit: the effects of burning on faunal remains. *Archaeozoologia* 3:51–64.

Spitz, W. U. 1993. Thermal injuries. In: Spitz, W. U., editor. *Medicolegal Investigations of Death*, third edition. Springfield IL: Charles C. Thomas, p. 413–443.

Staiti, N., S. Spitaleri, C. Vecchio, and L. Saravo. 2004. Identification of a carbonized body by DNA profiling. *International Congress Series* 1261:494–496.

Steele, D. G. 1970. Estimation of stature from fragments of long limb bones. In: Stewart, T. D., editor. *Personal Identification in Mass Disasters*. Washington, DC: National Museum of Natural History, Smithsonian Institution.

Stevens, P. J. 1977. Identification of bodies from fire. *Medicine, Science and the Law* 17:95.

Stewart, T. D., editor. 1970. *Personal Identification in Mass Disasters*. Washington, D.C.: National Museum of Natural History, Smithsonian Institution.

Stewart, T. D. 1979. *Essentials of Forensic Anthropology*. Springfield, Illinois: Charles C. Thomas.

Stiner, M. C., S. L. Kuhn, S. Weiner, and O. Bar-Yosef. 1995. Differential burning, recrystallization, and fragmentation of archaeological bone. *Journal of Archaeological Science* 22:223–237.

Stratton, S. U., and O. B. Beattie. 1999. Mass disasters: comment and discussion regarding the Hinton Train collision of 1986. In: Fairgrieve, S., editor. *Forensic Osteological Analysis: A Book of Case Studies*. Springfield, IL: Charles C. Thomas, p. 267–286.

Strom, C. M., and R. Svetlana. 1998. Use of nested PCR to identify charred human remains and minute amounts of blood. *Journal of Forensic Science* 43(3):696–700.

Stryer, L. 1988. *Biochemistry*, third edition. New York: WH Freeman and Company, p. 1089.

Suarez-Penaranda, J. M., J. L. Munoz, B. Lopez de Abajo, D. N. Vieira, R. Rico, T. Alavrez, and L. Concheiro. 1999. Concealed homicidal strangulation by burning. *The American Journal of Forensic Medicine and Pathology* 20(2):141–144.

Suchey, J. M., and D. Katz. 1986. Skeletal age standards derived from an extensive multiracial sample of modern Americans. *American Journal of Physical Anthropology* 69:269.

Sudimack, J. R., B. J. Lewis, J. Rich, D. E. Dean, and P. M. Fardal. 2002. Identification of decomposed human remains from radiographic comparisons of an unusual foot deformity. *Journal of Forensic Sciences* 47(1):218–220.

Sutherland, L. D., and J. M. Suchey. 1991. Use of the ventral arc in pubic sex determination. *Journal of Forensic Sciences* 36:501–511.

Suzuki, T., H. Takahashi, and K. Umetsu. 1995. Unusual aspirations in fire death. *Forensic Science International* 72:71–76.

Sweet, D. J., and C. H. W. Sweet. 1995. The DNA analysis of dental pulp to link incinerated remains of homicide victim to crime scene. *Journal of Forensic Sciences* 40(2):310–314.

Takayasu, T., T. Ohshima, T. Kondo, and Y. Sato. 2001. Intratrachial gas analysis for volatile substances by gas chromatography/mass spectrometry—application to forensic autopsies. *Journal of Forensic Sciences* 46(1):98–104.

Tatlisumak, E., G. Y. Ovali, A. Aslan, M. Asirdizer, Y. Zeyfeoglu, and S. Tarhan. 2007. Identification of unknown bodies by using CT images of frontal sinus. *Forensic Science International* 166:42–48.

Taylor, R. E., P. E. Hare, and T. D. White. 1995. Geochemical criteria for thermal alteration of bone. *Journal of Archaeological Science* 22:115–119.

Teather, R. G. 1994. *Encyclopedia of Underwater Investigations*. Flagstaff, AZ: Best Publishing, p. 186.

Teige, B., and J. Lundevall. 1977. Carboxyhemoglobin concentrations in fire victims, and in cases of fatal carbon monoxide poisoning. *Z Rechtsmed.* 80(1):17–21.

Ten Cate, A. R., G. W. Thompson, J. B. Dickinson, and H. A. Hunter. 1977. The estimation of age of skeletal remains from the colour of roots of teeth. *Journal of the Canadian Dental Association* 2:83–86.

Thompson, H. 1891. *Modern cremation: its history and practice.* 2nd edition. London: Kegan Paul.

Thompson, T. J. U. 1999. A preliminary investigation into the influence of burning on the ability to sex the human pelvis. Presented at the 46th Annual Meeting of the Canadian Society of Forensic Science.

Thompson, T. J. U. 2004. Recent advances in the study of burned bone and their implications for forensic anthropology. *Forensic Science International* 146:203–205.

Thompson, T. J. U. 2005. Heat-induced dimensional changes in bone and their consequences for forensic anthropology. *Journal of Forensic Sciences* 50(5):1008–1015.

Thompson, T., and S. Black, editors. 2007. *Forensic Human Identification.* Boca Raton: CRC Press, p. 518.

Todd, T. W. 1920. Age changes in the pubic bone: I, the male white pubis. *American Journal of Physical Anthropology* 3:285–334.

Todd, T. W., and D. W. Lyon. 1924. Endocranial suture closure: its progress and age relationship. Part I, adult males of white stock. *American Journal of Physical Anthropology* 7:325–384.

Todd, T. W., and D. W. Lyon. 1925a. Cranial suture closure: it progress and age relationship. Part II, ectocranial closure in adult males of white stock. *American Journal of Physical Anthropology* 8:23–44.

Todd, T. W., and D. W. Lyon. 1925b. Cranial suture closure: it progress and age relationship. Part III, endocranial closure in adult males of negro stock. *American Journal of Physical Anthropology* 8:47–71.

Todd, T. W., and D. W. Lyon. 1925c. Cranial suture closure: it progress and age relationship. Part IV, ectocranial closure in adult males of negro stock. *American Journal of Physical Anthropology* 8:149–168.

Trotter, M. 1970. Estimation of stature from intact long limb bones. In: Stewart, T. D., editor. *Personal Identification in Mass Disasters.* Washington, DC: National Museum of Natural History, Smithsonian Institution.

Trotter, M., and G. C. Gleser. 1952. Estimation of stature from long bones of American Whites and Negroes. *American Journal of Physical Anthropology* 10:463–514.

Trotter, M., and G. C. Gleser. 1958. A re-evaluation of estimation of stature based on measurements of stature taken during life and of long bones after death. *American Journal of Physical Anthropology* 16:79–123.

Trotter, M., and B. B. Hixon. 1973. Sequential changes in weight, density, and percentage of ash weight of human skeletons from an early fetal period through old age. *Anatomical Record* 179:1–18.

Tsaroom, S. 1996. Investigation of a murder case involving arson. *Journal of Forensic Sciences* 41(6):1064–1067.

Ubelaker, D. H. 1984. Positive identification from the radiographic comparison of frontal sinus patterns. In: Rathbun, T. A., and J. Buikstra, editors. *Human Identification.* Springfield, IL: Charles C. Thomas, p. 399–411.

Ubelaker, D. H. 1989. *Human Skeletal Remains: Excavation, Analysis, Interpretation.* Second Edition. Washington, D.C.: Taraxacum.

Ubelaker, D. H. 1990. Positive identification of American Indian skeletal remains from radiographic comparison. *Journal of Forensic Sciences* 35(2):466–472.

Ubelaker, D. H. 1999. *Human Skeletal Remains.* Third edition. Washington, DC: Taraxacum Press.

Ubelaker, D. H., and C. H. Jacobs. 1995. Identification of orthopedic device manufacturer. *Journal of Forensic Sciences* 40(2):168–170.

Ubelaker, D. H., and C. G. Volk. 2002. A test of the Phenice method for the estimation of sex. *Journal of Forensic Sciences* 47:940–943.

Uchigasaki, S. 2004. Forensic external examination before cremation—introduction of tile system in Hamburg. *Research and Practice in Forensic Medicine* 47:219–222.

Van Vark, G. N. 1974. The investigation of human cremated skeletal material by multivariate statistical methods, I Methodology. *OSSA* 1:63–95.

von Wurmb-Schwark, N., E. Simeoni, A. Ringleb, and M. Oehmichen. 2004. Genetic investigation of modern burned corpses. *International Congress Series* 1261:50–52.

Wagner, G. N., and R. C. Froede. 1993. Medicolegal investigation of mass disasters. In: Fisher, W.U., editor. *Spitz and Fisherès Medicolegal Investigation of Death: Guidelines for the Application of Pathology to Crime Scene Investigation.* Springfield, IL: Charles C. Thomas, p. 567–584.

Walker, P. L., and K. P. Miller. 2005. Time, temperature, and oxygen availability: an experimental study of the effects of environmental conditions on the color and organic content of cremated bones. *American Journal of Physical Anthropology Supplement* 40:216–217.

Warren, M. W. 1996. *The anthropometry of contemporary commercial cremation.* Paper presented at the 48th Annual Meeting of the American Academy of Forensic Sciences. Nashville, TN.

Warren, M. W., A. B. Falsetti, W. F. Hamilton, and L. J. Levine. 1999. Evidence of arteriosclerosis in cremated remains. *The American Journal of Forensic Medicine and Pathology* 20(3):277–280.

Warren, M. W., A. B. Falsetti, I. I. Kravchenko, F. E. Dunnam, H. A. Van Rinsvelt, and W. R. Maples. 2002. Elemental analysis of bone: proton-induced X-ray emission testing in forensic cases. *Forensic Science International* 125:37–41.

Warren, M. W., and W. R. Maples. 1997. The anthropometry of contemporary commercial cremation. *Journal of Forensic Sciences* 42(3):417–423.

Was, J., D. Knittel, and E. Schollmeyer. 1996. The use of FTIR microscopy for the identification of thermally changed fibers. *Journal of Forensic Sciences* 41(6):1005–1011.

Weaver, D. S. 1980. Sex differences in the ilia of a known sex and age sample of fetal and infant skeletons. *American Journal of Physical Anthropology* 52:191–195.

Wells, C. 1960. A study of cremation. *Antiquity* 34:29–37.

Wenham, S. J. 1989. Anatomical interpretations of Anglo-Saxon weapon injuries. In: Chadwick Hawkes, S., editor. *Weapons and Warfare in Anglo-Saxon England.* Oxford: Oxford Committee for Archaeology Monograph No. 21:123–139.

Wetherell, H. R. 1966. Occurrence of cyanide in the blood of fire victims. *Journal of Forensic Sciences* 11(2):167–173.

White, T. D., and P. A. Folkens. 2005. *The Human Bone Manual.* New York: Elsevier Academic Press.

Wickenheiser, R. A., C. E. MacMillan, and C. M. Challoner. 1999. Case of identification of severely burned human remains via paternity testing with PCR DNA typing. *The Canadian Society of Forensic Science Journal* 32(1):15–24.

Willey, P., and T. Falsetti. 1990. The inaccuracy of stature reported on driver licenses. Paper presented at the 42nd Annual Meeting of the American Academy of Forensic Sciences, Cincinnati, OH, February 19–24.

Williams, A. B., R. B. Friedman, and L. Lorton. 1989. A new algorithm for use in computer identification. *Journal of Forensic Sciences* 34(3):682–686.

Williams, D., M. Lewis, T. Franzen, V. Lissett, C. Adams, D. Whittaker, C. Tysoe, and R. Butler. 2004. Sex determination by PCR analysis of DNA extracted from incinerated, deciduous teeth. *Science and Justice* 44(2):89–94.

Williams, D. J., editor. 1996. *Color Guide—Forensic Pathology.* New York: Churchill Livingstone.

Yeshion, T. E. 1980. Thermal degradation of erythrocyte acid phosphatase isoenzymes in a case sample. *Journal of Forensic Sciences* 25(3):695–698.

Yoshida, M., J. Adachi, T. Watabiki, Y. Tatsuno, and W. Ishida. 1991. A study on house fire victims: age, caroxyhemoglobin, hydrogen cyanide and hemolysis. *Forensic Science International* 52:13–20.

Yoshino, M., S. Miyasaka, H. Sato, and S. Seta. 1987. Classification of frontal sinus patterns by radiography. Its application to identification of unknown skeletal remains. *Forensic Science International* 34:289–299.

Index